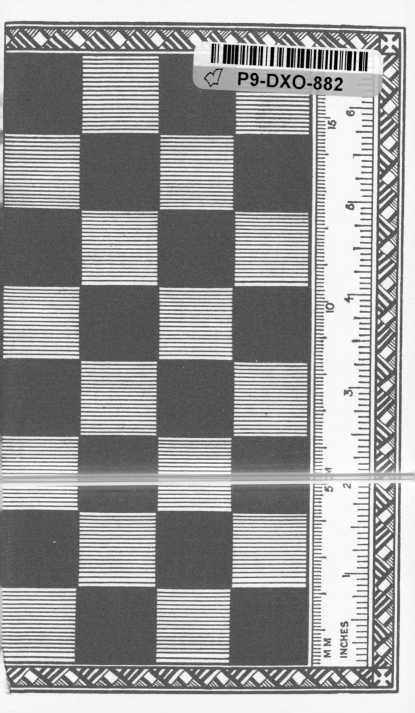

THE WEEK-END BOOK

The Week-End Book was first published in June 1924.
With various editions and alterations it was reprinted in
England thirty-four times. In 'criticism' of its commercial
success, Virginia Woolf once commented:

'The Hogarth Press may not make any money
– but at least we did not publish
The Week-End Book.'

The
Week-End
Book

Editor: Francis Meynell
Introduction by John Julius Norwich

A Nonesuch book
published by
Duckworth Overlook
London · New York · Woodstock

First published in 2006 in the United States by
Duckworth Overlook
in association with The Nonesuch Press

LONDON
90-93 Cowcross Street
London EC1M 6BF
inquiries@duckworth-publishers.co.uk
www.ducknet.co.uk

WOODSTOCK
The Overlook Press
One Overlook Drive
Woodstock, NY 12498
www.overlookpress.com
[for individual orders and bulk sales in the United States,
please contact our Woodstock office]

NEW YORK
The Overlook Press
141 Wooster Street
New York, NY 10012

Cataloging-in-Publication Data is available from the Library of Congress

ISBN 0 7156 3443 7 (UK)
ISBN 1-58567-813-9 (US)

Typeset by Ray Davies
Printed in the United States of America
2 4 6 8 10 9 7 5 3 1

WEEK-END

The train! The twelve o'clock for paradise.
Hurry, or it will try to creep away.
Out in the country everyone is wise:
We can be only wise on Saturday.
There you are waiting, little friendly house:
Those are your chimney-stacks with you between,
Surrounded by old trees and strolling cows,
Staring through all your windows at the green.
Your homely floor is creaking for our tread;
The smiling tea-pot with contented spout
Thinks of the boiling water, and the bread
Longs for the butter. All their hands are out
To greet us, and the gentle blankets seem
Purring and crooning: "Lie in us, and dream"

Harold Monro

The Publishers thank those readers who appreciate the effort made in this year 2005 to set a footprint backward into the past by including in this edition only pieces that have appeared in the thirty-four previous printings of this book, in other words, before twilight and sunset ended the British tradition. If the dawn has not completely come up, the publishers undertake to publish a new WEEK-END BOOK in 2006 with completely new material – we think both the countryside and everyone's aspiration to it will still be intact.

THE CONTENTS

INTRODUCTION

The Week-End Book and I are both children of the Twenties (although, having been born in September 1929, I only just scraped in). I remember it well as a child, teenager and young adult. Whenever you went anywhere for the weekend there always seemed to be a copy on your bedside table, and very welcome it was: you could open it anywhere, skim through the pages, pick out an item or two at random and then, as your eyelids grew heavier, lay it aside exactly when you wanted to, without there ever being a chapter to finish. From its very first appearance in June 1924 it had been a runaway success – the first edition sold out within days, and it went through five impressions in the next four months – largely because it instantly caught the public imagination: it was one of the first beautifully-produced books – if not *the* first – that had something for everyone. It's hard for us to remember, in these days of ubiquitous paperbacks, how heavy and bulky all books used to be: the future editors, Francis and Vera Meynell, setting off on an Italian walking tour soon after they had founded the Nonesuch Press with their good friend David 'Bunny' Garnett, staggered under the weight of their rucksacks. How wonderful, they thought, if they could pack just one book that would cater for all their needs. And so *The Week-End Book* was born.

A substantial part of it was devoted to poetry, largely selected by Francis himself. He did his best to avoid the obvious anthology pieces – there was even 'A List of Great Poems Not in this Book' – the intention, he explained, was to make it a supplement to, and not a competitor with, *The Oxford Book of English Verse*. But it was an anthology none the less; and only when the poetry stopped – often nearly half-way through – did the book show its true originality. From that moment on, anything could happen – and most things did. There was a selection of songs – chosen by the Meynells' friend John Goss, a professional singer – and a section on games compiled by Eleanor Farjeon. Vera herself dealt with food and drink; and a section on *First Aid in Divers Crises* included what Francis proudly described as 'a neatly disguised aphrodisiac'. (I'm still looking for it.) As edition followed edition there were minor changes: contemporary poetry was one significant breakthrough, astronomy another, ornithology a third. (I am delighted to see, incidentally, that this new edition has retained those brave attempts to reproduce birdsong by musical notation; I look forward to trying them out on the piano, *molto espressivo* of course, and always bearing in mind that 'the blackbird possesses a quite different emotional quality from the robin, being full of fears, suspicions and nervous reactions'.)

Looking at *The Week-End Book* again after half a century, I am surprised at the nostalgia it evokes; for it represents, of course, a vanished world. The last edition before this for the book trade was published as late as 1955, but essentially the whole concept reflects the years between the two world wars – years when English middle- and upper-middle-class society was very different to what it is today. There was more leisure, for one thing. Nobody worked as hard as they do now. With civil aviation still in its infancy, it was comparatively seldom that people travelled out of England. Even when they went away for the weekend they still tended to take the train, and when they did reach their destination they could be quietly confident that they would not be asked to make their beds or help with the washing-up.

And then, of course, they had no television to fall back on. They were expected to amuse themselves. At country-house weekends, as I remember, there was always a good deal of backgammon and bridge – and, in my early childhood, mah-jong with those lovely Chinese pieces, and bezique. And incidentally, whatever happened to bezique? It was Winston Churchill's favourite game (until he discovered canasta) and it had beautiful little scorers, with ivory teeth that you flipped up and down. After dinner one played pencil-and-paper games, ranging from Consequences (the least intellectually challenging) through Categories – also known, for some reason, as Guggenheim – in which one had to list diseases beginning with L or puddings beginning with W, to the composition of sonnets of which each player wrote a line in turn. Alternatively there might be charades, or that variant simply known as The Game, in which one mimed phrases like 'A Rolling Stone gathers no Moss' or – always good for a laugh – 'Doing what comes Naturally'.

Best of all, for me, was reading aloud. Does this ever happen nowadays, I wonder, at least among grown-ups? In my parents' life, and in my life with them, we did any amount of it. They never went on holiday without taking a book – usually Dickens or Trollope – which my father would read to my mother as she did her embroidery. In his diaries (which my wife and I have just been editing for rather belated publication), and especially in those covering the 1920s, there are constant references to readings-aloud after London dinner-parties, short stories by Wells or Kipling or Maugham, poetry – Keats and Meredith seem to have been particular favourites – or even Shakespeare plays, with everyone present allotted a part.

It was to this world – leisured, cultivated, intelligent but not particularly intellectual – that *The Week-End Book* most appealed. The Meynells certainly cast their net wide. Today I doubt whether they would have got away with those rather precious chapter headings – *The Fields and the Beasts Thereof, A Kalendar [sic] of Wild Flowers, Starshine at Night* (by Dr Fred Hoyle, no less, who begins 'The Earth is grilled by the Sun like a joint on a spit') – but they were very much part of the whole ethos of the book and I'm delighted to see them retained here. Nature-lovers were – and still are – particularly well served: the section in the 1955 edition could still begin 'Of Britain's 56 million acres 45 million are used for agriculture; one third of these are under the plough.' (Would that they were today.) In the New Forest, we were told, 'you will still find groves of oak and beech, where the dark shadows of the trees have scarcely shifted, and where the sunlight has not fallen on the leaf-mould beneath, since Domesday'. For the more musical, there were not only songs, but rounds and catches. In the seventeenth-century world of Samuel Pepys, people were always singing rounds and catches in the coffee-houses after dinner; how many people, I wonder, could manage them in the 1920s and '30s? Not many, I suspect, though probably a good deal more than today. I actually find it rather touching that the present editors have kept them in: I only hope their confidence in the musicianship of their readers has not been misplaced.

Suddenly, too – for the Meynells were nothing if not unpredictable – we were treated to a positive showerbath of statistical information. I was mildly disappointed not to be informed – as I had been by Charles Letts's Schoolboy's Diary in the 1930s – of the boiling-point of tallow; who, on the other hand, would have guessed that the average gestation period of an elephant was 600 days, as opposed to 64 for a guineapig, or that a moderately athletic worm travels at 10.5 feet per hour? We are told, too, that a puncheon of beer equals 72 gallons, which seems a little unfair when the same measure of brandy corresponds to 120. Precise instructions are given for the mixing both of a Satan's Whisker cocktail and of builder's concrete. Weather, finally, receives much attention; it was doubtless comforting to know that 'areas of high pressure are the precise opposite of low pressure'.

But even the 1955 *Week-End Book*, from which these last gems have been mined, is already half a century old. This new edition which you have in your hands is the first for those same fifty years; in other words, the gap between it and its predecessor is far, far longer than that separating any two previous editions. But the spirit, I am relieved to find, is unchanged. And the advice proffered remains as sensible as ever: 'DON'T cook and attempt to eat young bracken shoots because the Japanese do. What suits the hardy races of the extreme East may not suit you'. On the other hand, 'Mice cooked in honey should be imported from China, not prepared at home.'

So what, finally, *is* the 2005 edition of this extraordinary work? An exercise in nostalgia? A brave and brilliant attempt to present an old and tried formula in today's colours? Or something between the two? I will leave you to judge.

Have a good weekend.

John Julius Norwich

KALENDAR OF WILD FLOWERS

To see a World in a Grain of Sand
And Heaven in a Wild Flower.
William Blake.

A wilderness of sweets.

Milton.

In the green grass she loves to lie
And there with her fair aspect tames
The wilder flowers, and gives them names.
Andrew Marvell.

No season is dead. In January look for small weeds already flowering, and remember that a weed can be regarded as a flower out of place. GROUNDSEL (1) introduces gold to the year, SHEPHERD'S PURSE (2) has both flowers and seeds, and you will find the first tiny white stars of CHICKWEED (3). This is the main flowering time for CHRISTMAS ROSES (4), though in shelter they may have bloomed earlier. You will find WINTER HELIOTROPE (5) in an old garden and often outside it. YEW (6) and BOX (7) will stiffen a winter posy.

Though most of the dry stems are battered now and berries eaten, save for black IVY berries (8), long grasses still droop gracefully in the lanes. But the best prize is in a cleared patch of copse, for there you will find a few short-stemmed PRIMROSES (9). Pick HAZEL catkins (10) now, and they will soon treble their length and be spilling gold dust in a warm room.

February is often the worst month of winter; but if we use the poet's eye we shall see Spring as the infant that "flutters sudden 'neath the breast of Earth A month before the birth". First of the CROCUSES (1) is the orange; then comes the purple, then the white. There are drifts of SNOWDROPS (2); ACONITES (3) pushing up with the frills of their necks; GORSE (4) on the common, smelling almost warm and summery, and little BARREN STRAWBERRY (5) in the short grass. In the woods DOG'S MERCURY (6) is flowering and HONEYSUCKLE (7) is putting out the first leaves of the year. On chalky soil you will find SPURGE LAUREL (8) on a shady bank, shiny green and poisonous, and very rarely, you will find its sweet smelling cousin, DAPHNE (9). Towards the end of the month FERNS (10) uncoil and DAFFODILS come spearing up—look for one carrying a leaf on its point "stabbing winter at a blow" (11).

DAISIES (1) are out, "smell-less yet most quaint". Let them have first place on the page as on the lawn, where soon they will be beheaded. March is golden: KINGCUPS (2) by the pond; COLTSFOOT (3) along the roadside, and glistening LESSER CELANDINE (4) in the ditch. In the garden daffodils bend stiffly in March winds and, if you know where to look, you will find WILD DAFFODILS (5) in the copse. We may have "blackthorn winter" this month when the BLACKTHORN (6) is snowy, and dry frozen ground—but remember "a peck of March dust is worth a king's ransom". GREEN HELLEBORE (7), wild relation of the Christmas rose, is rare, but you may find it in a chalk wood of the South. Watch the trees: the ALDER (8) hangs down purple catkins, the POPLAR (9) red ones, and the ELMS (10), their twigs rosetted with small flowers, wear the pink-purple bloom of a ripe peach.

April is the great month in the weald. Spring is in the hazel copses, a green mist in the branches, soon to settle as clouds of new leaves. Walk delicately between cushions of primroses and constellations of ANEMONES (1). You will find the EARLY PURPLE ORCHIS (2) with spotted leaves; LADY'S SMOCKS (3) silver-white in the shade, but pinker where the sun can reach them; and DOG VIOLETS (4) and GROUND IVY (5), both purple-blue. There may be a patch of WILD GARLIC (6) but walk round it, for if it is bruised its onion smell will drown the better scents of spring. Watch for delicate WOOD SORREL (7) in a bed of moss, with its veined white flowers and the young leaves neatly folded down on their pink stems like a shut parasol. PERIWINKLE (8) likes a half-shady bank, and the brittle STITCHWORT (9) stars a sunny one. At the fringe of the wood look up for WILD CHERRY blossom (10), and shell pink CRAB APPLE (11) buds.

May is pink and blue and gold, with YELLOW ARCHANGEL (1) for her herald: BLUEBELLS (2) in the woods; magenta CAMPION (3) in the clearings; BUGLE (4) with its blue flowers and shiny bronze leaves, and YELLOW PIMPERNEL (5). You may chance on WOODRUFF (6), one of the Bedstraws, with white waxen flowers and leaves arranged in ruffs round the stem. The GREATER CELANDINE (7), no connection of the Lesser but really a poppy, is the early southern flower with yellow juice and because of that property it was, redundantly, used in treating jaundice. You will find it growing on a bank usually near a farm or village. A field pond may be shining white with WATER CROWFOOT (8), a buttercup, which gets the best of two worlds with sturdy leaves above and trailing threadlike leaves below the water. Notice small GERMANDER SPEEDWELL (9) under the hedge, with flowers of heavenly blue. Best of all, the COWSLIPS (10) are out.

In June hay rises to its flood, almost submerging the rose-embroidered hedgerows. It is the high month for daisies and buttercups and cloves, for grasses dusty with pollen as mauve as the FIELD SCABIOUS (1). But climb up past the hay, up the edge of the plough—you may find HEARTEASE (2) in passing—to the open down, and lie on a warm turf. There you will smell THYME (3) and, head near the ground, look down the purple veined throat of EYEBRIGHT (4) and watch butterflies on the pink stars of CENTAURY (5). The ROCK ROSES (6) will be out, their petals like crumpled yellow silk, and MILKWORT (7) crimson and blue. Perhaps you will find a BEE ORCHIS (8) or CLUSTERED BELL-FLOWER (9). Certainly there will be BUGLOSS (10), royal blue and scratchy, very hard to pick, and wine red SALAD BURNET (11). As you descend to the valley again through a dim hanging wood search for HERB PARIS (12)—one day you will find it.

In July, be proud, and walk nose in air for the scent of lime blossom. Wander by a fen river or chalk stream and you will find PURPLE LOOSESTRIFE (1) spearing up through the meadow-sweet. Look for handsome ARROWHEAD (2); FLOWERING RUSH (3); MIMULUS (4) cool and juicy with its feet in the water; little CREEPING JENNY (5) and water FORGET-ME-NOT (6) between the rushes on the edge of the bank. Or if the water meadows are

STRAWBERRIES (7) under a bower of HONEYSUCKLE (8).

But if you cannot go to the country at all, picnic on a bombsite near St Paul's before they are all built over. There among the willowherb and ragwort you will find EVENING PRIMROSES (9), and BINDWEED (10) with fragile snowy trumpets, using rusty wire for trellis. Next month the willowherb fluff will be blowing between the buses.

August is the month for the harvest flowers, though with cleaner seed much beauty has been exchanged for more bread. Cornfields seldom harbour POPPIES (1) now, nor blue cornflowers. The wine red CORNCOCKLE (2), once so common, is becoming rare. Look along the roadsides for WHITE CAMPION (3); golden spires of TOADFLAX (4); for great-mullein, grey Goliath of the hedgerow, and its smaller purple-eyed cousin, DARK MULLEIN (5). On the moors listen to bees in BELL HEATHER (6). Eat BILBERRIES (7) while you look for a small parasite, LESSER DODDER (8), wound on a furze bush like a pink cocoon. Squelch through a brown bog to seek GRASS OF PARNASSUS (9); pink BOG PIMPERNEL (10), and insect catching SUNDEW (11). A fly settling on a sundew leaf is caught in the sticky hairs, and the leaf curls over and digests it. In wiry turf there grow slender ST JOHN'S WORT (12) and blue HAREBELLS (13) that rustle if you shake them.

If you go to the sea in September and walk above the ride-rim you may find growing among dusty pebbles and dry seaweed and litter a golden horned SEA POPPY (1)—it has been flowering all summer and now its horns are long—and SEA HOLLY (2), which is really a thistle, all the colours of sea on a cloudy day. In crevices of cliff rocks SAMPHIRE (3) grows right down to high-water mark. It is a seaside relation of the parsleys with

flowers of THRIFT (4) and white SEA CAMPION (5) which had their gay season in June. In a marsh behind dunes you may come on patches of shrubby BOG MYRTLE (6) which smells sweet as you run your fingers through it. Up on the short grass of flanking headlands look for the little white orchis of September, the twisting LADY'S TRESSES (7). SEA LAVENDER (8) and PRICKLY SALTWORT (9) belong to the mud flats of the East coast.

11

October is the month of chestnut harvest. Who does not stoop for a CONKER (1)? SWEET CHESTNUTS (2) should be gathered too, and roasted if possible in a log fire.

The colour of the year is changing: scarlet, unseen in spring, rare in summer, is becoming the focal point of the hedge's colour scheme. The WOODY NIGHTSHADE berries (3) are shiny red and squashy, and SPINDLEBERRIES (4) have split to show the orange seed inside the bright pink cases. Unnoticeable in spring, Spindle is now the glory of any chalk lane. Look for WILD HOP (5) decorating the hedges; PELLITORY (6) growing between the stones of an old wall, and neat white SNEEZEWORT (7), last to bloom in the year's succession. The STINKING IRIS (8), growing on the edge of woods in a limestone district, had dully greyish-mauve flowers, but now its fat seed-cases have split into three parts, each showing a double row of brilliant orange seeds that will last through the winter in your room.

Squirrels must hurry, and we too, for the last of the hedgerow harvest. As you peer in the bushes to see if just one hazel nut has been left, look under the yellow leaves for spring catkins, packed tight for winter storms. You may find a few BEECH NUTS (1), but only every five or seven years is there a heavy crop of beech mast. Nuts may be scarce, but as birds have no storage arrangements there are plenty of berries still: scarlet HIPS (2) and claret HAWS (3), which will serve for food, but only in dull quantities, PRIVET berries (4), like old-fashioned packets of black-headed pins, and ELDER-BERRIES (5) hanging in heavy clusters. HONEY-SUCKLE berries (6) are rose-red and glassy, the berries of BRYONY (7) red and orange and yellow, and bitter black SLOES (8) are ripe. It is a very red and black and gold month. Trails of BLACKBERRY (9) make a good if scratchy decoration. Frothing over nearly every lane is OLD MAN'S BEARD (10). Another name for this wild clematis is Traveller's Joy.

A bunch picked in December has line, not colour, and is a prickly and fragile load. Seek HOGWEED (1) stripped like a scarecrow's umbrella, and bleached NIPPLEWORT (2), SELF-HEAL (3), still neat, and KNAPWEED's ragged cups (4). PLANTAIN (5) is as erect as ever and WOODSAGE (6) keeps its summer curve. These will make a brown etching on your mantelshelf and their shadows will double your design. You may find TEASEL (7) towering over some rough patch, with spines as fierce as when they protected the tiny mauve flowers from insects' feet in July—the "Fullers' Teasel", once used to raise nap on cloth. Stretch for a bunch of ASH seeds (8) and pick up a blown-down twig from the high SCOTS PINE (9). Though the beech trees are bare, the HEDGE BEECH (10) still has leaves to rustle, and OAK leaves (11) cling curled as if carved by Grinling Gibbons. Do not forget the Christmas-pudding HOLLY (12), and perhaps you can claim a sprig of MISTLETOE (13) from an old cottage apple tree.

14

ALL CREATURES THAT
ON EARTH DO DWELL

A dewdrop like a looking-glass. A hair like golden wire.

Great things are done when men and mountains meet;
This is not done by jostling in the street.

Blake.

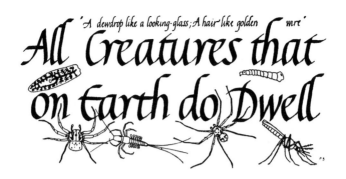

All Creatures that on Earth do Dwell

'A dewdrop like a looking-glass; A hair like golden wire'

SUPPOSE we go walking in the English countryside. Its pleasing pattern lies all about us: woods, meadows, valleys, hills. We are aware of the flowers in the hedgerows, the butterflies fluttering about them, the birds in the trees, the crops and beasts in the farmers' fields, the slow-meandering river, the close-cropped Downland, dotted with sheep and quarries, which rises out of the vale. We accept the pattern unquestioningly, in the same way that we accept the ubiquitous summer hum of countless tiny atomies; it is simply part of our background. Nevertheless it will be fun to ask and answer some questions, to try to project our sight *behind* the familiar landscape, into its origins and its history, and to consider how it came about: how geological factors sculpted it, how weather and climate shaped its contours, how living things painted the pattern upon it, and how the most ingenious, adaptable and (so far) the most powerful of these organisms made out of the wilderness his garden and his playground.

You and I are surveyors of these creatures; we had better begin with a moment's reflection upon our own place in the order of things.

Homo sapiens, despite the fact that he is the lord of the earth or at any rate the only creature capable of rationalising a belief that he is so, nevertheless is a newcomer and parvenu. The scientists' best guess is that life has existed on this planet for some 500 million years; Man has strutted here at most for one million, the greater part of which he has spent as a humble competitor with the beasts for a precarious livelihood. The period of his mastery and dominion is measured in mere centuries. It is rather less than a hundred years since he began to understand his own relationship to the innumerable creatures, ranging from the Protozoa consisting of a single cell to the Atlantosaurus 80 feet long, which preceded him upon the earth.

The remains of these creatures, which he has named and classified, are found in the rocks which form the outer crust of the planet. If you take a hammer and chisel to almost any quarry you can break open their sarcophagus, which is older by hundreds of million years than Tutankhamen's. They died in the lakes, seas and swamps of long ago, and the silt or sediment entombed them where they lay. Some rocks, such as chalk, are composed almost entirely of the tiny shells of marine molluscs; others of fish-scales and bones; others of coral; while the seams of coal represent petrified forests and petrified swamps.

These "sedimentary" rocks were deposited in layers, of mud, of limestone, of sand or gravel; so we are able to "date" them by their organic remains, which a Victorian geologist pleasantly described as the footprints of time. For instance, the earliest rocks of all contain the prototypes of Life—shrimp-like creatures, marine worms, Trilobites (resembling our King Crabs) and so on; later come the molluscs, the fishes, the first birds, the great lizards; and so the cavalcade marches on, to mouse and mammoth and at last to man.

From this record Darwin and others drew the conclusion that all existing and extinct creatures were manifestations of a continuous process of evolution. This evolution did not, of course, proceed in a straight line; it was more in the nature of a series of experimental gropings and questings, sometimes in this direction, sometimes in that, sometimes parallel, sometimes divergent. All the experiments did not succeed. The reptiles made two attempts to fly. The first attempt, conducted by the Pterodactyl, was remarkably similar to man's earliest efforts; it involved a launch from a high place and a glide or flutter to a lower one. It failed, so Pterodactyl paid the usual penalty for failure and ceased to be. The next attempt, by Archaeopteryx, was based on sounder principles and resulted in the birds.

Here and there nature's gropings seem to have run parallel

and reached different conclusions which nevertheless have something in common: for example the social communities in an anthill or a beehive, and the social communities in the crowded cities of man.

But it is misleading to use the word "conclusion" in connection with the processes of evolution; for their pattern is one of ceaseless trial-and-error and continual change. Change is the necessary consequence of the unrelenting struggle in which living things have been engaged ever since life began: the struggle of each different organism to adapt itself to the ever-changing environment. It may have taken a million years to modify a leg-muscle for faster running to escape a new foe or to catch a new prey; ten million perhaps to amend the operation of a digestive system to assimilate a new food; twenty million perhaps to get rid of a no-longer-necessary appendage, such as a tail! No matter, *if the amendment was made in time.* If it wasn't made in time, the creature concerned was thrown on the scrap-heap to which the signpost reads Extinct.

Such is the struggle for survival which has been going on ever since life began. *How* it began nobody knows, nor can confidently speculate.

THE SCULPTING OF THE SCENE

THE SCIENTISTS would perhaps have developed a Theory of Evolution a little earlier if the successive rock-formations existed in the form of a vast Neapolitan ice, layer upon layer each neatly superimposed in the order of their antiquity. The sedimentary rocks would of course look like that if earth's history had been a less turbulent one: if the heavings and convulsions, explosions and earthquakes, had not torn apart the strata, folded them, upended them, and here and there even turned them upside down. It is supposed that since the beginning of life there were three major earth-movements, widely separated in time and involving areas equivalent to continents. We cannot easily imagine them, for the earthquakes of today are but "the final murmurs of a great storm" (Professor Dudley Stamp). Those birth-pangs of Alps, Himalayas and Andes may each have continued for centuries. They threw up continents out of oceans; redistributed the seas on the face of the earth; and sent earth-waves running round the world like giant ripples. Such a ripple determined roughly the shape of that gently rolling Down which lies before us as we set off upon our walk in the country.

Its contours make for easy walking. This is generally the case where the rock beneath is of the "sedimentary" kind, fairly soft and easily weathered. But there is another kind of rock. Into the fissures and folds caused by the surface-splitting flowed lava, molten and plastic minerals, the "magma" of which the bowels of the earth are composed. Cooling, it formed the igneous (fire-wrought) and volcanic rocks, which are generally hard and uncompromising, good for climbers, bad for fossil hunters (for if any living things were engulfed in the molten flow the heat has utterly destroyed them). You will find such rocks as these in the West Highlands, in the Lake District, in the Pennines, in Ireland and Wales, and here and there (as at Malvern) rising unexpectedly out of a plain. Being so hard, they are necessarily rugged; the rain, ice and snow of long geological ages have failed to rub smooth their jagged outcrops and sharp peaks.

But upon the landscape as a whole the physical forces which we lump together as "weather" have acted powerfully to modify and amend the results of the ancient cataclysms. Expansion and contraction, due to heat and cold, have caused mountains to "peel" and split. The sand-papering action of moraines and glaciers has worn away the sides of the valleys. Rock-falls and silting have dammed rivers to create lakes. The polar ice has advanced and retreated, each time leaving behind it an altered scene. Seas have flowed in and out of the low-lying areas: estuaries have silted up, islands have emerged. Everywhere the watercourses have carved their hieroglyphs great and small.

Most of these processes are still going on. Mountains are being denuded, rocks laid down, and fossils formed, including those of our skeletal selves. But the contemporary eye is not equipped to record happenings so gradual. The geologist's understanding of time requires to be somewhat godlike: he must think of a million years as a very short space indeed. "A thousand ages in Thy sight Is like an evening gone."

THE LIVING THINGS

ALL THE TIME, while earth movements and climate changes have been going on, life has pullulated, evolving a series of organisms infinitely various in shape and function, "multiplex of wing and eye", furred, feathered, scaly, armoured, creeping, floating, swimming, flying, creatures of soil, sea and air—the mind boggles at their diversity.

Now the influences which *shaped* the landscape also determined what kinds of creatures should inhabit it: soil, rainfall, temperature, altitude and many other factors dictated the pattern of life in any given place. For instance, if we compare the sheep-cropped Downland, which we glanced at earlier, with our memories of similar hill-country in, say, Devon, Surrey or Scotland, we may wonder why no heather grows upon it. This is because heather likes an acid or peaty soil, and cannot grow on limestone, which is alkaline. In consequence our Downs will show us no heather-loving insects or birds. All living things exist in a complex relationship not only to their environment but to each other. They are competitors for food, space, water, air, sun; they are preyed upon or predatory, or parasites one of another; interacting, interdependent. Biologists use the term ecology for the study of these fascinating relationships. It is a comparatively new science, covering a huge field which we have only just begun to explore; but we cannot look at any country scene without being aware of the interacting relationships and seeing some of the effects of them.

For example, an extremely small organism, the virus which produces myxomatosis, has nearly wiped out the rabbit-population in many parts of England. The grass grows more freely in the

can also grow corn crops or vegetables in some places where it was too risky to plant them before; and thus, perhaps, the whole aspect of the landscape is changed. So much for the effects which we can *see*. But there must be other effects which we are as yet unaware of: the creatures which prey upon rabbits (foxes, badgers, buzzards) will be compelled to seek other food. They will prey upon other animals or birds, and possibly in time may seriously reduce the numbers, or even threaten the existence, of some species to which the rabbit stood in no direct relationship at all.

There is a very rare and lovely butterfly, the Large Blue, which exists in precarious colonies here and there in two or three English counties. The caterpillar feeds on wild thyme; but when autumn comes it falls to the ground and is picked up by ants, which carry it into their anthills not, as you might suppose, for the purpose of devouring it but to keep it alive as a source of some sticky sweet secretion which the ants love. For this reason they cherish their captive, feeding it upon their own offspring, the tiny ant-grubs which are less precious to them than the stuff which they "milk" from the caterpillars. In the spring the caterpillars crawl forth, turn into chrysalises, and ultimately hatch out as Large Blue butterflies. The butterfly therefore requires for its continued existence (a) the wild thyme and (b) the ant, to be present in conjunction; its caterpillar could not survive the English winter without the shelter of the anthill. Here is a very intricate relationship not of predator and prey but of mutual benefactors. It is called symbiosis. The butterfly, however, *is* the victim of a predator—Man with his butterfly-net; for it is now so rare that single specimens fetch 5s. each. The farmer with his ploughs and his tractors also threatens its existence, destroying both thyme and anthills. So the Large Blue, which has become too specialised to adapt itself to changing circumstances, may shortly join upon the scrap-heap the millions of failures labelled Extinct.

There is yet another relationship, of parasite to host:

Big fleas have little fleas upon their back to bite 'em.
And little fleas have lesser fleas and so ad infinitum.

The "wiser" parasites do not destroy their hosts: the louse which sucks the blood impartially of man and of man's foe the rat does little harm to either unless it happens to be infected with another and deadlier parasite, the bacillus of typhus. The Ichneumon fly allows its victims to live for just so long as it has use for them. It lays its eggs under the skin of the Cabbage Butterfly, the grubs hatch out and feed upon the caterpillar's tissues but do it no mortal harm until they are ready to vacate its dying body. Were it not for Ichneumons, Man would probably have found it impossible to grow cabbages; at any rate until he discovered DDT, which is another story.

Two parasites working in association are at present altering the appearance of much of the English landscape: the fungus which causes elm-disease, and the bark-boring beetle which carries the spores of the fungus from tree to tree. In the course of time the elms become rotten and unsafe; the gales bring them down or they are felled by the landowners. In many parts they were the only tall hedgerow trees, and their disappearance makes the country look very bare. One misses, too, the clamour of the rookeries in March. Possibly the passing of the great elms may result here and there in a local reduction in the rook-population: and fewer rooks may also mean more wire-worms and less corn, for ecological changes have chain-reactions of which we cannot easily predict the end.

Our stretch of Downland, dotted with quarries and sheep, provides perhaps the best example of a long chain of cause-and-effect. The limestone in the quarries is composed of tiny grains rather like fish-eggs and consequently called Oolite; it also contains the calcified remains of the creatures that swam in the seas 200 million years ago. Now this stone crumbles at the surface, where it is exposed to the action of the weather, into a reddish-brown soil which countrymen call foxes' mould because it is often seen piled up outside the earths of foxes. A particular kind of grass, called Fescue, grows best upon this porous, limey soil, and Fescue happens to provide excellent grazing for sheep. When the great wool boom occurred in the fourteenth and fifteenth centuries huge flocks were pastured on the Downs. Stone walls were built to keep them apart and later, when the wool-growers and wool-staplers had made great fortunes, the craft of the quarryman was employed to build the fine manor houses and the great churches of the Cotswolds.

They have a saying in those parts, that "the sheep built the churches". But we can go back farther than the sheep and see the churches as the end-result of a chain of circumstance which started with the little creatures swimming or floating in the Mesozoic sea:

Marine creatures—limestone—foxes' mould—fescue grass—sheep—rich men—

and so to the handiwork of the servants of the rich men, the noble square towers which lord it over "the hundred little towns of stone Which nestle in the western wold".

LANDSCAPE, then, is the product of circumstance: of geological happenings, historical accidents, and of the interaction of all the warring, struggling, fiercely competing organisms which at any moment make up the sum total of Life. But, as we remarked at the beginning, there is one organism which by its ingenuity and its predominance exerts a greater influence upon its environment than any other. That creature is Man; and the time has come to consider those aspects of the country scene which have resulted from the toil of his hands and the cunning of his mind.

THE GREEN AND PLEASANT LAND
AND HOW IT CAME TO BE SO

How blessed is he, who leads a country life
Unvex'd with cares, and void of strife!

Dryden.

A fool sees not the same tree that a wise man sees.

Blake.

A flowery, green, bird-singing land.

W. H. Davies.

the Green and Pleasant Land

*How blessed is he who leads a country life
unvex'd with anxious cares, & void of Strife'*

OF BRITAIN'S 56 million acres 45 million are used for agriculture; one third of these are under the plough. The uncultivated areas, the "highlands" and rough heaths, lie mainly to the west of a line drawn from the mouth of the Tees to the mouth of the Exe, which roughly divides the country into two halves. To the east of that line cultivation is practically continuous; pastoral England is really an immense garden. So in fact is a large part of the temperate and a small part of the tropic world. The landscape-gardener is Man. His necessities chiefly, to a lesser degree his sports and pastimes, and his aesthetic appreciation least of all, have dictated the design. In his self-appointed task he has been sometimes helped, sometimes hindered, by a host of his fellow-inhabitants of the planet: viruses, bacilli, plants, trees, insects, birds and beasts.

Possibly he has been hindered more than helped. There is a tale told of a country vicar who was congratulating one of his parishioners upon the tidiness and fertility of his little plot, recently reclaimed from a patch of wasteland. Next Sunday was Harvest Festival. We must go to church and thank God for these fruits of His bountiful earth." "Yes indeed," replied the gardener dutifully, "but you ought to have seen what this here piece was like when the Almighty had it on his own."

THE WILDERNESS THAT WAS

IN SUCH a condition was the greater part of Britain during Shakespeare's lifetime: when Michael Drayton surveyed it in his long topographical poem *Poly-Olbion*. Pastoral settlements were

27

scattered here and there, mainly in the neighbourhood of the towns; but these were not "farms" as we know them.

Probably the only areas which looked much the same as they do today were the sheep-raising Downs (though much of our present-day Downland is corn-growing); the rugged mountains and rough heaths of the north and west; and the great oak woods such as the New Forest—where you can still look upon scenes practically identical with those which would have met the eye of a shipwright in, say, 1580, as he searched for stern-posts for the ships which eight years later destroyed the Armada.

But although Elizabethan England was much forested, tended woods with tall trees were comparatively few. The charcoal burners had made inroads upon them; and great tracts of the country were covered with tangled scrub composed of hawthorn, small birches, brambles and stunted, crooked oaks. This was the "woodland waste"; and you may imagine it as resembling that "part of a Heath with a Hovel" in *King Lear* which was Edgar's home: "*Through the sharp hawthorn blows the cold wind.*" The lower grounds consisted of bog, malarial fen and rushy marsh; for the rivers which we now confine in deep narrow courses ran much shallower, and spilled over a wider area, often dividing into separate rivulets. In winter and early spring the silted channels could not carry away the mass of water that poured down from the hills, and the floods spread far and wide. Even in the places unaffected by flooding the lack of drainage caused rainwater to lie for months. These areas became reed-beds, impenetrable as jungles except by the fowler with his punt; you can see what they looked like at Wicken in Cambridgeshire, which is now preserved as a sanctuary for the disappearing fauna and flora of the Fens.

Nowadays we think of the "unspoilt countryside" as something idyllic: it was not considered so in Shakespeare's day. Blasted heaths, bogs, and the nearly-impassable roads through the forest were regarded with dismay, and travellers were pitied whose paths lay among them. The lord's demesne, with its safety and its orderliness and a good high wall enclosing it, was the kind of "country" that was most admired; and the well-tilled fields of peasant farmers came a good second. When Shakespeare in *Henry the Fifth* described the war-wasted fields of France he found no loveliness in the "fallow leas" which

> The darnel, hemlock and rank fumitory
> Doth root upon,

and it was always Man's handiwork, not Nature's, which seemed beautiful to him:

> The even mead, which erst brought sweetly forth
> The freckled cowslip, burnet and green clover,
> Wanting the scythe, all uncorrected, rank,
> Conceives by idleness; and nothing teems
> But hateful docks, rough thistles, kecksies, burs,
> Losing both beauty and utility.

Those lines describe precisely the condition to which the land returns if even for a season the husbandmen cease to till it or to graze it with their beasts. Within two or three seasons the scrub encroaches upon it and, as the drains become blocked, the marsh-vegetation begins to claim the low-lying areas. If husbandry suddenly ceased in Britain, Nature would win back her wilderness in less than ten years: woodland waste on the higher ground, reeds and bogs in the parts which lie in flood's way. Such is the patter of "unspoilt Nature" in temperate climates; and it does not make a green and pleasant land.

THE COLOURED COUNTIES

FOR CONTRAST, let us now look about us at the modern scene—at that stretch of pleasant, pastoral and gently undulating countryside somewhere in the heart of England which we chose for our leisurely walk on a summer's day. Within it, Nature is expelled, whenever necessary, not with a fork only but with a tractor-drawn plough, a bulldozer, a rotary cultivator or a poison spray; and we take good care that she does not come back again.

The underlying theme, the *motif* of the landscape is the green-brown-yellow of "mixed" farming: smallish fields growing a rotation of crops, divided by hedges chiefly of hawthorn. But England is a hotch-potch of scenery as it is of soil, and often

29

within a few miles the pattern of the fields changes half a dozen times: from arable to meadowland, from orchards, say, to hopyards, from market-gardens to Downs. Scattered here and there in between the cultivations are the relics of a previous landscape: some left-over fragments of that England of the squires which was not wholly agricultural. For instance there are parks with isolated trees and ornamental shrubberies of rhododendrons, woods laid out for the convenience of a Master of Foxhounds, avenues planted perhaps to celebrate an heir's coming-of-age, spinneys situated so as to please a lordling's eye or to conceal from his windows the distasteful sight of human habitation other than his own. There are also occasional furzey commons and village greens which somehow survived the Acts of Enclosure. There are osier-beds, willow-fringed pools, disused canals, slow-running rivers in the vale and swifter trout-streams in the hills. Railways with their flowery cuttings and embankments, old lanes and newer motor-roads, criss-cross the land. There are villages built of stone, brick, flint, half-timber-and-thatch; churchyards with their grave chestnuts and yews, churches with towers or spires, farmsteads, byres, barns, oasthouses, rickyards, cottages …

The sum of all these familiar things makes up the pattern which we know as the English Countryside. We are so used to it that we are apt to forget it is a very recent pattern; even the patchwork of the fields has existed for less than two centuries. The oldest man-made features in our landscape are probably the churches; a few are Saxon, many are Norman, but the majority were built later than 1400. We shall be hard put to it to find many traces of man's presence on the scene before the time of William the Conqueror. Here and there ancient burial places are marked by barrows and tumuli; here and there as at Stonehenge the old altars still stand. There are the White Horses on the Downs, and the enormous Long Man at Cerne Abbas, a naked giant 200 feet high brandishing a club. These are much more than mere scrawls on the green turf and the white chalk; they are man's first signature upon the scene. It was a primitive scene, in which he lived precariously among wild beasts, devils and gods; he put his bold mark upon it in affirmation that it was his. The White Horse at Wantage is nearly 400 feet long, and you can see it for 15 miles.

It is thought to have been set there by Alfred the Great to commemorate his victory over the Danes. More than a thousand years later his countrymen, being threatened by another invasion, were put to some trouble and expense to cover it up lest it serve as a landmark for their airborne foes.

Fortifications, both Roman and British, have left a few scratches on some of our hilltops; some sections of Hadrian's Wall and Offa's Dyke remain. There are also the great military roads of the Romans, which run like steel rulers across the country: Ermine Street, Akeman Street, the three Watling Streets, the Fosse Way. They look straight on the spot but not on the map— for they were sighted line by line from one hilltop to another. Sometimes two gangs working in opposite directions failed to make good their meeting-place, and there was a kink in the road—a kink which remains in the modern motor-road that we have built on top of it.

In places these Roman roads have disappeared, under the plough or in woodland; but even so you can often trace their course from the air. Flying over them, you see what a hovering eagle might have seen, in the time of the Emperor Claudius! To a small extent they have had a share in the shaping of our modern landscape; not only do they form part of our road system, but they have determined the siting of some of our towns. It is doubtful if Cirencester would stand where it does today if the Fosse Way and the Akeman Street hadn't happened to intersect at a spot which the Romans called Corinium.

But for the most part, the marks which man's handiwork left upon the landscape in Roman, Saxon, and even Norman times were scattered, few and faint except in the neighbourhood of the towns. The "country" remained under nature's stern dominion; and we scarcely began even to challenge that dominion until the Middle Ages had gone by.

THREE BAGS FULL

THE FIRST effective weapon which man employed in his battle with nature was not his spade, his axe, or even his wooden plough, but his domesticated herbivorous animals. The grazing of cattle, horses and especially sheep won more acres from the wasteland than all his digging and ploughing. So the first great

31

change which came over certain parts of England in the fifteenth and sixteenth centuries was due to the wool boom which occurred when the exiled Huguenots taught their first English pupils the arts of weaving. The flocks grazing on the uplands cropped close the rank grasses and fertilised the thin chalky soil: furze, bracken and scrub retreated before them. The shepherds began to build their dry-stone walls, getting their stone from the handy outcrops or hewing it from quarries. These stone walls gave to the landscape of our Downs a distinctive character which hasn't changed much since 1500; probably many of them follow the same course today over the hills' broad shoulders as they did then. The craftsmen in stone were ready at hand when (as we have seen) the wool-merchants grew rich and sought to spend their new wealth on the lovely and lasting things. So the bare hills blossomed during those two centuries which were England's spring: the tall churches sprang up, the manor-houses four-square to all the winds that blew; the little grey villages huddled about them. If you stand on Cotswold now your view will be much the same as that which William Grevel, *flos mercantorum*, looked upon as he watched the sheep grazing in his huge pastures (about the time when Chaucer was writing *The Canterbury Tales*) and followed with his eye the straggling line of the stone-walls to the great tower of his own proud church at Chipping Campden.

WHEN ADAM DELVED

EXCEPT where the sheep flourished, farming continued to be localised, scattered and on a primitive scale.

During the Middle Ages the Black Death had decimated the rural population, and it took a century to recover from that disaster. Thereafter the recurring plague, typhus and the enormous infant mortality, kept down the numbers to about 4 million, which was the total when Elizabeth I came to the throne.

(Here are some more examples of very small organisms producing a large effect upon their environment. The virus that caused the Black Death, the bacilli of Bubonic plague and typhus, the louse that carried the latter, the black rat that carried both, caused the deaths of so many peasants that there were not enough left to cultivate even the small acreage which they had won from the waste; and some of this land slipped back into its weedy anarchy.)

During the next two centuries the population increased; but agricultural methods remained primitive, communications and transport were appallingly difficult, and even the main roads were often impassable in winter; so the face of England did not change much except in a few places where the multiplying peasants were able to steal back a piece of good land from the waste, or a prosperous landowner with plenty of labour at his disposal decided to increase the area of his demesne. In the seventeenth and early eighteenth centuries the process of bringing land under cultivation went on very slowly in relation to the increase in population; it was a gradual erosion, a nibble here, a nibble there, and much less extensive than the deforestation caused earlier by the charcoal-burners. There was no radical change in the practice of farming. When at last it did happen it was sudden, thorough-going and complete, and it transformed in about 80 years the whole aspect of England.

TRANSFORMATION SCENE

EVEN as late as 1700 the proportion of arable land was very small in relation to the pasture. Sheep grazed the Downs, as we have seen, and the river meadows, enriched by winter flooding, provided summer grazing for cattle as well as hay; the woodland afforded acorns and beech-nuts for swine. The arable, mostly in the neighbourhood of villages, consisted generally of three largish unfenced fields cultivated in parallel strips. Each season one of these fields would be sown with wheat or rye; another with oats, barley, beans or peas; the third remained fallow, providing a triennial rotation of crops.

Here and there in England you still can see traces of this open field cultivation in the curved ridges or "lands" which run lengthwise down some of our pastures. When you walk across a field which has a surface resembling a series of waves, you can be pretty sure that this was one of the pieces of arable.

The peasant-farmers did not hold adjacent strips, but separate ones in different parts of each field, so that every individual had his share both of the good and the less good land. The strips were divided by baulks or unploughed strips of green turf; these are

33

the "ridges" which you see today. There were no fences or hedges. Consequently there had to be common agreement about how the land should be used; for of course animals could not be turned into any part of the field until the last crop had been gathered in. There was therefore little natural manuring, and drainage was to say the least of it chancy, since any strip-owner by negligence or malice might block the outfall of his neighbours' ditches. Now towards the end of the seventeenth century, when the rise in population increased the demand for produce, the strip-owners began to find an advantage in cultivating all their strips together. There was less waste (for the baulks could be ploughed and cultivated) and when each man's land was fenced he was free to use his piece in whatever fashion best profited him. So the separate strips were exchanged for adjoining ones (doubtless after some hard bargaining) and the first hedges appeared. The cultivated part of the landscape—still a very small proportion—began to take on the patchwork appearance which gives the countryside its character today. What had been essentially a feudal landscape (though continuing long past feudal times) became suddenly a capitalist landscape; and each little patch, differing from its neighbours in size and shape, became an expression of the individuality of the little capitalist who cultivated it.

At first the process was slow and the changes local; but here and there between 1680 and 1750 there began to emerge a shape and pattern which we should have recognised as a sort of blueprint of the modern English scene. The "parallel" landscape was broken up, and became a higgledy-piggledy one; not only were the big open fields divided into rectangles and even triangles, but a new diversity entered into the farmers' methods and their choice of crops. In 1724 turnips were first grown in the fields as winter-feed for cattle; clover suddenly came into favour for the same purpose. The fresh green of the turnip leaves, the warm reddish-purple of the clover and vetches, alternated with the rusty yellow of the ripening corn as it does in England today. The land lost its sameness, and the "coloured counties" became a fact.

During the next 70 years the pace of these changes quickened, as diehard farmers and diehard landlords faded from the scene. Evolution became revolution. Early in the eighteenth century

Jethro Tull invented his new plough and the first effective seed-drill. Lord Townshend, nicknamed "Turnip", introduced the Four Course system of cultivation which substituted for the year of fallow a crop of turnips and so increased the productivity of the land by a third. Meanwhile Bakewell of Leicestershire began his campaign for the improvement of the English flocks and herds. He bred for uniformity, quick maturing, and good meaty joints, and created the first modern breed of sheep, the Leicester. The brothers Collins on Tees-side followed suit with cattle, and by careful selection established the breed of Shorthorns. A great landlord, Coke of Holkham in Norfolk, demonstrated how to reclaim a sandy waste by heavy manuring and by planting shelter-belts of trees. (His trees still stand at Holkham, his living memorial.) An ingenious fellow called Small, who was not a farmer, turned his attention to the old-fashioned plough and invented a vastly improved one.

It has been said that Tull produced the bread and Bakewell produced the meat which made it possible for Britain to become an industrial country. In fact these lively-minded and far-seeing countrymen not only changed the whole aspect of rural England but created the conditions which resulted in the dark satanic mills, the slag-heaps and the pit-heads of the Industrial Revolution.

The immediate effect of their inventions and improvements was to treble or quadruple the productivity of any given piece of land. In theory Britain could already support a large population; in practice the cultivated land was not available. But as food prices rose it became worth while for the first time to bring into cultivation the waste and the marshes, where large-scale drainage now proceeded apace. The commons and the open fields were enclosed, and the peasant farmers, who could not afford the new machines, were mostly dispossessed and became labourers upon what had been their own land.

For those who lived through it the transformation of England must have been astonishing indeed; no scenic change has ever happened so quickly. Within a man's lifetime most of the fens and much of the woodland disappeared, the countryside became criss-crossed with a myriad hedges, the new multi-coloured crops filled the new arable fields, barns and byres,

35

hayricks and straw-ricks grew up like mushrooms where none had been before, and for the first time in English history fat cattle and sheep went to Christmas market down the muddy lanes. The services of Peter Piper with his peck of pickled pepper were no longer required; for it had ceased to be necessary to kill off in autumn the stock which was not needed for breeding and to salt and spice the meat so that it would keep until the spring.

The revolution, of course, brought prosperity to a few but misery and poverty to many more. The Acts of Enclosure which ruined the peasant farmers made petty squires enormously rich. A lampooner wrote:

> The law locks up the man or woman
> Who steals the goose from off the common,
> But leaves the greater villain loose
> Who steals the common from the goose.

Here and there, as a direct consequence of the Enclosures, whole villages ceased to be. Oliver Goldsmith in 1770, complaining that "all the bloomy flush of life is fled", wrote of a *Deserted Village*:

> But a poor peasantry, their country's pride,
> When once destroy'd, can never be supplied …

and he went on to praise the pleasures of the frugal country life which, he imagined, the simple peasant had enjoyed before:

> For him light labour spread her wholesome store,
> Just gave what life requir'd, but gave no more;
> His best companions, innocence and health;
> And his best riches, ignorance of wealth.

If this were so, he could be ignorant of wealth no longer. He could see all round him how rascals thrived, greedy men prospered, little tyrants became great tyrants, while poor and honest men went down. The history of the English countryside during those 70 hectic years is one of cut-throat competition resulting in the survival of the fittest—or perhaps the most acquisitive. It is a tale of neighbours' squabbles, endless litigation, and plain rapine: an unlovely turmoil out of which emerged the lovely pattern of pastoral England.

THE LEGACY OF LEISURED FOLK

HUSBANDRY was the main though not the only cause of the transformation. When the huge task of feeding 10 million people instead of 4 million had been achieved with the aid of new inventions and new ways, some other factors came into play which helped to shape the modern countryside. The most important of these were rich men and sport. Both the Agricultural and Industrial Revolutions threw up *nouveau riche* classes, some of whom invested their quickly-earned money in great estates. These new landed gentry were very much richer than the old squires and even the old nobility had been. (It was the view of the Meltonians about 1820 that a man could "jog along all right on ten thousand a year".) They possessed the large extravagance which comes with easy money and those of them that were not entirely preoccupied with horseflesh have left their mark upon the land in the form of great country houses, elaborately laid-out gardens, stables, kennels, weird hilltop "follies", spacious parks and so on. They introduced from abroad ornamental trees and shrubs, some of which (such as rhododendrons and certain conifers) have flourished and multiplied. The laying out of parks, with appropriate vistas, mazes, lakes, woodland walks, spinneys and copses was an expensive hobby which has left us a legacy of great loveliness: and when we consider the relation of man to his environment it is amusing to reflect that we owe many delightful clumps of trees to the fact that some arrogant squire couldn't abide the spectacle of his upstart neighbour's new and pretentious dwelling glimpsed across the intervening fields.

The ecology of rich men makes a fascinating study; it is deeply involved with sport. Foxhunters, for example, require largish scattered coverts, good galloping country in between, jumpable but difficult fences, adequate gates, and the absence of barbed wire. Pheasant-shooters must have woods also, but they tend them differently, cutting rides in certain places and using wire-netting for fencing, which foxhunters abhor. They try to arrange the whole lay-out of the coverts in such a fashion that the birds can be driven high over the guns. (There was a lord who conceived the strange desire to drop a pheasant, shot from his favourite stand, upon his own greenhouses at the other side of the valley. He achieved this feat in the end, but it involved planting a completely new covert at the top of the hill to make the pheasants fly high enough!)

Grouse-shooters need very large moorlands upon which they burn the heather from time to time in accordance with a carefully worked-out plan. Deerstalkers demand the preservation in their natural state of the almost tree-less "forests" of Scotland; and so on.

It happens that much of the beauty of the countryside is a direct consequence of the activities of these thoughtless and rather selfish individuals. We are indebted to a few thousand country squires and to their love of guns, dogs and horses for most of our loveliest woodlands, for the preservation of moors, for the fine "bullfinch" sloe-hedges of the Shires, and for the rides and bridle-paths which make it so easy for a walker to go where he will in the country. Other kinds of sportsmen have given us race-courses and golf-courses—and the golfers at any rate have saved thousands of acres of cliff-top, heath and warren from haphazard "development" by the jerry-builder. The cricket field, too, has its place in the country scene; and when cricket is played on village greens we see a reflection of those Acts of Enclosure, for the greens were often pieces of grassland given to the villages in compensation for the expropriated "strips". Cricketers, incidentally, exert another influence upon the landscape, where willows are grown commercially for the purpose of making cricket-bats.

Even fishermen have left their marks upon the scene, for the monks made stew-ponds for their carp, and in recent years salmon-anglers have built weirs and salmon-ladders, and trout-anglers have dammed or diverted small streams, cut waterweeds and reedbeds and trimmed the growth on the banks.

WATERWAYS AND WATERWORKS

ON THE WHOLE the pattern of our rivers and streams is less artificial than that of the land. The great rivers, Humber and Tweed,

Thames and Severn, run much the same courses as they did 500 years ago; Shakespeare's Avon goes down from Stratford through the Vale of Evesham by the same winding way which he knew well. But dredging, better drainage, locks, weirs and flood-gates enable us to control the flow, so that there is less winter flooding and the rivers hold a good head of water even in dry seasons. At Stratford and most of the other "fords" you must cross by the bridge or swim; the river is ten or twelve feet deep where once it was possible to drive a wagon across it in summer-time.

If we have not greatly changed the old waterways, we have at any rate contrived some new ones. The canals by which, until a few years ago, a barge could travel right across England from east to west or north to south provide a curious man-made landscape of their own, utterly different from the landscape of natural streams and rivers. Their low banks are treeless, but have been colonised by the loosestrife and the willowherb which in places form two parallel purple hedges between which the canal runs as straight as a Roman road. There are no pools or rapids; but here and there the unruffled water is gently lifted over a gradient by a series of locks like the steps of a ladder. All the way the towpath goes beside it, like a footpath beside a main road.

These canals were important means of communication before the railways superseded them. A few are still in use; but many have fallen into disrepair, they are choked with weeds, banks are falling in, the locks are broken, and you feel, when you come upon them unexpectedly, as if you had found the remains of an old lost civilisation—which indeed they are.

The engineers who work with water found a bigger job to do long before their canals ceased to be profitable. The population of the great growing cities demanded not only food, but also water from the lakes and rivers. There was rarely enough in the neighbourhood of the cities; so the mountain watersheds must provide it. Thus, to ensure the water supply of Birmingham the engineers blasted away part of a hillside in Wales, built great dams, inundated a valley, obliterated some farms and made at Rhayader a chain of lakes lying between steep hills covered with conifers: a Swiss landscape rather than a British one. Glen Affric in Scotland has been dammed to provide the electrical power for towns hundreds of miles away; other huge schemes are in progress. So industrial man's necessities work changes upon the landscape not only where he lives and labours but on the high hills and bleak moorlands to which even the Agricultural Revolution brought no change.

THE EFFECT OF COMMUNICATIONS

INDUSTRY demanded, as well as food, water and (later) electric power, a network of roads and railways between the cities. MacAdam, Telford, Stevenson played their parts as architects of the modern scene. As each innovation occurred there were sober and thoughtful people who prophesied that it would destroy the countryside. When Mr MacAdam's new roads, about 1800, caused a revolution in travel which enabled the London to Edinburgh mail-coach to do the journey in 62 hours instead of 82, heads were shaken over the possible effects of the fumes of tar. When the railways began to stretch out their tentacles the early Victorians visualised a landscape intersected by steel rods along which the engines snorted between blackened fields. Horses would bolt, cattle stampede, crops would be set on fire. The later Victorians, smelling their first whiff of petrol, predicted that the very herbs of the roadside would droop and wither and the hedges die on account of it. None of these catastrophes happened; and this is worth remembering when we look gloomily into the future and see certain destruction of many a lovely scene. The man-made landscape inevitably changes as man's habits change; but the changes are not always as destructive as we fear. The railways did not spread soot over the fields, the petrol-fumes did not kill the roadside grass; the new pylons that spider the Downs do not, as many predicted, ruin their loveliness. The eye grows used to them, they become a part of the pattern like the railways and the roads.

There are gains as well as losses. The railways have their own characteristic fauna and flora; what child has not been tempted into trespassing past the black notice-board with its forty-shilling warning because of a summer spectacle of poppies and harebells, brimstones and blue butterflies, upon a gorse-dotted embankment beside the line? As for the roads, wherever one runs across country two hedges accompany it. Out of the hedges grow up trees; along the hedge-roots spring up flowers. Some wise and public-spirited authorities plant saplings along the verges, or shrubs in the grassy ribbons between the traffic-lanes. Where this happens, we probably gain more than we lose.

THE EVER-CHANGING SCENE

ONE THING is certain: that we cannot arrest the process of change however much we may wish to do so. For while man holds his dominion over it, landscape is but a reflection of his changing ways. It mirrors his science and his sociology, his customs, sports, economy, his evolutions and revolutions. Every piece of scenery has a tale to tell about these changes. We have seen, for instance, how the stone-walls are related to the economics of sheep-breeding in the fifteenth century, how an avenue of chestnuts may be the legacy of a man who grew rich out of the East India Company, how the hedges are hieroglyphs which explain the Acts of Enclosure, how a spacious park fallen into ruin may be a consequence of the rising surtax during the 1930s.

The story is not ended; and if we now take a look about us at the countryside as it is today we shall see the new changes are taking place and history is still being written upon the farms and the fields.

THE FIELDS AND THE
BEASTS THEREOF

We are assured that the compassion of Heaven will
not be wanting to them.

This is the farmer sowing his corn,
That kept the cock that crowed in the morn.
Nursery Rhyme.

A painted meadow, or a purling stream.
Joseph Addison.

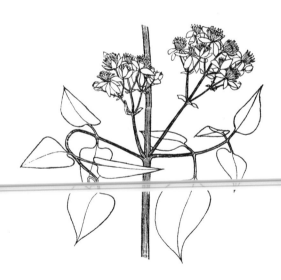

HARVEST
from "The Land" by V. Sackville-West

An English cornfield in full harvesting
Is English as the Bible, though no more
(These clanking times) the gleaners following
The reapers by their rhythm rapt
Plunder the gavels for their little store;
Or the sickle cut the poppies and the corn,
Save when the crop is tangled by a gale,
Beaten by rain, twisted like murdered hair:
Then comes the sickle to its old avail
Crook'd as the young moon in her narrowest horn,
And steals in the poor broken tangle, where
Straightforward knives are parried, and the apt
Inventiveness of man shall not prevail.
Then to the simplest shapes of his first craft,
—Livelihood wrested from the earth that bore,
Cradled, and coffined him,—man shall repair;
Shapes copied from the sky, with cutting edge;
Natural shapes, to meet the natural hitch
Of hindering weather, the permanent enemy;
Then, with the noonscape, underneath the hedge,
His fingers blistered by the rubbing haft,
His shoulders propped by hedge, his feet in ditch,
The random reaper drains his pint of ale.

Look to your stooking, for full many a field
Of hearty grain and straw runs half to waste
Through heedless stooking, and the proper yield
Leaves half its measure to the rook and daw.
But if you'd have full grain and ripened straw,
After a week of drying fit to cart,
Stooker, take up a sheaf in either hand,
Between the ears and band,
And swing them clear, and bring the butts apart
Sharply to ground, ears sloping to a peak,
(Ten sheaves for Kent) clashing together, braced,

So that the little ridge be thatched and sleek,
Firm to the wind, secure to rain and hail,
That winnower and that flail,
Those thieves of harvest, pilfering what they can
In last-hour larceny from rival man.
For nature gives, and nature takes again,
Therefore be eager of her liberal hours;
To drought succeeds the flood, to calm the gale,
And winter's frost lays low the summer's flowers.

Therefore, you harvesters, before the rain
Trample your crop with roguish feet,
Wring what you may, and if too fast and fleet
Even the summer sun describe his arc
Leaving you with your shocks but half-way set,
Be prouder than the punctual rigid clerk,
And stickle not to labour after dark,
For you take nature's orders, he the clock's.
The cooler night shall spare your noonday sweat;
The breeze shall whisper in the rustling shocks;
The moon above the thorn
Rise harvest-tawny on the stubble shorn,
And in the bending lines of girls and men
Some snatch of song be born.
Lovers shall find their magic then,
And jolly farmers wink at privilege;
Only the moon shall look behind the hedge,
Confederate of youth;
Only the moon shall hear the whispered pledge,
Great lyric liar, to a lovelier truth
Transcending, setting purport free,
And touching all things with her alchemy.

The Fields, and the Beasts thereof

'We are assured that the compassion of Heaven will not be wanting to them'

Key: *a* Water Vole; *b* Fox; *c* Otter; *d* Grey Squirrel; *e* Brown Rat; *f* Wild Cat; *g* Fallow Deer; *h* Stoat; *i* Badger; *j* Hedgehog. The drawings are not to scale.

THE ENGLISH HEDGE

BEFORE we look over the hedge at the growing crops and the grazing beasts let us glance for a moment at the hedge itself.

It is really a narrow strip of the natural "forest floor" of England adapted to man's needs. Hedges grow best in those parts of the country which were originally clothed with the "woodland waste" (and to which, if husbandmen ceased to toil, the "woodland waste" would swiftly return). In the places which were bare, or covered with very light scrub, we have to use some other means to divide our fields—stone-walls, for instance, if the quarries are handy. But in most of pastoral England the hedge is the cheapest form of fencing. You do not need to plant it; you have only to prevent the beasts from grazing in the place where you want it to grow. Then up springs the hawthorn and the other sturdy and indestructible plants and shrubs which grow in association with it; the ungrazed, uncultivated strip goes back to its natural state, and within ten years your rough and ready hedge is ten feet tall.

However, the farmer generally improves on nature's version by "laying" his hedges. The stems of the bushes are "nicked" and bent over horizontally, all facing in the same direction *along* the hedge, and then are woven between upright stakes driven in at intervals. This makes the hedge stronger. It is done as a rule every three or four years. The hedges of good farmers are also trimmed

47

every season, which gives them a sturdier growth. Nowadays this job is often done by an ingenious machine which moves parallel with the hedge and chops off the top with rotating knives. A disadvantage of the machine is that it may not spare a likely sapling here and there, as good hedge-cutters generally do, and its use may mean that in a score of years there will be very little hedgerow timber.

The main constituent of most hedges is hawthorn, which of all our native trees loves best the English soil. In some places, notably Leicestershire, it is replaced by the sloe or blackthorn, which makes those great "black" hedges that test the courage of hunting men. ("How on earth do you manage to jump them?" asked an awe-stricken visitor to the Shires about 1820. "We throw our hearts over first and then we follow as best we can.")

Mixed with the hawthorn and the sloe there are generally at least a dozen other shrubs and climbers which have woven themselves into the homogeneous whole: within a few score yards, sometimes, you will find elm, elder, bird-cherry, ash, spindle, sycamore, sallow, willow, dog-rose, privet, wayfaring-tree, honey-suckle, bryony both black and white, bramble, dewberry, and old man's beard. These diverse components paint the hedge a different colour as each season goes by: orange-pink of sallow twigs in the early spring, wine-purple of elm, then the fresh green of the crinkly hawthorn-leaves, sprinkled snow of blackthorn-flowers, curded cream of the may, shell-pink dog-rose in high summer, red autumnal leaves of sycamore, scarlet berries of bryony, purplish-black of elder, pink of spindle—and then when winter comes the fluffy grey-white of the old man's beard.

The hedge, in fact, probably contributes more loveliness to the English scene than any other single feature; what a dull sameness the landscape must have had before the Acts of Enclosure!

But there are fewer hedges in England than there were only a dozen years ago; very soon there may be fewer still. The increase in market-gardening and arable farming generally is partly responsible for this; there is no need for a fence to protect the wheat from the brussels sprouts adjacent to it, and where there is intensive cultivation hedges are wasteful of land. Another cause is the invention of electrified fencing. A single strand of wire, carrying enough current to give a harmless electric shock, can keep a whole herd of hungry cattle from a patch of luscious-looking kale. The advantage to the farmer is that his wire fence is *moveable*. He can change every season, or if he likes every day, the shape and pattern of his fields. He can let his cows into any part of his kale-patch, and bar them from the rest; so that they eat it bit by bit as they need it and do not trample and spoil the whole field. Moreover, because the electrified fence is moved so frequently there is no risk that the thorn and the thistle, those native daemons of the English soil, will spring up beneath it, creating an unwanted hedge—which happens whenever a permanent wire fence prevents the beasts from grazing along the line of the wire.

It is possible that in a few years' time electrified fencing may completely alter the appearance of the land; and that the pastoral scene (coming full circle, as it were) may look much the same as it did when peasant-farmers cultivated the "open field" three or four hundred years ago. Here and there, in the great market-gardening areas around Evesham or Wisbech, you can see what is conceivably the shape of things to come; for the hedges have already disappeared. For the most part, however, the effect of electric fencing is local and confined to the bigger farms; and the lovely patchwork of farming England remains.

THE PATTERN OF THE FIELDS

THIS patchwork pattern is always changing. The large trends of commerce change it: our economics, our emergencies. During world wars we plough up the grassland to grow corn and potatoes; in slumps, when the price of wheat falls steeply, the arable land is turned back to grass. But there is also an annual change in the pattern of any given farm, due to the Rotation of Crops.

Different crops "rob the soil" of different constituents. (For ___ cereals use up a lot of nitrogen, peas and beans use hardly any). So if the same crop is grown on the same patch year after year the soil becomes poor in the particular plant-food which the crop needs most. Also the pests which are specific to that crop flourish and multiply. Therefore the farmer arranges his cropping-plan so that each year for at least four successive years every arable field grows a different crop. The usual "four-course system" runs like this:

Wheat – Turnips – Barley – Clover and Grass.

But there is no hard-and-fast rule so long as the chosen system of cropping does not, as the farmers put it, "take the heart out of the land". The kind of soil, its texture and its thickness, even the weather, may cause a variation in the plan; and some farmers adopt six or seven year rotations such as "oats – beans – wheat – roots – barley – grass".

THE YEAR'S WORK

THE ROTATION of crops also enables the farmer to make the best use of his labour. A year's work in the arable fields may go something like this, but it varies considerably from one district to another and there is no set pattern for the whole country:

January and February:	Carting muck; ploughing
March:	Sowing oats and barley
April:	Planting potatoes and spring wheat
May:	Sowing turnips and swedes
June:	Singling roots: hoeing and other summer cultivation
July:	Haymaking
August:	Corn harvest
September:	Corn harvest and potato lifting
October:	Potato lifting and ploughing
November:	Root lifting and sowing winter wheat
December:	Ploughing and carting muck once again.

That is a fair sample, and it takes no account (for instance) of sugar-beet, nor of silage-making which is now becoming common on many farms throughout the summer.

You must not suppose, however, that these are the farmer's only jobs. His stock must be fed and tended, his cows milked, his machinery kept in order. He must buy and sell, either at market or privately. And his other major tasks include hedgetrimming and laying, ditching, draining, spreading artificial fertilisers or lime, spraying crops and fruit trees, fruit picking and so on. He must be handy with at least ten different sorts of tools and a dozen more or less complicated mechanical implements. He must be a rough carpenter, motor-mechanic, wheelwright, blacksmith, and a bit of a meteorologist, chemist, botanist and biologist as well.

THE CROPS IN THE FIELDS

UNTIL about 1700 the only important farm crops grown in Britain were cereals, beans, peas, and of course, hay. Lord Townshend, whom we mentioned earlier, added turnips to the rotation, and later William Cobbett sang the praises of swedes with as much enthusiasm as that with which he cursed what he called "the ever-damned potato". Despite him potatoes (which had long been a staple crop in Ireland) took their place upon the English farms wherever the land suited them; and during the next 100 years a variety of crops unfamiliar to Englishmen painted the fields as many-coloured as Joseph's coat. Unless you are country-bred you can hardly expect to recognise them all; for even a countryman, unless he looked very carefully, would not easily tell the difference between winter wheat and winter oats pricking the brown fields in spring. Here are some notes, however, which may serve as a rough guide:

Root-crops include turnips, swedes and mangolds, sugar and fodder beet, and kohlrabi. You can tell swedes from turnips because the former have a reddish-purple tinge in the stems and leaves. Turnip leaves are rougher and much less glossy-looking than those of fodder beet, and of mangolds (a cultivated variety of the wild sea-beet) which are also called mangel-wurzels, a bucolic-sounding name which, however, comes from the German and means "root of scarcity". All these roots provide winter feed for stock; they are often stored in clamps which look like long barrows. When the clamps are first opened the young blanched shoots are indistinguishable ... caught the eye of the poet Edward Thomas who promptly wrote his poem "Swedes":

> They have let in the sun
> To the white and gold and purple of curled fronds
> Unsunned. It is a sight more tender-gorgeous
> Than when, in the Valley of the Tomb of Kings,
> A boy crawls down into a Pharaoh's tomb

And, first of Christian men, beholds the mummy,
God and monkey, chariot and throne and vase,
Blue pottery, alabaster and gold ...

Sugar-beet is sent to the factories as soon as the permits arrive after it has been lifted and any time between October and January. Only the tops are fed to the cattle and sheep. As you see it growing in the field you cannot, at a glance, distinguish it from either fodder-beet or mangolds. Kohlrabi is grown only locally, chiefly in Suffolk and Essex. It is a cabbage-like plant with a large white fleshy swelling (erroneously called the root) at the base of the stem. This is the part which is eaten by cattle and sometimes, we think misguidedly, by human beings.

Forage-crops are generally fed to stock in their fresh green state. They include cabbage and kale (like a giant cabbage with crinkly leaves), clover (red or white), lucerne (purple-flowered, grown chiefly on limey land in the south east, fed to milking-cows), vetches, sainfoin (rose-red flowers, chiefly fed to sheep), rape (belongs to the cabbage family, has glaucous smooth leaves like a swede, its seeds are rich in oil), and mustard (bright yellow cruciferous flowers). Mustard is often fed to stock but it also used for "green manuring"—that is to say it is grown simply for the purpose of ploughing it back into the land to increase the content of humus. It grows so fast that it can be put in as an "extra" between a normal rotation; such crops are called *catch-crops*.

Potatoes are grown chiefly for human consumption; only the small ones are used for stock-feed. Almost everybody can recognise a growing crop of potatoes, moulded up into "ridges", but if you present a friend with a single potato-flower, divorced as it were from its context, he is quite likely to pronounce, after careful consideration, that "it is probably an exotic nightshade, grown in a greenhouse". Few people ever really *look* at a potato flower. It is as pretty as many a garden favourite, and is in fact a nightshade, closely related to the Deadly one and also to the tomato. Its berries are said to be poisonous.

Field peas when grown by themselves nowadays are generally for canning or drying; but they form part of some mixed crops which are used for stock-feed, e.g. peas, vetches, oats and beans grown together, which combination in Scotland is called by the pleasant name of Mashlum and in England Dredge Corn.

Beans, called Horse Beans to distinguish them from the garden variety, advertise themselves by the sweet smell of their flowers and the perpetual murmur of bees among them. They are fed to stock, especially to working horses, milch cows and pigs; horses eat the bean straw and it is also used for litter. As a farm crop, beans are less grown than formerly; they were excellent fuel for horses, but are no use in the tanks of tractors.

Grain-crops, the most important next to grass, include wheat, oats, barley and rye. Wheat has an ear of largish grains without long "whiskers" and goes rust-red, almost the colour of a marmalade cat, when it is really ripe. Barley varies very much in the colour of the grain but the "whiskers" will always identify it; a field ready for cutting ripples like a cat's fur when it is purring. The best grains are bought by the brewers for malting, and make our beer and whisky. The least breeze causes the barley to sigh in a fashion quite different from the swishing sound made by oats, which bear their separate seeds on branched panicles (like quaker-grass) and are ash-blonde when ripe. Rye has a seed-head, or ear, rather like wheat, but slenderer, longer, and more compressed. It is grown very little in Britain, mainly on the sandy soils in the east.

THE CORN HARVEST

UNTIL well into the nineteenth century corn was cut by hand with scythes or sickles and the harvest was a long toil that rarely finished before October. In 1826, a Scottish minister, of all people, invented the first reaping machine, which was the ancestor of the modern binder. Even the binder looks antiquated today, an Emmet-like contrivance with ... revolving wooden bars somewhat reminiscent of a waterwheel, and its place is being taken by the combine harvester, which threshes and bags the corn as it cuts it.

When the combine is at work there are no sheaves thrown out behind the machine to be stacked by hand into the lovely "stooks" which used to stand in the field until they were dry enough for ricking. The combine moves steadily over the field like some great juggernaut, devouring all. We miss the stooks

53

which used to delight the eye when their long shadows fell across the golden stubble in the evening and the pigeons fluttered about them, taking their tithe of the corn; but the combine enormously speeds up the business of harvesting, and is capable of cutting corn beaten down by rain and wind, which otherwise would have to be gathered in the ancient way, with a scythe. We still see the binder at work here and there, for it can reap when the corn is too wet to be threshed in the combine; also the combine is too expensive a machine for very small farmers.

The corn-rick (which was generally a round one) is disappearing as the combines become more numerous. Thus each new invention has its effect upon the agricultural scene—and also, incidentally, upon the population of animals and birds. The harvest-mouse, our tiniest mammal, which weighs less than half an ounce and can climb up a corn-stalk without bending it, was common enough in the days when men harvested by hand; but the binder and the combine reap its little nest with the corn, and it is now extinct in all but a few of our eastern counties. The corncrake, whose insistent sawing used to match the sound of the whetstones rubbing the reapers' scythes, has become a rare bird for the same reason. The partridge, on the other hand, probably benefits from the introduction of combines; for these machines leave a longer stubble than the binder did, providing the partridges with good cover.

CHEMICAL WARFARE IN THE FIELDS

BUT it is our chemical inventions, rather than our mechanical ones, which affect the fauna and flora most. Nowadays most farmers spray their crops at various stages of their growth, against pests, fungi or virus diseases, and also to destroy the weeds which grow among them. The invention of DDT put into man's hands a weapon with which any trifling rebellion of the insects could be instantly quelled; probably without DDT and other insecticides we could not grow enough food to support the increasing world-population of mankind. Hormone weed-killers, which kill certain plants by over-stimulating their growth, gave us a similar weapon against the weeds. It is roughly selective, acting chiefly on broad-leafed plants upon which the spray can settle, and hardly at all upon narrow-leafed upright plants such as cereals and grasses. Thus for the first time the farmer can kill the weeds in his cornfield without killing the corn. The thistles, nettles, docks and tares which compete with the corn for plant-food and sunlight disappear almost as if a magician had waved his wand; the poppies which used to stain the oatfields blood-red are vanishing from the scene.

We have, however, possessed these very deadly weapons for a very short time; and their long-term effects are uncertain. For instance, if we kill the caterpillars of the cabbage butterfly with DDT in the autumn, their parasites, the grubs of the Ichneumon fly which live within them, will certainly share their doom; a fresh immigration of cabbage butterflies from the continent next year may produce a plague of caterpillars in the absence of the parasite which normally controls them. Likewise the sprays which kill aphis or "blight" deal impartially with the ladybirds which live upon aphis. Among the weeds which we destroy in the cornfields are numerous "host-plants" of beneficent insects; pests may multiply if these insects which prey upon them become rare. Grain-eating birds, which live mainly upon weed-seeds, may alter their habits in the absence of their natural food; they may be compelled to feed upon *our* grain. Insect-eating birds, many of which are killed by the chemical sprays, may become too few to control this pest or that one.

These are *risks* only; and we must beware of prophesying woe to those who "interfere with the balance of nature" because "the balance of nature" is a meaningless phrase. What we really imply by it is the arrangement which best suits ourselves; for every operation upon the farm interferes with "Nature" to a certain extent and if "Nature" is left to herself in England, the land ~~would~~ ~~as we~~ ~~...~~ ...ght forest and scrub. So when the farmer sprays his crops to get a larger yield the small incalculable risk of inconvenient long-term consequences is certainly justified. When County Councils spray the grass verges and roadside hedgerows simply to save the wages of a few roadmen it is a different matter. A "weed" has been defined as "a plant growing in the wrong place"; and the beautiful plants of the roadsides cannot be described as weeds. The hormone blackens and withers not only the thistle and the nettle, but the delicate lacy hedge-parsley, the stitchwort with its sprig-muslin petals, the sweet violet, the exquisite meadow cranesbill. It may indeed extinguish forever a few rarities which have their last refuge by the sides of the road; replacing them with the tidy suburban sameness of lawn-like turf.

The roadman with his scythe cuts the herbage from time to time, but does not permanently destroy the plants. It will be sad if the destructive sprayer takes his place; for the beauty of our roadsides has an imponderable value, and cannot be measured in terms of a halfpenny Rate. Incidentally the roadman, nowadays, is generally an oldish man who uses a scythe with the graceful ease which he learned in his youth from his father, perhaps, who would go into the hayfields at four o'clock in the morning and cut his acre of grass before dusk fell.

THE HAY HARVEST

FOR HAY was mown by hand, here and there, within the memory of old men. The mowers would start at the first light, when the dew was on the grass and the scythe cut clean; they would break off when the sun rose high, eat their bait and drink their cider, sleep a little, and start again in the cool of the evening; from six o'clock, say, they would work till dark. Each man's scythe was his personal, cherished possession, upon which his livelihood partly depended: he would not lend it to another man, nor dream of using it to cut rough bents or thistles, for which he would use an old, discarded blade. When haymaking was over he would hang it in a tree; the dews would rust it; but the rust would enable him to get a better edge on it, when the corn harvest came round. The scythe, the rake and the pitchfork, all very ancient tools, were the only instruments of haymaking up till the last quarter of the nineteenth century, when they gave place to the mowing-machine, the horse-rake, and the tedder, a machine which kicks up the swathe of hay behind it and turns it over, leaving it loose so that the wind can dry it. Later came other inventions, such as the haysweep which collected up the hay and the elevator which lifted it on to the rick. Haymaking was speeded up, but the pattern of haymaking was unchanged. The hay was still cut in swathes when it was "ripe" (i.e. ready to seed), the sun and the summer air dried it, and it was ricked as soon as it was ready. The hay harvest was still a job needing plenty of labour; the fields were populous with the men in their broad straw hats, the women in their floppy white ones, the arms and faces of all burned brick-red by the sun.

But the modern fashion does away with this busy scene. As a rule nowadays the hay is baled by a machine as soon as possible after it is cut. You can see the bales lying about in the fields, some oblong, some cylindrical, according to the kind of machine which the farmer uses. Later the tractor with the big trailer goes round and picks them up; and they are stored until they are needed, generally in a Dutch barn.

Many farmers do not make hay at all. Either they cut their grass when it is still very young and fresh, to make silage; or (on very big farms) they feed the grass into a grass-dryer, whence it emerges in the form of powder or pellets. The grass-dryer costs several thousand pounds; so the silo is more general. It is a simple pit (occasionally a tower) in which the grass is packed tight when green and mixed with molasses. The resulting silage provides the milking-cows with a much richer winter feed than hay. Incidentally as you walk through the country your nose will possibly tell you when you are in the neighbourhood of a silo. If it is not very well made it gives off a sourly unpleasant smell.

These more profitable ways of using grass may soon cause haymaking to be a thing of the past. Silage also cuts out the climatic risks of haymaking. The hayrick may disappear, as the loaded wain, so beloved of landscape painters, had gone into limbo already. Perhaps our grandchildren, as they glance at old paintings some twenty years hence, will point at the hayricks and the wagons and ask: "What are those funny things?" Film-producers on location, trying to recapture Ye Olde Englishe ~~~~~ build rickyards at colossal expense out of plastics in order to convey "the atmosphere of the period".

MEADOW AND PASTURE

A WORD about grassland. To the townsman, and indeed to many countrymen, all green fields look more or less alike. The farmer's eye sees differences in the type of pasture and the kind of herbage which composes it. There is the rough grazing of the uplands; there is the permanent pasture, some of it unploughed for many years; there are water-meadows which are artificially flooded each season; and there are the "leys" in which grass is sown just as cereals or turnips are sown, as part of a rotation. The "leys" remain under grass for one, two, three or more years; and are then ploughed up again to grow a different crop. They have one great advantage over permanent pasture; we can choose what kind of grass-mixture we shall grow, and can provide for a long grazing season. There are hundreds of species of grasses, and many varieties of each species artificially produced at the plant-breeding establishments; so that modern "ley" contains a mixture of the sorts most suited to a particular soil, climate and purpose (e.g. silage, grazing, hay). It contains as well as grasses other nutritious plants, such as wild white clover and the pretty blue chicory, which makes available to cattle certain "trace-elements" which they need for their well-being. So even the meadows, nowadays, have little to do with "Nature", but are the product of highly-specialised scientific research, a far cry indeed from the green fields which Falstaff babbled of.

THE BEASTS OF THE FIELDS

IF YOU chance to come across an old print of a Champion Ram or a Prizewinning Fat Cow you will stare in astonishment at a weird and wonderful creature utterly unlike the animals you see on the farms today. The artist was not at fault; for within the last two hundred years we have learned to mould the very beasts we feed on to match our changing whims. When the consumer demands a smaller joint or a leaner joint, a richer milk or a greater quantity of milk, our farmers do their best to breed the kind of animal which meets the demand; and nowadays our knowledge of genetics enables them to do so within a very few years. Selective breeding is a process similar to natural evolution, but with Man standing in the place of God, the Life Force, or what you will.

You would think that breeding to match the consumer's needs would lead to standardisation: and that we should achieve, perhaps, a People's Milch Cow or a Common Man's Lamb. We have done nothing so totalitarian; for certain kinds of beasts seem to suit certain soils, climates and conditions of farming, and some which thrive in their native county turn out to be bad doers elsewhere. The Danes have gone to great trouble to produce a pig which represents the common denominator of their needs; the Irish are trying to do so, and have made it illegal to possess any other than the "Government pig". But in Britain we still breed 13 different kinds (not counting crosses) which perhaps express the individualism of our farmers as well as demonstrating the diversity of conditions under which they farm.

Pigs

Most of the pig breeds are quite easy to recognise. The SADDLE-BACKS are black with a white "saddle" across their shoulders which runs down to their forelegs. The GLOSTER OLD SPOT is white with black spots. The TAMWORTH is sandy with a fine coat, and claims descent from the original Wild Boar of Britain. The MIDDLE WHITE is a pork pig, trimmer and smaller than the baconers, with a somewhat squashed-in and pug-like face; its ancestors came from China. The BERKSHIRE is like a black version of the Middle White. The LARGE BLACK and the LARGE WHITE are as their names imply. A favourite cross is between white and black, which produces "blues", the white pigs with blue-grey mottlings.

A female pig is called a gilt or hilt or yilt until she has had her first litter (i.e. farrowed); thereafter she is a sow. A good litter is ten or twelve. A pleasing phrase in a book designed to help novice pig farmers runs "see that your sow is equipped with at least twelve teats"—suggestive of a visit to the spares shop for supplying any deficiency... A sow suckling her piglets (which arrange themselves neatly in two layers) is a pleasing sight. Not until all the piglets have found their places, each with a teat, will she let her milk down. Then, all squealing ceasing, the sow's talkative grunts and the suck-suck of the piglets combine to make a very satisfactory sound. Sows are in general gentle creatures. They like to be talked to. A sow who has her belly rubbed will almost always respond by slowly rolling on her side, emitting pleasurable grunts. Very occasionally a sow will become fierce at farrowing. It should be remembered that it is not a good idea to turn your back on a near-by boar.

Sheep

Sheep breeds are much more difficult; you can divide them roughly into Shortwools and Longwools, White-faced and Black-faced. The kinds you are most likely to see during your country walks are:

SHORTWOOLS: *Southdown* (white woolly faces); *Oxford* (grey-brown faces with a woolly topknot); *Dorset* (horned, with pink noses); *Suffolk* (black faces and black feet, no wool on either); *Hampshire* (woolly faces, black noses and black round the eyes, woolly legs).

LONGWOOLS: *Leicester* (white-faced); *Lincoln* (white-faced, much larger than Leicester); *Wensleydale* (black-faced).

MOUNTAIN SHEEP: smaller and lighter in build than most of the other breeds. *Welsh Mountain* have slightly-tanned faces and legs, and the rams are horned; *Scotch Blackface* are shaggy and both sexes are horned; *Cheviots* (pronounced with a long "e") are white-faced with a longish coat of very white and lustrous wool, which is the raw material of Scotch Tweed.

Tegs are yearling sheep; teg-wool is the wool of the first shearing. Gelded rams are called wethers. Ewes in lamb are described by countrymen as being in yean; lambing is yeaning.

Cattle

Cattle can be divided into those bred for beef, those bred for milk, and those which are "dual-purpose". The beef sorts include:

HEREFORD, white-faced, fierce-looking (though in fact they are exceptionally gentle) with somewhat downward-curving horns. They have thick coats of rich red which match the red Hereford soil; rather curly hair, especially on the forehead. They were originally used as draught-oxen.

SUSSEX, deep red with wide spreading horns and very short hair.

GALLOWAY, black, hornless, rather shaggy, very short-legged; bred mainly in Scotland.

ABERDEEN ANGUS, black, hornless but smaller and smoother coated than the Galloway.

WEST HIGHLAND, very shaggy with huge spreading horns; variously coloured, red, dun, yellow, cream, black and brindle. The closest breed to the original wild cattle of Britain and now confined to the north west of Scotland and the Outer Isles.

The following kinds are bred mainly for milk:

AYRSHIRE, dapple, red, brown or black with irregular white patches; udder rather flat and not at all pendulous; long up-turned sickle-shaped horns. Certainly the most delightful breed from the aesthetic point of view.

BRITISH FRIESIAN, black and white in patches; short horns. Gives the highest yield of milk but not of the best quality. There are also Friesian steers.

JERSEY, yellow-fawn to silver-grey, very small with a rather deer-like look. Forward curved horns. Its milk is richer in butter fat than that of any other breed.

GUERNSEY, bigger than the Jersey. Variously coloured, dun, fawn or reddish-fawn often with white patches.

KERRY, an Irish breed of black with very thin upward curving horns.

The dual-purpose cattle, which produce good quality beef and also plenty of milk include:

DAIRY SHORTHORNS, largish cattle with flesh-coloured muzzles, short coats of red, white or roan, and short upward curving horns. There are also Beef Shorthorns.

RED POLL, brown-red, hornless.

There are some other very local breeds, e.g. LINCOLN RED, WELSH BLACK, and DEXTER which are the smallest cattle of all; a Dexter cow is not much taller than a Great Dane.

Cattle which normally bear horns are often "de-horned" to prevent them from injuring each other. A young cow remains a heifer until after her second calving. A bullock is a gelded male. A steer is a fat bullock. It generally takes 30 months to produce a fat beast from a calf—which is why beef can never be a cheap commodity.

Bulls are often docile but no countryman would care to cross a field where a strange bull was at large. There is no panacea against bulls except to run faster than they do. A lady in a red coat is in no special peril since bulls in common with all mammals except apes and man are colour blind; any rag, and not only a red one, will provoke them.

MARKET GARDENS AND ORCHARDS

THERE ARE a few places in rural England where you can walk for miles without seeing any beasts of the field save perhaps a working horse or two. These are the areas given over entirely to market gardening. The gardens present a higgledy-piggledy landscape, quite unlike the bold pattern of the farms; it is a landscape dictated by short-term expediency rather than long-term planning, for if the farmer is a strategist the market-gardener is a tactician, matching his crops and cultivations to swiftly-changing conditions. It doesn't matter very much if the corn-harvest is a fortnight late; but if a crop of radishes comes a fortnight late and misses the "early trade" it may be more profitable to plough them back into the ground than to pull them for market. Supply and demand fluctuate from day to day, depending on weather conditions, imports, the public's whim. The cost of growing market-garden produce is high; much more labour, much more fertiliser, is used per acre than on the farm. Rewards and penalties are greater too. A single lucky crop may bring in £250 an acre; but there are proportionately more bankrupts among market-gardeners than among farmers.

The scenery of market-gardening is dreary and dull. Sprouts, parsnips, spring onions, carrots, cabbages, cauliflowers, lettuces do not decorate the landscape as farm crops do. But here and there are patches of warm colour: red pickling cabbage glowing in a glint of sunshine on a winter's day, kidney-beans in flower— an orange-scarlet furnace—gillyflowers grown for bunching in the spring, sweet williams in high summer. Where asparagus is grown there is a transformation in July and another in

September. The growers cease to cut their "grass" in late June, and let the fern grow tall. Its feathery greenness delights the eye; but as it fades to tawny it takes on an autumnal splendour and a large patch of it just before it is cut down looks almost like a field on fire.

Many market-gardeners grow soft fruit as well as vegetables, and often the gardening areas merge into orchard-country where the chief crops are apples, pears, cherries and plums. This is so in Kent and in Worcestershire, where the orchards are set amid the sprout-fields and the bleak landscape blossoms suddenly in the spring. The plum-blossom comes first (the end of March to the middle of April, its climax often coinciding happily with Eastertide). Unless the season is very late it comes on the bare black boughs, and is like a lace curtain drawn across the orchard-land. The pear and the cherry come in together.

> Loveliest of trees, the cherry now
> Is hung with bloom along the bough,

wrote Housman; but of pear and cherry who shall say which is the lovelier or set either above the apple; shell-pink when fully open, rose-pink when in bud? Incidentally the most free-flowering apple-trees are the cider sorts, which produce hard, sour, belly-aching apples; and the loveliest pear-trees, tall snowy pyramids in April, are not the kinds with aristocratic names (such as Williams Bon-Chretien and Doyenne du Comice) but the ones which bear little rough perry pears. The demand for home-made cider and perry seems to be declining; and every year a few more of the old beautiful orchards are cut down.

Frost in May is the fruit-grower's ever-present fear. It is the invisible slayer that creeps among the branches at dead of night and blackens the hearts of the blossom or the tiny green berries of the setting fruit. Frost tends to "flow" downhill and gather in the valleys and the sheltered places, just as water would do; so nowadays the orchards are planted on the exposed slopes of hills rather than in the hollows. You will notice that the trees are planted in parallel rows in line with the slope of the land, to give good "air drainage" when the frost flows between them. Even peaches will grow well in the open in England on a southward facing slope if they are clear of the frost-pockets.

63

There is not much defence against frost; but some growers build bonfires around their orchards and light those on the windward side on nights when frost is expected. The smoke forms a sort of protective canopy and sometimes the fruit is saved. Oil-burning orchard-heaters are also used in places sheltered from the wind.

By June, in England, the risk is past; and the growers, as they put it, "feel safe to get their ladders mended", ready for picking time. In most fruit districts cherry-picking comes first, beginning in mid-June. The plum harvest comes next, beginning with the Early Prolifics, which are small sloe-like purple plums; the yellow egg plums follow, and are mostly picked green for stewing or jam-making; then come the big purple eating plums, such as Czar, Victoria, Monarch—in that order. Cherry-picking may go on into early August in some parts, running on into the pear and apple time. Beauty of Bath and the bright scarlet Worcester Pearmains are the earliest apples; Blenheims are not picked till October and the old-fashioned russets will cling to the trees long after they are bare and last till next spring, staying sound though their skins are as brown and wrinkled as an old country-man's face.

The names of apples roll splendidly round the tongue: Duke of Devonshire, Lord Lambourne, Newton Wonder, King o' the Pippins, Laxton Superb, Cox's Orange Pippin. But by contrast there are some humble and as it were cottager's kinds, as Annie Elizabeth, so named after the two daughters of the man who first produced it.

HOPS

THERE is one more crop of local importance, though it is only grown on a large scale in four of our counties: Kent and Hampshire, Hereford and Worcester. Its harvest is the merriest of all; and the hopfields (gardens as they are called in Kent, yards in Herefordshire) have at that season a somewhat Bacchanalian air, for the beautiful leaves of the hops are very like those of the grape and the green bines that drape the poles and the strings made a frieze like that on a Grecian vase. The word "bine" is only a local variant of "vine".

The landscape of hopfields has a derelict appearance for eight months of the year, when the poles alone are seen in the bare fields; but the other four months make up for all. The hops begin to run up the strings in early May—in an anti-clockwise direction, which is contrary to the way of most vegetable climbers—and they grow on the average 2 inches in 24 hours, reaching 14½ feet by mid-June. They are ripe and ready by the first week in September, when the hordes of hop-pickers arrive in the districts where they are grown: cockneys and gypsies in Kent, Welsh and Black-country folk as well as gypsies in Hereford. The picking lasts for 3 or 4 weeks. Whole families, with their children, spend their holidays in this way and are paid at piece rates, so much a "bushel" though the bushel-basket which measures it varies in size from district to district or even from farm to farm. Each family or group of pickers is allotted an area to pick in which must be cleared before they move elsewhere. This is called a "drift" in Kent, a "house" in Hereford. Hop-growing has its own quaint vocabulary. The special hoe used in the early cultivations is called a kerf. The yellow resinous dust that is found in the hop-flowers and gives them their distinctive smell is called the Gold. The two most popular sorts of hop are named respectively Bramblings and Fuggles.

On many of the bigger hop-farms nowadays picking is done by machine. Although the machine is complicated and very expensive, it saves a great deal of labour and avoids difficulty with education regulations; and in a few years, alas, the hop-picking holiday may be a thing of the past.

Hops, by the way, do *not* make beer stronger. Their only purpose is to give it a bitter flavour. Ground ivy was used for this purpose before hops were introduced into England, about the middle of the sixteenth century. According to an old rhyme

Turkey, carp, hops, pickerel and beer
Came into England all in a year.

THE WOODLANDS

WE HAVE wandered leisurely through the farmers' fields and glanced at the domestic beasts and crops which occupy about 85 in every 100 acres of Britain. The remaining 15 is accounted for by urban areas, aerodromes, uncultivated mountainsides, and woods. There are more than 3 million acres of woodland. Much of this is owned by the Forestry Commission, which pursues a policy of planting the "marginal land", which is unsuited to agriculture, with quick-growing softwoods; 92 per cent of all its plantings consist of various conifers, firs, larches and pines. These new woods look somewhat alien in our countryside; "natural" forest of Britain is a mixture of hardwoods, mainly oak, beech, elm, birch and ash. Savernake, Sherwood, Dean and the New Forest were the famous woodlands of England, and not much is left of Savernake, only a fragment of Sherwood. The Forest of Dean and the New Forest are "Royal" Forests, in the charge of the Commission, which has indulged its passion for planting conifers here and there. For the most part, however, the oaks remain; and as we walk among them we can imagine ourselves in the ancient Greenwood of England. We owe the New Forest to a king's inordinate addiction to sport. William the Conqueror is said to have "loved the red deer as if he were their father". He made for the deer a sanctuary, and for himself a hunting ground, of nearly 100,000 acres upon the thin and hungry soil of Hampshire; and that county would look very different today but for the accident that a ruthless, hard-swearing, hard-riding Norman who loved his deer, his horses and his hounds much better than he loved his conquered people. Although modern forestry has altered the appearance of a good deal of it, you will still find there groves of oak and holly where the dark shadows of the trees have scarcely shifted, and where the sunlight has not fallen on the leaf-mould beneath, since Domesday.

"Greenwood" was the poets' word; "Black Wood" might have been more fitting, for in the Middle Ages the Forests were dark and savage places hedged about by dark and savage laws. Certainly they were playgrounds for kings (though the game was sometimes a grim one, as Rufus discovered) but they were by no means playgrounds for the kings' subjects. Unless a man had business there he was wise to shun the Forest lest he lose his right hand for the crime of shooting an arrow with it, or his eyes for the sin of looking covetously at the fat hinds. "Hunting in Forest, Chases, and suchlike privileged places of pleasure", wrote Manwood in his *Forest Laws* (1598) "is only for Kings, Princes, and great worthy personages, and not for mean men of mean calling or ambition". Despite the ghastly penalties, there seems to have been a good deal of poaching, and presumably a black market in deer-flesh was not unknown; for there is a proverb in Latin which was common in the Middle Ages: *Non est inquirendum unde venit venison.*

In Shakespeare's *As You Like It* we find the sunlight breaking into the black wood at last; the fear of the deep woods is lifted, perhaps because Man as well as the sunlight was beginning to break into them. There must have been a great deal of felling during the reign of Elizabeth and much more during the fifty years after her death; John Evelyn in his *Sylva* (1664) complained of the ruin of the woods in England. Since then there has been a steady erosion which has left us a few islands of old woodland widely scattered in various parts of the country. None is so large as the New Forest, and none gives you such a good idea of the kind of scenery among which the wolf and the wild boar roamed, even as late as 1500.

The great oakwoods are rich in fauna and flora: you will find in the New Forest, for example, most of our 71 sorts of butterflies, including the great Purple Emperor which sails high among the treetops yet deigns to descend to the ground now and then to settle on carrion, which it loves. You will find more representatives of our 2218 different sorts of moths than in any other area of the same size. You will find three species of deer, most of our other mammals. (We still possess 75 kinds, having made extinct during historical times only 5, the wolf, the wild boar, the brown bear, the beaver and the reindeer.) You may even come across creatures weird and wonderful, for instance an adder with its belly of beautiful porcelain blue; the great naturalist W. H. Hudson found such a one basking upon a Forest heath.

oaks; beechwoods in contrast are barren, for their wide-spreading branches keep out the light. It is only in the glades and open spaces that the bluebells grow, and the foxglove, which is surely the typical flower of the oakwoods, is hardly ever seen among the beech. The beech (like the box) is really a tree of the chalk; and where it grows well it forms still and lovely woods of soft green shade, in which few birds twitter, and which have a quiet cathedral air. The botanist, finding little to interest him under the trees, will do well to hunt along the edges of the wood; the chalk-loving flowers include some of the quaintest and most local of our orchids, the Musk, Frog, Wasp and Bee, and the rarest of all, the Red Helleborine of the Cotswolds.

Flowers, incidentally, provide the best indication of the kind of soil in any particular area; wherever you find the foxglove, the ling, the whortleberry, the rhododendron you may be sure you are not on chalk. But wherever the Traveller's Joy or Old Man's Beard drapes the hedgerows, you will know that you are back on the limestone, for in common with about a dozen other plants (the Bloody Cranesbill and the Kidney Vetch are the best known) it will not grow anywhere else.

Many of our woods are "mixed": they contain oak, birch, hazel, sycamore, alder and aspen growing naturally together. When from time to time such woods are felled, the stumps are left in the ground to sprout again and form new woodland in a few years' time. This is called "natural regeneration", and the new growth is described as coppice.

Now and then, in the course of our wanderings, we may come across a small patch of woodland, perhaps on the slope of a hill, which consists of old birch trees, rather widely scattered, hawthorns, occasional hollies, and stunted, crooked oaks. These oaks, when the winter gales have ripped the leaves off them, seem to hold out gnarled arms in gesticulation to the sky. We have a sense of something primitive, druidical; for this is a fragment of the ancient, original scrub. By chance it has survived the encroachment of man. His plough has never ripped open the soil, his axe has never been wielded here. All around us, north, south, east and west, is spread out the garden that man has made; but we have come full-circle, and where we stand is the woodland waste, that once was England.

Left to right: Annual Meadow Grass; Couch Grass;
Italian Rye Grass; Cocksfoot; Timothy;
Meadow Fescue; Crested Dogtail.

BIRDSONG AT MORNING

Yes, I will spend the livelong day
With nature in this month of May;
And sit beneath the trees, and share
My bread with birds whose homes are there.
W.H. Davies.

Crave the tuneful nightingale to help you
    with her lay,
The ousel and the throstlecock, chief music
    of our May.
Michael Drayton.

To hear the lark begin his flight
And singing startle the dull night.
Milton.

Thou was not born for death, immortal
    Bird!
No hungry generations tread thee down;
The voice I hear this passing night was
    heard
In ancient days by emperor and clown:
Perhaps the self-same song that found a
    path
Through the sad heart of Ruth, when sick
    for home,
She stood in tears amid the alien corn,
The same that oft-times hath
Charm'd magic casements, opening on the
    foam
Of perilous seas, in faery lands forlorn.
Keats.

Bird engravings by Bewick (1753-1828)

Bird Song at Morning

... And sit beneath the trees, and share my bread with birds whose homes are there.

...that al the wode rong
So sodainly, that, as it were a sot,
I stood astonied...
        ...until late and long
Ne wist I in what place I was, ne where;
The birdes song was more convenient,
Than mete or drink, or any other thing.
                        Anonymous, 15th Century.

The following pages are designed for the unfledged student of birds. By the weekend's end, perhaps, he will be a fully fledged Birdwatcher. No longer can birds be safely and conveniently lumped together as small brown birds, large black birds and sea-gulls; no longer can a glib literary allusion to "the sea-blue bird of March" or "a small hot bird" be accepted in lieu of ornithological exactitude. For this is an age of specialisation, and anyone who looks at a bird today calls himself a Birdwatcher and must submit to all the rigours of that dedicated life, whether he watch for reasons of aesthetic appreciation, scientific enquiry, artistic endeavour, or merely from curiosity.

Bird-watching, advised a famous Field-Marshal, is the ideal hobby for all young officers. He probably had in mind the encouragement of some of those qualities desirable in both military and ornithological operations: the quick eye, the scientific assessment of the field, patience, and a passionate belief that the end justifies the means, that the ten-mile walk into the east wind, the scaling of the unscalable cliff, the crawl on hands and knees over wet mud, are worthwhile for the sight of one small bird disappearing into an impenetrable bramble bush.

A hundred and thirty million years ago the chase would not have been so arduous. The blundering flight of *Archaeopteryx*, with his toothy jaws and claw-tipped fingers and long pointed tail, would have been easy to identify. Even among the rapidly changing forms of avifauna in the Eocene period, from sixty to forty million years ago, it would not have been difficult to pick out the huge head and tiny wings and large arched beak of 7-foot *Diatryma*. But with 8,500 species of birds in the world today—and over 450 of them on the British list—the Birdwatcher has a life's work before him.

How shall he begin, in a brief weekend?

HOW TO WATCH BIRDS

First, he must equip himself with the right tools. Of these, the essentials are field-glasses, a library, and a note-book. Refinements such as hides and cameras can be added later as he becomes more proficient.

FIELD-GLASSES. This is the only really expensive item of the Birdwatcher's equipment, and it will pay him to get the best he can afford, for a good pair of field-glasses will last a lifetime. Ross, Barr and Stroud, Kershaw, Zeiss, and Leitz are the best makers. As well as price, consideration must be given to magnification, field of vision, illumination, weight and durability.

For bird-watching, a magnification of not less than 6 and not more than 9 is desirable. (The sign 6 x on a pair of field-glasses means that the object is magnified 7 times.) With a higher magnification, the field of vision is smaller and it is more difficult to follow a quickly moving bird. The higher powered glasses are also heavier, and they magnify the shake of one's hands as well as the size of the image. Only people with steady hands and strong eyes and the ability to support a millstone round the neck should use 10- or 12-power glasses. On the other hand, if the glasses are very light, as in the case of those made of some of the new lightweight alloys, durability will be sacrificed.

Some binoculars have a centre focusing screw, and others have independent focusing of each eyepiece. Although the former is slightly heavier it is to be preferred, as it can be quickly altered with one hand.

Many of the modern field-glasses are made with "coated" lenses, which provide a more brightly illuminated image. They are especially useful in a poor light.

To sum up: the best field-glasses for a Birdwatcher will be 6 to 9 magnification; they will have the widest possible field; they will have coated lenses, central focusing and will be both light and strong.

Such an expensive toy must be properly cared for. The lens should be carefully wiped after use with a soft silk handkerchief or cleaning tissue. If the strap suspending the glasses is too long, they will swing out against fences and rocks as the wearer bends over or climbs up and will become chipped and dented. The strap should be shortened to avoid damage—and this will also take some of the strain from the neck and will make it easier to raise the glasses quickly to the eyes. It is also advisable to cover the glasses in some way when they are not in the case, either by protecting the eyepieces from rain by a piece of leather or rubber fitted over them, or by tucking the glasses into the jacket.

LIBRARY. This will also depend to some extent on the size of the Birdwatcher's purse. The library could be extended indefinitely. The most essential requirement, however, will be a good field-guide – one that will go into the pocket. The best of all guides is *A Field Guide to the Birds of Britain and Europe* by Roger Peterson, Guy Mountfort and P.A.D. Hollom. Then, even if he cannot afford it, the serious Birdwatcher will never be satisfied until he has acquired the 5-volume *Handbook of British Birds*, an avian *Who's Who, Kelly's* and *Debrett* combined: it contains every-thing of importance that is known about every bird on the British list. If he does not have the *Handbook* he will probably substitute *The Birds of the British Isles* (3 volumes) by Coward. Books to guide him in the art and science of bird-watching should include James Fisher's *Watching Birds*, and, if he can get hold of it, *A Guide to Bird Watching* by Joseph Hickey (published in USA). And he would be well advised to listen again and again to the recordings of *Songs of British Birds* by Ludwig Koch until he has them by heart.

NOTEBOOK. For whatever reason birds are watched, notes

should be taken of the observations made. Even if the Birdwatcher has no other motive than the enjoyment of a delightful hobby, he will want to recall the details of exciting and memorable moments. A small notebook should always be carried in the pocket, and observations should be jotted down in this on the spot. Details should be as full as possible: the kind and number of birds seen, where they were seen, their behaviour, particulars of the light and weather, and so on. Sketches should be made whenever an identification is in doubt. These rough notes should be written up at home as soon as possible, while the experience is still fresh in the memory.

The permanent record can take various forms. The sentimental beginner will probably confide his emotions to a rather colourful diary: "A dainty little bird watched me with bright eyes from the branch of an oak tree. It made a pretty picture against the young April green. Could it have been a willow warbler? The sad little song reminded me…" But with practice his style will tauten, his observations will expand, and he will become altogether more scientific. He will probably abandon the diary in favour of a card-index system or a large loose-leaf notebook, either of which will allow for indefinite expansion. The arrangement will be a matter of the Birdwatcher's temperament and his own particular interests, but each species should have a separate heading, with others for Song, Behaviour, Plumage, Nests, and so on, and there should be plenty of cross-references. Very soon our Birdwatcher, if he is worth the salt he has attempted to sprinkle on the tail of many a rare bird, will be writing to the press—and then his Notebook will be indispensable.

WHAT TO WATCH FOR

Now that the Birdwatcher is fully equipped, the really difficult part of the business begins. How will he recognise a bird when he sees it? He has his field guide—but birds do not always sit still enough for comparison with the coloured plate. He must learn what to look for.

There goes a bird! It is flying across a meadow, too far off for us to see clearly the details of its plumage. What size is it? It seems to be larger than a sparrow, smaller than a blackbird. How does it fly? Its flight is undulating, in long curves. It might be a finch of some sort: undulating flight is an identifying field mark of most finches, our guide book tells us. Or it might be a lark. It is unlikely to be a warbler, so far from the trees—and anyway the flight is too strong, the bird too large. It cannot be a starling, whose flight is swift and straight. Now the bird is down on the ground. It is against the sun, so still we cannot see its markings. But we can make out that the bill is long and slender, not short and stout as it would be on a seed-eating finch. Nor is the bird hopping on the ground, as a finch would; nor walking with the slightly waddling gait of a lark. It is running, with an occasional little hop into the air after an insect. And now that we can see the long tail wagging up and down as it runs, we know for certain that it is a wagtail. The tail is not long enough for a grey wagtail: it will probably be either yellow or pied, and when we get closer to the bird we can make out the black and white patterning of a pied wagtail.

These, then, are some of the questions the Birdwatcher must ask himself. What size is it—as big as a dodo, or smaller than a humming-bird? What shape is it—thick or thin, long or short? What is the shape of its beak, its wings, its tail? How does it behave? Does it walk or hop or run or climb trees or bury its head in the sand? How does it fly—with a straight or undulating flight, rapid or slow or flap-flap-glide? Does it hover or dive or soar or wade? Is it alone or is it in a flock? Has it got a kind face, or does it look rather predatory? What colour is it? What are its distinguishing field marks? Has it wing-bars? White in the tail, or on the rump? And eye-stripe? Where is it found? Every bird has its own niche, and is unlikely to be found out of it, except on migration. A wood warbler will not be found in a ploughed field, and it is no good looking for a sky lark in a wood. When is it found? Some birds will be summer migrants, others will be seen only in winter.

WHERE TO WATCH

In his selection of terrain, the week-end Birdwatcher may have to confine himself to his own home ground. If he is free of ties, however, he can choose to spend his week-ends in a wide variety of localities, in each of which he will find a different group of birds. He can also extend his hobby by visiting one of the Field

Study Centres, where bird-watching courses are held several times a year under the direction of experienced ornithologists. Then, as his interest grows with knowledge, he will be able to stay at some of the bird observatories round the coast of Britain at which the study of migration is carried on.

Wherever he may be, the Birdwatcher will find scope for his activities. He may live "in the highlands, in the country places"; by meres or moors or marshes, or in the middle of a turnip field; in a cottage in a wood or a mansion on a hill. Whichever way his path lies, there will be birds on either side of it. There will be warblers in the woodlands and waders on the mud-flats; finches in the stubble and hawks on the hills and titmice at the milk bottles on his doorstep. Even a city, if he cannot escape from it, can be an excellent place for watching birds, in the parks and public gardens, at the reservoirs and along the rivers. There can be few keener pleasures for the city-dweller than to watch a pair of blackbirds building a nest against a drain-pipe oblivious of the clamour of the crowded street below; or to follow the daily movements of a kestrel that owns the bombed church at the end of his square; or to lie awake in the dark and suddenly to recognise the lonely call of a golden plover high above the city on its migratory passage. Many large towns possess a Natural History Society or similar group which organises bird-watching walks and trips at week-ends.

But the best place for the beginner to learn his birds is undoubtedly in his own garden. (And those who prefer to do their bird-watching with a minimum of effort can manage quite well from a deck-chair on the lawn or an arm-chair at the window.) Here he can watch the story of his birds unfold from month to month, and here he can even combine his hobbies, and dig for birds. There is much that a good bird-gardener can do, by planting the right fruit- and seed-bearing shrubs and plants in the right places, to attract to the garden birds that would otherwise pass it by. The berried lure of hawthorn, mountain ash, cotoneaster and elder will prove irresistible. If possible a corner of the garden should be devoted to weeds and allowed to run to seed, and the more thistles there are the more goldfinches there will be. Cover is important, too, both for nesting purposes and for protection from the wind and sun and from natural predators.

Beech, privet, yew and holly afford good cover. If the garden is large enough to contain a wild patch of brambles, briars and bracken, this will bring in warblers. Well-placed nesting boxes will provide homes for birds that normally nest in holes, such as tits, nuthatches and even woodpeckers—and also for the sparrows and starlings who will try to "gate-crash" on them; and a roofed-over tray sort of affair will often appeal to robins, spotted flycatchers, blackbirds and thrushes as a nest-support. The provision of water in the garden is very important, both for drinking and bathing, and if there is no pool or pond a bird-bath should be provided. Dripping water is a great attraction to warblers. And of course there will be a bird table in every Birdwatcher's garden. Set with breadcrumbs, suet, nuts, seeds, berries and scraps from the human table, it will be an excellent place for observing birds. Here at close range the details of their plumage and behaviour can be studied during the lean days of winter, so that when the seasons of courtship and nesting and migration follow in their cycle, the Birdwatcher's eye is already "in". Here, too, in his own melodious plot he can familiarise himself with many of the best songs, and this branch of birding can often—especially on Sunday mornings—be most successfully conducted from his bed.

The following pages give a brief description of some of the birds the week-end Birdwatcher is likely to find in his own garden.

HOUSE SPARROW, Philip Sparrow, Spug or Roo-Doo. Length, 5¾ inches.

Because it is present in every garden in Britain, the sparrow heads the list of garden birds, but it is very far from being first in the affections of either gardener or bird-lover. Wherever man goes, the sparrow follows—but there is no disguising the fact that he makes use of us in the most impudent manner and gives nothing in return. He takes over our houses, eats our food, disturbs our sleep with his noisy quarrelling, and delights in the wanton destruction of our peas and crocuses; but he refuses to make friends and remains aloof and suspicious. The sparrow is always bustling about, hopping perkily or in fussy flight, but a good deal of his activity appears to be entirely aimless. This is evident even in the ardour of courtship, when several males will hop jauntily round a female indulging in every form of noisy display and then, apparently losing interest, will all suddenly fly off together. The sparrow's incessant two-syllabled chirp of *phillip* earned him the old nickname of "Philip Sparrow". The male has a brown back streaked with black, a

dark grey crown to his head with chestnut nape, a black throat and greyish-white underparts. A country cock sparrow, free of the grime that camouflages his city brother, is a handsome bird; but his hen, brown above and dingy white below, is undeniably dowdy. The nest, which is an untidy mess of straw and rubbish thickly lined with feathers, is merely a lining to a cavity when it is built under the eaves or stuffed into a hole in the wall or in ivy or a drainpipe; but when no house is available and a tree site is used, the nest is domed with a side entrance. The eggs are "spickled and spackled" with black, brown or grey on a white ground: they vary both in colour and size.

ROBIN, Redbreast or Ruddock. Length, 5 ¾ inches.

There are certain birds which show a preference for the society of man and take advantage of his curious activities to make their habitations in the neighbourhood of his own. Of these the robin is the most intimate. The reason for the universal recognition of the robin in England is not merely his friendship for or indifference to the presence of man, but also his strong personality. It is his original departure from the timidity characteristic of the race of small birds which endears him to us and invites us to woo him—especially with the irresistible bait

of the meal-worm—to familiarities we can achieve with no other species. In defence of his territory he is exceedingly pugnacious towards his own kind. His alarm note is as explosive as his nature, and sounds like the tocking of a grandfather clock. The song follows no set pattern, being at once ringing, exultant and full of timbre, but at the same time a kind of musing recitative with a sad and beautiful undersong.

The robin's flight is low and somewhat jerky, and he does not fly far without alighting. On the ground he progresses in swift long hops, pausing occasionally to draw himself up with almost military precision. He is easily recognised by his challenging red breast above white underparts. The rest of his spruce form is olive brown. Young robins have spotted breasts up to the first moult and so deceive the uninitiated into thinking them a

81

different species. There is no difference in the sexes' colouring. A roughish nest of dead leaves, grass and moss interwoven with hair and a few feathers is built pretty well anywhere and in anything from a tin kettle to an orthodox hole in a tree or bank. Five to six eggs, white in ground colour with freckles of light red, are laid in it.

BLACKBIRD, Ousel, or Amsel. Length, 10 inches.

The blackbird possesses an emotional quality quite different from that of the robin, being full of fears, suspicions and nervous reactions. He is almost as conspicuous about human dwelling-places, but never reposes in man the same degree of confidence. His loud chuck of alarm is a sign of his volatile and unstable temperament; anger, rufflement, uneasy protest change in a moment to the most taking airs of gallantry to his brown mate. His movements, too, are typical of his character. In the air, over a short distance, his flight is weak and wavering, though he seems to gather courage and strength over a longer distance; and on the ground, where he proceeds by hopping and running as a thrush does, he makes a great show of jerking his tail and wings in a nervous and excitable manner. When the blackbird begins to sing in February his low fluting is unrivalled for its pure and mellow tone, and is delivered with a leisureliness which draws out the full value of each note.

The brown female has not the distinction of the ebony male with his golden dagger of a bill. She builds very early, and her shack is an untidy affair of grasses, roots, and herbs, lined with finer grasses and mud-plastered within. The eggs are four to six in number, greeny blue in colour, smeared with light brown.

MISTLE-THRUSH or Stormcock. Length, 10 ½ inches.
SONG THRUSH, Mavis or Throstle. Length, 9 inches.

Temperamentally there is much kinship between thrush and blackbird; but the thrush's song is far less moving in musical quality than the blackbird's, being at once more powerful and

83

more strident—so much so that at close quarters it can be very harsh. The melancholy tenderness of the blackbird's flute is quite absent. If one may express it in human terms, the thrush's song seems to represent unreflecting joy and the blackbird's the fulfilment of experience. No singer lives more in his song, for he will persist in repeating, from a bold and commanding perch, old phrases and experimenting with new ones for hours at a stretch and in all months of temperate weather.

On the ground the thrush will run or hop a little way, then stand still, his head cocked to one side, as though he were listening to secret movements within the earth. In reality, however, he turns his head the better to detect the worms or insects on the surface. Snails are a favourite food, and a snail-stone will be found in most gardens, surrounded by the splintered shells of the victims who have been battered to pieces. The thrush's flight is direct and swift, with a rapid wing movement. The nest, which may be found in any imaginable site, is unlike the blackbird's in the use of small twigs and moss and of a final smooth lining of rotten wood for the interior. The eggs, usually four to five in number, and laid two or three times during the season, are of a fine blue tinged with green and stippled with black spots. Both sexes are alike.

A predilection for mistletoe berries gave the Mistle-thrush this name; but his other name of Stormcock is even more expressive, for that is how most people remember him—a bold, conspicuous figure blowing his bugle of a song from the bare topmost boughs across a wintry sky. The loud notes of his ringing challenge have a blackbird-like quality, but the forceful manner of their delivery helps to disguise the fact that his short phrases are really rather monotonous and repetitive. His call note is a harsh and grating chatter.

On the ground the mistle-thrush behaves very like a song thrush, but in flight his action is stronger, with a distinctive long closure of the wings, and he flies higher. In appearance he is easily distinguished from his relative: he is much larger and greyer, and the spots on his breast are bigger and bolder. In fact, he is a bolder bird in every way, quarrelsome and intolerant of competition, and fearlessly aggressive in defence of his large grassy nest, which is usually conspicuously sited in the bare fork of a tall tree. The eggs are cream or greenish white blotched with brown and mauve.

DUNNOCK, Hedge-Sparrow, Shuffle-Wing, Creepie, Darby or Hatcher. Length, 5 ¾ inches.

The dunnock, as he is now officially called, is more familiar to many as the hedge-sparrow, though he comes of a family entirely unrelated to the house-sparrow—that of the Accentors, who, as the reality implies, are concerned with singing, and sing he does, more or less all the year round, a bright, jingling, high-pitched little song which sounds remarkably like *weeso, sissi-weeso, sissi-weeso, sissi-weeso*. His call note is a monotonous shrill "peep". The dunnock is not exactly secretive, but he very often passes unnoticed as he creeps and shuffles about unobtrusively among fallen leaves and under hedges. He always seems to be busy, in a quiet way, and minding his own business. When he flies it is on rapid, purposeful wings, and he never goes far.

85

His nest is what you would expect of him—or, rather, of her, as it is built by the hen alone—an efficient job of woven grass, moss and roots, neatly lined with hair or wool. It is usually placed in a thick hedge or shrubbery, or in a faggot stack. The main consideration seems to be that the site should be private and impenetrable. The eggs are of a very lovely shade of clear deep blue. The sexes are alike: dark brown back finely streaked with black, slaty grey head and neck and slaty grey beneath. The fine pointed beak, hallmark of an insect eater, is enough to distinguish the dunnock from the house sparrow with his short thick seed-eater's beak.

BLUE TIT, Tom Tit, Blue-Cap, Billy-Biter, or Nun. Length, 4½ inches.

GREAT TIT, Saw-Finch, Saw-Sharpener, Black-Capped Lolly, or Sit-ye-Down. Length, 5½ inches.

The titmouse forces his minute presence upon our attention not only because of his slightly supercilious fearlessness of man, his intense vitality and handsome colouring, but from the eccentricity of his ways. There is no other bird in the calendar who so far succeeds in defying the humdrum in movement, performing an endless variety of unnatural postures on branch or twig with such topsy-turvy agility that only the most patient observer is able to record the sight of a titmouse motionless on his perch. In winter, for there is a roaming and gregarious but not definitely a migratory impulse through the dark days, fat or coconut will bring him within arm's length.

The blue tit is perhaps the most familiar in the garden and is certainly the most endearing of this troupe of acrobats. He possesses a spring song of a very bright and limpid trill which has been compared to a musical escape of water. As few as five eggs and as many as twenty (pure white with spots and freckles of vandyke brown) may be laid in a convenient cavity of a wall or tree or stump or letter-box, into which the cock bird helps the hen to bundle a surprising quantity of moss and dry grass, with wool, hair and feathers for the lining. The bird himself is richly and strikingly coloured with a blue crown rimmed with white, and his cheeks are patterned with the same chequer, while a fainter blue is suffused into the wings and tail. The back is olive-green, and the under-parts are yellow crossed by yet another dark blue line.

The great tit is the largest of the common tits. He can immediately be distinguished from his relatives by the broad black band which cuts down the centre of his sulphur-yellow breast. His head and neck are glossily blue-black with white cheeks. His back is olive-green and the wings and tail are blue-grey. He shares with the other tits a number of similar call notes, of which his own repertoire is the most extensive, but his song is individual and distinctive—a metallic and rasping "saw-sharpening" of *teacher, teacher, teacher*. The siting and construction of the nest and the number and colour of the eggs are very similar to the blue tit's, but the eggs are larger. Both species will hiss with anger if disturbed on the nest. Both species, also, move in the same manner: on the ground, with a jerky hop, and in the air, by swift and undulating, though rather laboured, flight from tree to tree.

The COAL-TIT and MARSH-TIT, though more confined to solitary places, will often be seen in the larger gardens, the former particularly on conifers. Both have black heads and white cheeks, but the coal-tit is distinguished by a large white patch on the nape of the neck. A family party of tiny pussy-faced LONG-TAILED TITS may also pass through the garden, apparently utterly oblivious of the presence of man, however close.

CHAFFINCH, Spink, Shilfa, Scobbey, Skelly, or Shel-Apple. Length, 6 ½ inches.

The chaffinch frequents human habitations more closely than any other bird except the house-sparrow, and so is seldom noticed as he really is, a bird of lustrous and even gaudy plumage, suiting the rollick of his song and his mettlesome disposition. His jovial rattle is one of the most copious and familiar set songs between February and June, and its first tentative rendering is one of the earliest signs of spring. His flight conforms to the undulating finch type, but is less volatile than the goldfinch's or the linnet's, though more buoyant than that of the hawfinch or bunting. On the wing he delivers a sibilant double note not

unlike the pied wagtail's, and his alarm cry is a sharp *ping*. He prefers the ground more than all other finches, except brambling and house-sparrow, and in winter joins the mixed companies of roaming flocks in the fields.

The nest, which is built entirely by the much drabber female, is fashioned perfectly, felted without of mosses, lichens, grasses, wool and other very soft substances deftly woven. It is compacted with cobwebs and lined with hair, feathers, and the down of plants. Four to six rather variable eggs, pale bluish green or reddish brown in ground colour with streaks and freckles of black or purplish brown, are laid twice in a season. The forehead of the male is black and the rest of his crown and nape a greyish sea-blue, with chestnut pinkily diluted on the cheeks, while the same blend of pink, deepening to reddish brown, suffuses the under-parts which fade into white. The rump is green, the back a warm chestnut, while two bands of white on the brown wings make a conspicuous recognition mark.

Other finches of the garden are the GREENFINCH, with a toy golden sword strapped to his side and constant twittering talk; the stocky BULLFINCH, despoiler of orchard buds, with his tender pipe, velvety black head and wonderful rose-madder breast; the GOLDFINCH "pausing upon his yellow flutterings"; and the rarer, bulky HAWFINCH, very shy and very handsomely plumaged, with an adze-like bill.

WREN, Stumpy, Jenny Wren, Titty Todger, Tit Meg, or Stag. Length, 3 ½ inches.

The wren is as individual a bird as the robin, and his haunts are much the same, except that the wren's distribution is a little more extensive. You will see a wren creeping mouse-like among the stalks from your window and you will see the same movements, the same upcocked tail, and hear the same blast of song from the undergrowth of the wildest and most desolate moor, cliff or forest. The quaintness of the wren comes from his exceeding small size and secret elusive ways in contrast with his vigorous and brave personality. The latter shows itself in his song, a bright clear gush of notes hastening to a trill and wonderfully heartening on grey winter mornings, for the wren is almost as abundant a singer as the robin or thrush. It is delivered with

extraordinary virility and indifference to the presence of an observer. His excitement note resembles the ticking of a clock sharply anxious to be much faster than other clocks, and when he flies his blunt wings whirr like clockwork, which is all too soon unwound. No bird is so much at home in the densest maze of undergrowth, threading the labyrinth with a dexterity rivalling the most cunning movements of any small mammal, and emerging upon a free spray to sing his song.

The wren's energy is also vented in building more nests than are ever used, while the regular nest, wedged into holes or crevices in houses or faggots or other odd litter, or woven in bush-tangle, ivy, rock-shelter or heather, is larger than that of birds twice his strength. The external structure is domed of moss, dead leaves, lichens or grasses, which usually match the surroundings, though hardly with intent, since wrens' nests are often so conspicuous; and the snuggery within is warm with moss, hair and feathers. From four to nine, or occasionally even thirteen, eggs are laid twice in a season, of white lightly and ruddily splashed. The plumage is a warm rufous above, a greyer brown below, and barred and mottled with a pale streak through the eye.

PIED WAGTAIL, Water Wagtail, Trotty Wagtail, Polly-Wash-Dish or Devil's Bird. Length, 7 ½ inches, including the long tail.

The pied wagtail is a duodecimo edition of the magpie, both in the variegated black and white (greyer in winter) of his plumage and the inconsequence of his ways. The term "water" wagtail is far too narrow, for he is as happy on the lawn or in the farmyard as he is by pond or stream. He is also particularly fond of hawking flies on the sun-warmed roof of the house. The pied wagtail is never in the same posture for a minute at a time. He trips nimbly to and fro, whirrs round upon himself, leaps into the air after an insect, goes tittering across the grass so swiftly that the movements of his feet are lost, stops dead and then bounds off into a dipping switch-back flight with a double note of *tschizzik* and *tzi-wirrp*.

The nest of the pied wagtail is a hole packed with welded grass-roots, leaves and other material lined with hair, wool and feathers. He will build it in almost any imaginable site, in a bank, against a wall, among rocks, under a clod, at the roots of a tree, between railway sleepers, in an old nest of the magpie. The eggs, four to six in number, are correspondingly variable and capricious in colouring, the more normal having a bluish white background streaked and flecked with greys and browns. Some of the birds migrate in winter. The sexes are more or less alike in plumage.

91

SPOTTED FLYCATCHER, Post-Bird, Egypt Bird, Old Man, Beam-Bird, Cobweb, or Bee-Bird. Length, 5 ½ inches.

The spotted flycatcher, who, in May, is almost the last of the summer visitors to arrive, is nothing much to look at. His back is ashy-brown, his brown head streaked with darker brown, his whitish breast streaked lightly—an unremarkable effect. His behaviour, however, is so distinctive that he can be recognised immediately. He sits, bolt upright, silent, absorbed, perched like a little monument on a bare branch, post, or fence before some open space. Here he appears almost indifferent to his surroundings; but in reality nothing is escaping that bright eye, and at the chosen moment he will sally out to seize some passing insect in mid-air, twisting and turning in aerial pursuit before he takes it with an audible snap. He seldom misses.

Spotted flycatchers prefer a solid support for their nest in the vicinity of buildings, on the ledge of a window, on a beam, in a hole, or in a climbing shrub or trellis against a wall. They will also build in the old nest of another bird. They are wise to choose some solid foundation, for their own nest is a flimsy affair, loosely constructed of trailing grass, moss and cobwebs. The eggs are bluish white, spotted and blotched with red. The sexes are alike.

WILLOW WARBLER, Willow Wren, Willow-Biter, Peggy Whitethroat, Banty-Jug, Tom Thumb, Willie Muftie, Sallypecker, Pettichaps or Grass Mumruffin. Length, 4 ½ inches.

A slender, graceful, greenish-yellow little bird, glimpsed momentarily among the boughs unfolding their spring buds, will be one of the three "leaf warblers". They are easily confused: the CHIFF-CHAFF is usually slightly browner than the willow-warbler, and has black legs, while those of the willow-warbler are light brown. The WOOD-WARBLER is brighter and yellower than the other two, and has much longer wings: he is, moreover, a bird of the woods and is unlikely to be seen in a garden. But all of

them keep closely to the trees, and only occasionally is their jerky, flitting flight visible as they pass from one tree to another. Sometimes they will make an aerial pounce on a passing insect, or hover to investigate the under-surface of the leaves. The best way to distinguish between the chiff-chaff and the willow-warbler is by their song. The *chiff-chaff-chaff-chaff-chiff-chiff-chaff-chaff* of the former is unmistakable; and so will soon be the song of the willow-warbler to anyone with half an ear. It is a tender, lyrical, simple song and has a dying fall, so sweet, so sad, that even in its beginning one is reminded of its end. The chiff-chaff is the earliest of these summer visitors from Africa, arriving in March, but the willow-warbler's song is not normally heard until the middle of April. The nest of the willow-warbler is usually built on the ground among grass, at the foot of a tree or by a path or hedgerow. Moss, grasses, stalks and dead leaves are neatly interwoven to form a domed nest with a side entrance and a cosy lining of feathers. The eggs are white blotched with red. There are several other warblers whose joyous recognition of mate and kingdom gladden any garden. The BLACKCAP's is one of the loveliest songs, a rich, liquid jet of melody. The tone resembles the blackbird's, but the utterance is very rapid and much more confident. The song will probably be heard from the depths of some dense shrubbery at the bottom of the garden. The black cap of the male and the rich chestnut cap of the hen bird will distinguish them at sight from other warblers. The song of the GARDEN WARBLER is very like that of the blackcap, but more breathless and not so rich in tone; and the bird himself is not unlike a plump blackcap without the cap. The WHITETHROAT, unlike the other warblers, will often go out of his way to advertise his presence: he is a great scold at any passer-by. The boundary hedge will be the place to look for him. From here he may suddenly shoot into the air, to descend with open wings in song—a brisk, cheerful but often rather unmelodious song of varying quality. The NIGHTINGALE is not properly a bird of the garden, but a large garden with a thick copse and plenty of tangled undergrowth on the outskirts could easily harbour a nightingale.

SWALLOW, Length, 7 ½ inches.

HOUSE MARTIN, Easing Swallow or Martlet. Length, 5 inches.

The swallow leads a double life, his own and a symbolic one in human imagination. Not the voices of all the warblers that announce the spring can evoke its presence and banish winter so surely as the sight of the first swallow. His habits are so universally known as to need no description, but the song, delivered in full air or from a gable, stump, telegraph wire, or coign of vantage, is, though a very abundant music, less familiar. When the swallow sings from a perch, he will often conclude his warm, warbling stave by rattling the mandibles in a self-appreciative clap.

The first swallows arrive on our coasts towards the end of March, but the first clutch of from four to six white eggs, freckled with reddish brown and grey, is rarely laid before early May, though the nesting season may continue until October. The beam or joist of a barn is a favourite site, and the saucer of mud is lined with grass and feathers. Old hats, shrimp-pots on shelves, and even boughs of trees may also become homes for the swallow.

He is a far more brilliantly coloured bird than the house martin, wearing a many-coloured dress of steel-blue above with a rich chestnut on the throat and forehead, a band of blue across the chest, buff underparts and a greenish gloss on the wings and tail.

95

The easiest way to tell a house martin from a swallow when they are in flight is by the conspicuous white rump of the house martin. His underparts are also white, and his back, wings and tail are black—but these details are not so noticeable in the air. Another identifying mark is the tail, which is short and forked and lacks the streamers of the swallow. It is the house martin which builds the enclosed mud nest under the eaves of the house, but it is extraordinary how many people refer to this familiar spectacle as a swallow's nest. Both sexes assist in its construction, but work is often interrupted for a playful interchange of billing at the edge of the muddy cup or to quarrel with a sparrow who may be attempting to take over the unfinished nest for his own use. House martins are sociable birds and often nest together in considerable numbers. The eggs, usually four or five, are white. The first clutch is not laid until early June, but it is often followed by another two, and sometimes the last late nestlings are left to starve while the parents gather for their return flight to Africa.

STARLING, Stare, Sterlin, Chepster or Jacob. Length, 8 ½ inches.

The starling, a bird belonging everywhere, and especially to buildings, presents on first acquaintance a rough-and-ready manner and hobbledehoy appearance. Only at close view and in the spring can his iridescent coat be seen, the feathers of a beaten-out metallic gleam throwing a lustre of black, purple, blue and green reflections changing colour at different angles and in striking tone with the lemon yellow of his bill. In autumn the tipping of the feathers with buff and white dulls their brilliance. His morning and evening song, time-keeper of the dawning and failing light, for all its hotch-potch of melodious and instrumental sound, its squealings, whistlings, chatterings, clickings, smackings and bubblings, for all its casual mimicries, has a very beautiful and moving effect, especially when uttered in chorus. The autumn flocking of the starling is one of the seven wonders of Britain. Along well-defined lines, starting sometimes from as far as thirty miles from their roost, thousands, and in favourable places hundreds of thousands, of birds converge in swift, direct flight and perform as one bird a number of rapidly changing figures on rapid triangular wings. Then as the dusk

thickens they fall like hail upon trees or buildings or reed and osier beds and burst into a shrill massive chanting.

On the ground the starling walks with bustling, jerky gait, and when it flies. The nest is built in a cavity in a tree, cliff, water-spout, chimney, haystack, ruin, barn, quarry or spire, and is a mere litter of straw, twigs and grass, lined with soft substances. The eggs are pale blue and from four to seven in number. The female is more spotted than the male.

CUCKOO, or Gowk. Length, 13 inches.

This famed and enigmatic bird looks on the wing something like a disconsolate hawk, and his flight, though powerful, is at

97

(QUICK 4)

times uncertain in direction and unsteady in poise. Poetic associations have invested the male cuckoo with a symbolic romance as the messenger of spring, on account of the soft flute-like major third of his call, first heard on his arrival in mid-April. But scientific interest centres in the female, who diverges from avian custom in her promiscuous mating and in her habit of depositing her eggs in the nests of pipits, wagtails, robins, dunnocks and various warblers, at the same time removing one of the eggs from the chosen nest in her bill. The nestling, a very ill-conditioned young oaf, has an irritant surface to the hollow of the back which enables it to pitch the other inmates out of the nest on to the ground, where they perish.

The "song" of the male cuckoo needs no description: the female employs a bubbling cry rather like water poured out of the neck of a bottle, and a strange howling note. Occasionally one bird will use both calls. On the ground the cuckoo is a clumsy, waddling walker. Both sexes are very greedy and irritable. Five or six eggs are laid at intervals of several days between each egg, and though these are often similar in size and colouring to those of the species victimised, there is no evidence that the cuckoo deliberately chooses a clutch to match the eggs she lays. Even more curious than the behaviour of the cuckoo is the apparent willingness of the foster-parents to play the role assigned to them without hitch. It has been suggested that the young cuckoo has a mesmeric power in its voice. Another point of interest is that the old birds depart for Africa a month or six weeks earlier than the young.

The sexes are alike in their handsome plumage, bluish-grey above, lighter on the neck and breast and darker on the wings and tail, whitish on the underparts with dark transverse bars. The long, rounded tail is spotted and tipped with white. The feet are yellow and the inside of the mouth is orange.

GREEN WOODPECKER, Yaffle, Rain-Bird, Woodall, Woodspite, High-Hoe, Hew-Hole, or Pick-a-Tree. Length, 12 ½ inches.

It is difficult to believe in the green woodpecker as an English bird, what with his bold tropical colouring, so foreign to the subdued tones of our landscape, his piercing cry, his oddly demoniac appearance, and his superlative animation. The green woodpecker, digging his trunk-dwelling, will be heard over the length and breadth of the land, and his movements seem to match that blithe laugh which, for those who love him, makes him the bird of liberty.

This indeed is true in fact as well as impressive, for the yaffle displays his independence by being one day a bird of the woodlands, flying in huge drooping loops and crests among the pillars of the trees to seek his food from their bark and branches; and the next a bird of the open spaces, getting his livelihood entirely from ants' nests on the ground. As an instance of this change of habit, due in part to the increasing scarcity of old timber, the green woodpecker is heard nowadays in open parkland and the margins of meadow and woodland as much as in deep woods, and often he is to be seen in gardens, where he will sit bolt upright on the lawn, stooping to plunge his dagger of a beak up to the hilt again and again into the ground in his fanatical quest for ants.

The nest is hammered out of a trunk that has begun to decay, though it often gives no visible sign of it. Chips of wood are laid on the floor of the hole as a bedding, and five to seven polished oval white eggs are laid upon them. The bird's colours are disposed in an abrupt and sharply contrasted manner. His face is black, his crown, moustaches and back of the head are crimson, his rump is bright yellow, his wings have the outer webs barred black and white, his back is olive green, and his underparts run to green with an infusion of yellow. The sexes are alike, except that the female lacks the crimson in the moustachial stripe.

BARN OWL, Billy Wix, Cherubim, Gilly Howlet, Oolert or Jenny Owl. Length, 13 ½ inches.

Many misconceptions of the nature and behaviour of birds have originated in the poetic imagination. Just as the nightingale has been inescapably branded as the broken-hearted lover who sings only at night, so has the owl come to symbolise death and disaster and the darker side of witchcraft. A bird that passes invisibly on

silent wings and wakes the sleeping world with an unearthly voice must expect to be misunderstood to some extent by the ignorant populace; but the poets have certainly made matters worse by referring to him as "the rude bird of hate", the "gibbering", "baleful", "deadlie", "ghastly owle", the "bird of omen dark and foul". Even the most desperate need of a rhyme cannot excuse that last epithet.

Of the three common species, the one most likely to ~~~~~~~ from the garden is the barn owl, which has a partiality for the vicinity of human habitations. As dusk softens the outline of landscape, his pale and ghostly form will materialise suddenly in silent wavering flight like some enormous nocturnal butterfly. It is his habit to quarter the ground systematically, flying some ten to twenty feet above it, in search of the rats, mice, voles, and shrews on which he feeds. He will also take small birds, particularly house-sparrows, from the ivy where they roost. He is indeed a useful ally to the farmer, who in former days recognised this

101

when he built a barn by always leaving for the owl an opening high in the barn wall.

The barn owl's voice, a weirdly horrible shriek, together with the loud hissing and snoring noises with which he finds it necessary to express his feelings, do not prepare one for the beauty of his person. He is the loveliest of owls, with his flat white heart-shaped face and large black eyes, his satin-white underparts and orange-buff back spotted with grey and white. The barn owl makes no nest, but will lay four to seven matt white eggs on a layer of dry pellets (of the undigested bones and fur which are regurgitated by all owls), among the rafters of a house, or in a barn or belfry, or a church tower or dovecote or in any ruined or unoccupied building. The eggs are laid at intervals of several days but are incubated from the start, so that a nest will contain young of varying ages and sometimes eggs at the same time.

The TAWNY OWL, although mainly a bird of the woods, is also often heard in the garden. Heard, but seldom seen, for he is a thoroughly nocturnal species. His melodious *hoo-hoo-hoo...oo ...hoooooooo* is the familiar hoot which many people wrongly attribute to any and every owl. The LITTLE OWL is much more a bird of agricultural country, and can sometimes be seen during the day sitting on a post or fence or telegraph wire.

'WEEK-ENDING' BIRDS

Apart from the common and not-so-common birds which can be expected in their own habitual environments, there is always the tantalising possibility for a Birdwatcher of spotting a distinguished casual visitor from the Continent, from Greenland or Iceland or even from America. These transient, "week-ending" birds, some of them drifting with unfavourable winds, or perhaps deficient in that magnetic sense of direction which guides a migratory bird from one latitude to another, turn up from time to time in any and every corner of the country. Their appearance marks the red-letter days of the Birdwatcher's calendar. The following are a few of the more conspicuous among them.

HOOPOE or Dung Bird. Length, 11 inches—slightly larger than a mistle-thrush.

This spectacular bird—which possesses the splendid Latin name of *Upupa epops epops*—is one of the most regular "week-enders" from the Continent and has visited most parts of the British Isles at some time or other, even in winter. In fact, several times he has stayed on to nest in the southern counties, and he would undoubtedly become one of the regular British breeding birds if allowed to do so. But the Hoopoe is tame to the point of stupidity and an easy prey to the man with a gun. His plumage is pinkish cinnamon brown, with boldly barred black and white wings, and a striking crest tipped with black which, when erected, gives the bird the appearance of a Red Indian brave. His diet consists of the larvæ of insects, worms, woodlice, ants and beetles, and he is often seen probing for these with his long curved bill on lawns and manure heaps.

This exploratory operation, carried out with the head bobbing up and down in a rather portentous way, accounts perhaps for the superstitious awe in which "The Doctor Bird" was held by the Arabs. They believed that it possessed remarkable medical qualities and also that it had the power of water-divining. Its head was once in great demand as a charm and in the practice of witchcraft.

BEE-EATER or Gnat Snapper. Length, 11 inches—slightly larger than a mistle-thrush.

The bee-eater summers in southern Europe and winters in Africa, and it is hard to understand what attraction an English summer could hold for such a bird. But he is obviously of a

irregular intervals in all the south and east coast counties, usually in small parties. When the weather is fine he spends much time on the wing hawking for insects, and often perches on telegraph wires. This is one of the most gorgeously attired of our "week-enders": the back is a rich chestnut-brown and yellow, the tail and wings and underparts are metallic green and blue, the throat is brilliant yellow. The middle tail feathers project well beyond the others, and this feature makes the bird easy to identify in flight. The beak is long and curved. The bee-eater really does eat bees, and he will even perch outside a hive and eat the bees as they emerge.

GOLDEN ORIOLE or Golden Thrush. Length, 9½ inches—midway between a blackbird and a song thrush.

This dazzling visitor is more often heard than seen, though once seen the male oriole is easily recognised and is not easily forgotten. But he is of a shy and exceedingly secretive disposition, and were it not for his unmistakable loud clear musical call (which sounds rather like *We'll owe it you*), his week-ends would often pass undetected in the depths of his aroboreal hotel. The oriole is essentially a bird of the trees, and is seldom seen in the open or on the ground. The male is brilliantly yellow, with black wings and a black tail patterned in yellow; the hen bird is greener, and might be confused with a green woodpecker. The oriole usually visits England in the spring, coming from the Continent. Very occasionally he stays to nest. He is usually seen in parks, old gardens, woods and copses. He eats mainly insects in spring, taking cockchafers, grasshoppers, bumble-bees and spiders; but in autumn he is a great fruit-eater, and enjoys mulberries, grapes, figs and every sort of berry.

GREAT GREY SHRIKE, Great Butcher-Bird, Murdering Pie, or Mattagess. Length, 9 ½ inches—midway between a blackbird and a song thrush.

In contrast to the exotic appearance of the last three visitors, the great grey shrike strikes a somewhat sinister note, with his grey head and back, black and white wings and tail, whitish breast and bold black eye-patch. But this lonely butcher-bird is, nevertheless, a conspicuous and easily identified figure as he stands sentinel on his watch tower of telegraph-wire or tree-top, waiting to pounce on a meal of other bird, mouse or insect. The shrike perches upright, rather like a hawk; and, again hawk-like, hovers over his selected prey before the final pounce. And like all shrikes, the great grey uses a larder of thorn-twig or barb of wire-railing on which to impale and dismember his victim; and often the rapacious bird kills and suspends more than he can use, leaving the bodies to decay. The great grey shrike is an inhabitant of northern and eastern Europe and visits Britain regularly, usually in autumn and winter.

SNOWY OWL. Length, 21-26 inches—slightly larger than a buzzard.

On the rare occasions when a snowy owl souths to Britain from his Arctic home it would be difficult not to notice such a large and conspicuous stranger, for the almost white plumage which camouflages his activities in Greenland, Northern Scandinavia and North Russia, in this country renders him visible, literally, a mile off. He is, moreover, a bird of open country, and hunts by day. He usually perches on the ground, preferably on a rock or log, and seldom on anything higher than twenty feet. He is seen most often in the north of Scotland and the Scottish islands, but has also been reported from a number of English counties. The snowy owl arrives here for a long "week-end" when food in the Arctic is scarce. His diet while in Britain consists of rabbits, mice, insects and small birds. In the far north he is said also to be an experienced fisherman.

OSPREY, Fish Hawk or Mullett Hawk. Length, 20-23 inches—about the same as a herring gull.

"And the Lord spake unto Moses and to Aaron, saying unto them, Speak unto the children of Israel, saying … these are they which ye shall have in abomination among the fowls; they shall not be eaten, they are an abomination." The unfortunate osprey

It was not for this reason, however, that he was exterminated as a British resident (the last Scottish eyrie was deserted in 1911), but because jealous fishermen and game preservers grudged his fishy diet, and eager gunners finished him off as he grew more scarce. Now the osprey is a rare but regular "week-ender" from Scandinavia to the coastal and inland waters of most parts of England and Scotland. The fish hawk is a handsome bird: dark brown above, except for the white head, slightly crested, with a conspicuous black cheek stripe; and snowy white beneath, with dusky breast-band. The wings are narrow, long and angled. When fishing, the osprey sails about thirty feet above the water, frequently hovering like a kestrel before plunging, feet first, on to his prey. The captive fish—trout, bream, perch, roach, carp or grey mullet—is then carried, head foremost in the talons.

BIRDS IN COMPANIES

A sege of herons and bitterns.

A herd of swans, cranes and curlews.

A dopping of sheldrakes.

A spring of teals.

A covert of coots.

A gaggle of geese.

A skein of geese (flying).

A bevy of quails.

A covey of partridges.

A congregation of plovers.

A walk (or wisp) of snipe.

A fall of woodcocks.

A murmuration of starlings.

An exaltation of larks.

A watch of nightingales.

A badelynge of ducks.

A sord (or sute) of mallards.

A muster of peacocks.

A flight of doves and swallows.

A building of rooks.

A brood of hens.

A host of sparrows.

A nye of pheasants.

A cast of hawks.

A plump of wildfowl.

A desert of lapwings.

A company of widgeon.

A chattering of choughs.

BEASTS ALSO IN COMPANIES

A pride of lions.

A lepe of leopards.

A herd of harts, bucks and all sorts of deer.

A bevy of roes.

A sloth of bears.

A singular of boars.

A sownder of wild swine.

A dryft of tame swine.

A route of wolves.

A harras of horses.

A rag of colts.

A stud of mares.

A pace of asses.

A baren of mules.

A flock of sheep.

A tribe of goats.

A sculk of foxes.

A cete of badgers.

A richesse of martens.

A fesynes of ferrets.

A huske (or down) of hares.

A dule of turtle.

A nest of rabbits.

A clowder of cats.

A kendel of young cats.

A shrewdness of apes.

A labour of moles.

A mute of hounds.

A cowardice of curs.

A drove of kine.

TRAVELS WITH A DONKEY

But all sorts of things and weather
Must be taken in together,
To make up a year
And a sphere.

R. W. Emerson.

Whoso hath but a mouth
Shall ne'er in England suffer drought.

Anonymous.

I Wisdom dwell with prudence
And find out knowledge
Of witty inventions

Proverbs VIII. 12.

"Write that down," the King said to the jury, and the jury eagerly wrote down all three dates on their slates, and then added them up, and reduced the answer to shillings and pence.

Lewis Carroll.

THE WEATHER (SCIENTIFIC)

Before making an irrevocable decision to spend the week-end out of doors, the would-be camper is well advised to consult the Weather Forecast which appears in his morning paper, in order to prepare himself against the worst vagaries of the climate.

A distinction must be made, however, between reading any weather forecast and reading the weather chart which appears in *The Times*, *Daily Telegraph*, etc. The first is almost useless, as third-hand information; the chart is at second-hand from the minute and accurate records kept at the Government Meteorological Office. It gives a simplified map, of England and parts of Europe, showing the condition of the atmosphere surrounding that part of the earth.

Everybody knows that the atmosphere is constantly in a state of flux, partly because the world goes round, and partly because water (e.g. seas and lakes) is always either condensing or evaporating, owing to the action of the sun's rays. As a result of this changeability, the degree of atmospheric pressure on the earth varies with place and time; this is shown in the barometric charts made by meteorologists. They have discovered a variety of tricks performed by the atmosphere, each of which has a specific bearing on the weather in the locality in which it is performed. The star turn, so to speak, is the pattern formed by a small circle of low pressure surrounded by several circles of greater and greater pressure. (We speak in terms of the chart, on which areas subject to the same weight of air are linked together by circles, or irregular, but always closed, forms, known as *isobars*. No such pattern exists, of course, actually in the air.) The effect of this condition of "circles" of low pressure is that the air tends to level itself by rushing into the defaulting gap. Nature, remember, abhors a vacuum. Further, it generally happens that the inrushing air is of a different temperature, and the result of the contact is rain. Maxim: avoid an area of low pressure, unless it is forecast that it will move away. For the habit of these meteorological "patterns" is to move about, as well as to widen or to become narrower, to "put out a tongue" or put it in.

Here we arrive at a second point of interest to the chart-reader. Namely, the wider apart the circles of different pressures (isobars) in a low pressure or a high pressure area, the less forceful the wind, whereas the closer the isobars the more violent the wind. Winds tend to blow along the isobars, with a slight deviation inwards in low pressure, and outwards in high pressure areas. They are often marked on charts by arrows, giving velocity (in miles per hour) in circles attached to the head of the arrow.

Areas of high pressure are (strange to say!) the precise opposite of low pressure; they consist of a small circle of high pressure surrounded by circles of less and less pressure toward the extreme circumference. There is thus little encouragement to atmospheric movement, and generally fine weather, unless there are unusual conditions of moisture, i.e. prevailing clouds (moisture that will condense on small provocation). The several degrees of pressure are given by figures close to the isobars.

Nobody knows precisely why these patterns happen at the time and place they do: it seems that they are governed by the movements of the upper air, which is not yet open to systematic study. Only the experienced map-reader can say that, according to his experience of sequences, he expects such and such a change to take place consequent on what he now observes. Therefore, if such a one forecasts that a given atmospheric "pattern" will move in such and such a direction at such and such a pace, trailing sun, wind, or rain in its wake, it is not incumbent on anyone to believe him, but it is more than probable that his experience will stand the test of events.

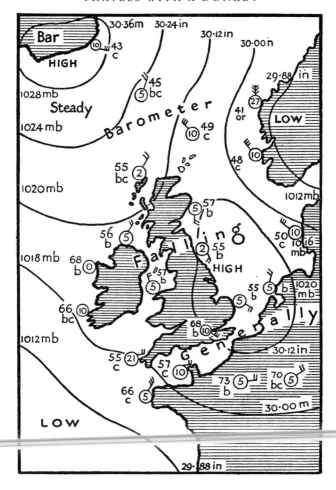

The map-maker usually gives the general character of the weather by the following conventional signs:

b = blue sky
bc = blue sky partly cloudy

113

c = generally cloudy
d = drizzle
e = wet air
f = fog. F = thick fog
g = gloomy
h = hail
l = lightning
m = mist
o = overcast sky
p = passing showers
q = squalls
r = rain. R = heavy rain
rr = continuous moderate rain
roro = continuous light rain
s = snow
rs = sleet
t = thunder
u = ugly, threatening
v = unusual visibility
w = dew
x = hoar frost
z = dust haze

The sign / divides what is from what has gone before, e.g. bc/r = fair weather after rain.

To supplement the instruments of science, there is the traditional wisdom of the countryside, or

THE WEATHER (POETIC)
★

If Candlemas-day be dry and fair
The half of winter's to come and mair:
If Candlemas-day be wet and foul
The half o' winter's gane at Yule.
        (Candlemas-day is Feb. 2nd)
★

If the oak be out before the ash
The summer will be but a splash:

If the ash be out before the oak
The summer will be all a soak.

★

St. Swithin's Day if thou dost rain
For forty days it will remain:
St. Swithin's Day if thou be fair
For forty days 'twill rain nae mair.
    (St. Swithin's Day is July 15th)

★

September mild, October gold,
Are followed by November cold.

★

An air' winter
A sair winter.

★

Ice in November enough to bear a duck,
All the coming winter will be mud and muck.

★

A green Christmas makes a full church-yard.

★

Rain before seven,
Fine before eleven.

★

Between one and two
See what the day will do.

★

Red at night is the shepherd's delight.
Red in the morning is the shepherd's warning.

★

Mackerel skies and mares tails
Make great ships carry low sails

When the wind is in the East
'Tis neither good for man nor beast:
When the wind is in the North
The skilful fisher goes not forth:
When the wind is in the South
It blows the bait in the fishes' mouth:
When the wind is in the West
Then it is the very best.

OF CAMP EQUIPMENT

If, in spite of the weather-chart, and in spite of the weather (for it has by now become apparent that these are not precisely identical terms), you determine to embark on the preparation of a camping outfit, *Be Prepared* for every emergency of weather and of distance from habitation by making your camping outfit as comprehensive as possible, but as little burdensome and inconvenient *en route*.

THE TENT

is, in England, the primary safeguard of the person, as the mosquito net is in finer and warmer countries. Tents range from the *extended cottage*, a magnificent structure of walls, roofs, door and porches, to an *Itisa* which will fold neatly into a pocket, the choice naturally depending on whether the expedition is pedestrian, cyclist or motorist. Most modern tents are made of finely woven cotton, some even of silk material, all of which are found perfectly waterproof. The tent, however, will be sure to leak if it is touched during the rain *even on the inside*. As extra security against cloudburst waterproofing solution can be purchased or concocted. A tent complete with poles and pegs may weigh as little as 5 lbs and they can with some difficulty be obtained in colours. They should be provided with *fly-sheets* which give extra protection from sun and rain as well as ventilation.

THE BED

is a scarcely less important protection to the wary camper than the covering overhead. To prevent chills from the damp which never fails in any weather to rise from the ground, a waterproof groundsheet of a light weight oiled fabric (which has superseded mackintosh) should be the foundation of the night's rest. It should be of a size to cover the floor of the tent, and may perhaps be spread over with a light ground blanket of cashmere or wool. If the ground sheet is the sole article of bedding, it is a very good plan to make a "*hip hole*" underneath it in the ground, but the hole must be large enough to make sure of not falling out and failing to find it again in the course of the night. Better still, a

116

palliasse case can be carried and filled with straw and grass, or these can simply be spread under the ground sheet and thrown away in the morning, in case of soddenness. *A scout's substitute bed is made by running two poles down the sides of two large canvas bags, placed together lengthwise and slit at their seamed ends. The ends of the poles are placed on logs, and should be wedged apart with a cross-pole to keep the canvas taut.*

For the rest, blankets are a heavy burden of superstition. An old eiderdown sewn into a bag is far less bulky and gives the warmth of three blankets. Incidentally, an eiderdown sleeping-bag, which has the appearance of a long green cocoon fitting closely to the person, may be bought. When rolled up it occupies the minimum of space, and in an ordinary quality weighs only 1 lb 15 ozs. The wool sleeping-bag weighs from 5 to 8 lbs, is not so easily washable nor so warm. If you use blankets instead of a sleeping-bag, remember that without a mattress you need as many under as over you.

THE KITCHEN

should include a stove, since the incontinency of the climate makes it advisable not to rely for the satisfaction of the appetite on an open camp fire. Of stoves, the very best and easiest to handle is the *Primus* paraffin air-pressure variety, preferably the roarer, which is less easily stopped up, though noisier. Petrol stoves are also perfectly satisfactory. To complete the kitchen outfit, say, for four, there are needed not more than three saucepans, fitting one into the other, a big frying-pan, a kettle with tea-infuser, a milk-can with top, and, for luxury's sake, a toaster. If the frying-pan is provided with a lid, it does duty for baking purposes. The pans should be of aluminium with wire handles (detachable). Paper

plates save washing, but paper cups impart a "mousy" flavour, especially to hot drinks. Lastly, one or two buckets (of canvas) serve for carrying water and washing-up. Cases can be bought containing knife, spoon, fork and tin-opener. In any circumstances, whether cased or no, do not forget the tin-opener. No camper has ever been known to open a tin with his teeth. It is reported that tins can be boiled to such a pitch that the metal becomes soft and pliable, but it seems probable that more of it would be deposited in the food than spooned or wrenched off after this treatment. Here, however, is a method of opening a bottle without a corkscrew. *Tie round the neck of the bottle a piece of string or other inflammable material, and set it alight. Where the glass is heated it will break in a clean line.*

If it is hot have a tin lined with glass for the butter.

FOOD QUANTITIES

should be calculated in liberal allowances, seeing that the open air notoriously whips up the sluggard appetite. It is suggested that of the following essential articles one person will require at least the following quantity per day:

Bread ..	1 lb.	Sugar			2 ozs
Butter ..	3 oz.	Meat (adding sausages,			
Jam / Marmalade	2 oz.	etc., for breakfast *ad lib.*)			10 ozs
Milk ..	¾ pint	Potatoes			½ lb

Tea, cocoa, cheese, rolled oats, flour, suet, biscuits, etc., etc., can be kept in tins in quantities which meet the demand for variety. Bacon is a useful standby, and its grease will provide fat for cooking. If it is inconvenient to carry or fetch milk, either dried or sweet condensed milk can be made to serve. (Beware of such as have a passion for eating such milk neat with a table-spoon.)— Similarly, dried eggs suffer no great loss of dietetic value by being treated in this way. They are easy to carry but nasty to eat. One pound of powder represents four dozen eggs.

You can tell the age of a *real* egg, without cracking the shell, by looking at it against the sun or any strong light. If you frame the egg in your hands or any opaque material, the shell will be sufficiently translucent for you to see the size of the air space in the egg. The older the egg, the larger the air space.

ON FINDING THE WAY

When he has provided himself with all his equipment, the camper will require to find his way from place to place by map and compass.

The only way to read with any advantage such maps as are not printed square with the points of the compass is to orientate them so that the North that is marked coincides with the North given by the compass. In the absence of a compass, a watch should be held horizontally with the hour hand pointing at the sun. The South then lies along a line exactly halfway between the hour hand and the figure XII, and the map can be faced South to correspond with this line. Supposing neither sun nor compass is to hand, the only thing to do is to turn towards some well-marked feature of the landscape, and, having identified this feature on the map, set it to give the hill, wood, or whatever it is, in the same direction. You may then pick out the direction of your objective. The wanderer at night must rely on the somewhat improbable appearance of the stars, and particularly of the Polar, or North Star, to direct him in his paths. The moon is of no assistance whatever.

There is no foundation for the popular belief that one can tell which way London lies by the placing of telegraph posts on one side or other of the road, for they sometimes appear on the left and sometimes on the right going towards London. *But the cross-bars are placed on the London side of the poles.*

ON CAMP SITES

Coming upon a desirable locality, the camper must yet be practical in the choice of his site. A camp should be pitched in the open, and not under trees, because there may be a visitation of lightning; and there quite probably will be rain. While trees protect for some time from the rain, after a while they shower heavy drops on the tent, and mixed with these drops is a certain amount of acid which causes canvas to rot much sooner than the hopeful purchaser is led to expect. The camper may, however, protect himself by placing trees between his tent and the wind, the direction of which is easily discovered by watching the bend of boughs or twigs, by lighting a piece of paper to see where its smoke is carried, or by wetting the finger and exposing it.

The best situation of all for a long stay is one open to the South and protected to the North and East. A clay soil should be avoided because it is cold and damp, whereas chalk and, even better, gravel, drain water away. Long grass indicates a place where ground is usually damp, and therefore better left alone; and even if the weather is undeniably dry, long grass is not a good site for a camp because it is much beloved of things that

119

creep and crawl. Naturally, high ground is better drained than low, and is the wiser choice unless it is unduly exposed.

It is sometimes imagined that the tent should be "ditched" all round, but this is an unnecessary precaution unless there is to be a tropical downpour. Moreover, in that case the ditching would have to be supplemented by a series of channels to carry off the floods. A well-drained site does not give any encouragement to these feats of engineering. A most important precaution, however, is to loosen all guy lines at night since they shrink considerably in the rain and will otherwise pull a mass of soaking canvas down about the sleeper's ears. If the soil is not very firm, the pegs to which the ropes are attached can be kept in position by placing logs or stones across them: in a gale the ropes can be attached to logs buried a foot or so deep.

While the tent is packed up the ropes should be rolled round their pegs, otherwise they will become inextricably entangled.

ON KNOTS

The following knots will do whatever else is necessary to keep the camp in its place:

The Reef-knot, for joining two ends of equal size.

The Double Sheet Bend, for joining ropes of different thicknesses.

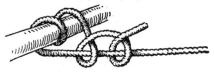

Two Round Turns and two Half Hitches, for fastening a boat, horse, dog, etc., to a horizontal rail.

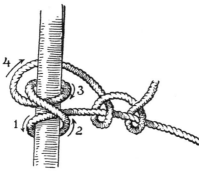

Two Clove Hitches and two Half Hitches, for hanging anything from a vertical post.

The Bowline, for slinging a hammock, or lowering anything from a height.

OF WATER

Above all, the camp should be pitched near water, if possible, running water. If the purity of the water is at all doubtful, it should be boiled for half an hour and afterwards strained through a piece of cloth, before drinking. The correct position for drinking from a pool is kneeling on one knee with the other leg stretched behind. Nothing is more uncomfortable than being flat on the stomach, which in this position is incapable of providing proper accommodation for the water. If the pool or stream is inaccessible to the mouth, you may still drink by the following method, if you happen to have a piece of paper in your pocket.

121

AN IMPROVISED CUP

These directions following have (we are told) saved many a bold pioneer from death by thirst at a cupless but otherwise well-equipped oasis.

A cup of convenient size may be made of a piece of paper 7 to 9 inches square (or smaller with less convenience).

To make a square from any rectangular sheet of paper, fold the paper diagonally so that the top edge is exactly super-imposed on the side edge. Cut or tear off neatly that part which is not covered by the folded piece.

You then have a square folded about the line A B into two triangles.

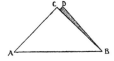

Fold over thus:

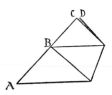

Turn the whole thing round, and fold over the other corner:

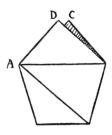

Bend back the flaps, and fold them into the lateral slots
D flap goes into A pocket, and C flap in B pocket:

122

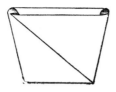

FUEL AND FIRE

The other primary necessity of the camp is a supply of fuel for the camp fire. A fire should be lighted first with dry grass or leaves, and next very small dry sticks: last only should the larger sticks be thrown on. Birch bark, since it contains oil, makes excellent kindling; so does standing dead wood, or even prostrate decaying logs, of which fine dry shavings from the inside are certain to start the fire successfully.

To light a fire without matches, use a petrol cigarette lighter. Only if you are improvident enough to lack all modern appliances should this exasperating method be attempted. *Set a hard pointed stick in a hole in a softer one, first filling the hole with sand or other gritty substances. Set tinder, such as very, very dry grass, or wool if you can find any, near the point of operation, and drill until such sparks as you may bring to life leap onto the tinder and start a blaze.* The operation takes half an hour at least, and will probably cost you the skin of your palms, unless you can do the drilling with a bow made of wood on one side and elastic (twisted once round the drill) on the other. If there is any sun, a lens (such as a magnifying glass or the glass of a cycle lamp), set so that the rays of the sun shine through it helps to heat the tinder. A concave mirror or a lamp reflector can be set to reflect the rays, but is not so effective. Plain glass is no earthly use.

Your fire should be made on the lee quarter of the camp, i.e. with the camp between the fire and the wind. It is important in dry weather to cut away all grass, bracken and suchlike surrounding the fire—particularly, of course, on the side to which the wind is driving.

A cooking fire should be only very small; in fact, it should be slightly narrower than the frying-pan or saucepan, so that this may be balanced on stones set at either side. Cooking is easiest over red cinders.

123

It is not necessary to lift the lid of the pot in order to discover whether the water is boiling (just as it is not necessary to eat all the peas to find out if they are tender). Hold the end of a stick or a knife to the pot and you will feel it vibrating when the water boils.

Most of your refuse can be burnt; but tins and other non-inflammable remains should be buried in a small pit—*not* thrown into the nearest thicket.

ON RIGHTS OF LAND

The last precaution, which might well be in fact the first, is to make sure of proper permission to use the site you have chosen. *No piece of land* in the British Isles is available for camping without express permission from its owner. Even "common land," so called, is not the property of the world at large; while paths and rights of way are allowed to be used only for passage. (See Section on The Law.) This is the only general rule that can be made, except that to obtain permission to camp is not such a difficult thing, provided that the landowner, probably the butcher or other strong man of the village, is approached with diplomacy and an order for meat or whatever may be his wares. He will probably, if assured that no damage of any sort will be perpetrated, discourse on the picturesque nature of the situation. However, on almost any of the large commons throughout the southern counties there is little strict observance of the law. It is asserted that the police may bring to court only persons who light a fire on the turf. No mention of this proviso is to be found in the Property Acts, but it is said to be a matter of common practice.

CHECK-LIST OF EQUIPMENT

Tent.

Ground sheet, quilts or eiderdown sleeping-bags, pillows.

Primus stove (*not forgetting the cleaning needles*), paraffin.

Three saucepans, 1 frying-pan, kettle and tea-infuser, milk-can, cups and plates, 2 canvas buckets, knives, forks, spoons, tin-opener, and corkscrew. (The fun of choosing a really adequate equipment at Woolworth's for next to no money may prove the best part of a rain-sogged holiday!)

Food in sufficient (indeed *more* than sufficient) quantities.

Map and compass.

Rope, axe for fuel, spade, candles or electric torch, matches. And then more matches.

Towels, dish-cloths, soap, soda, dish-mop, wire-brush for frying-pan, Lux for "washing-up" in general, brandy-flask, vaseline for sore extremities.

First Aid Kit (see page 254).

RULE OF THUMB

It is sometimes convenient to be able to measure by rule of thumb—literally. The following figures are those for that elusive character "the average man":

Span of thumb and index finger	7 inches.
Span of thumb and little finger	9 "
Nail joint of index finger	1 inch.
Wrist to elbow	10 inches.

The average size of a shod foot is presumably a foot.

KITCHEN MEASURES
Liquids.

1 teacupful	¼ pint
1 breakfast-cupful	½ pint
1 tumbler	½ pint

WEIGHTS AND MEASURES FROM COINS

Five pennies in a row measure just over 6 inches.
One halfpenny measures 1 inch.
One sixpence measures ¾ of an inch.

⌐⌐⌐⌐⌐⌐ and a threepenny piece	¼ oz.
2 halfpennies and a farthing	½ oz.
3 pennies	1 oz.

LINEAR MEASURES

7.92 inches	= 1 link
12 inches	= 1 foot
3 feet	= 1 yard
5½ yards	= 1 rod, pole or perch

4 poles	= 1 chain
10 chains	= 1 furlong
8 furlongs/1,760 yards/	
5,280 feet	= 1 mile
100 links	= 1 chain
6 feet	= 1 fathom
100 fathoms	= 1 cable length
6,080 feet	= 1 nautical mile
1 nautical mile	= 1.15152 land miles
4 inches	= 1 hand
9 inches	= 1 span
5 feet	= 1 pace

A GEOGRAPHICAL MILE is the length of one minute of Latitude. As the earth is a spheroid, the length of a minute increases from 6,046 feet at the Equator to 6,108 feet at the Poles. The length of the geographical mile is held to be 6,076.8 feet (2,025.6 yards).

THE LEGAL MILE in the British Empire and the United States is 1,760 yards, but in Scotland and Ireland, on the Continent and in Scandinavia the "mile" is very variable. Fior instance, the Scottish mile is 1,976.5 yards; the Irish 2,240 yards and the Swedish 11,000 yards.

A CRICKET PITCH is 22 yards (1 chain) between the stumps.

A LAWN TENNIS COURT is 78 x 36 feet (double) and 78 x 27 feet (single).

SQUARE MEASURES

144 sq. inches	= 1 sq. foot
9 sq. feet	= 1 sq. yard
30¼ sq. yards	= 1 sq. rod, pole/perch
40 sq. rods	= 1 rood
4 roods/4,840 sq. yards/	
10 sq. chains	= 1 acre
640 acres/3,097,600 sq. yards	= 1 sq. mile

126

CUBIC MEASURES

1,728 cu. inches	= 1 cu. foot
27 cu. feet	= 1 cu. yard

MEASURES OF CAPACITY

60 minims	= 1 fluid dram
8 fluid drams	= 1 fluid ounce
5 fluid ounces	= 1 gill
4 gills (20 ozs.)	= 1 pint
2 pints	= 1 quart
4 quarts	= 1 Imperial gallon
2 gallons	= 1 peck
4 pecks (8 gallons)	= 1 bushel
8 bushels	= 1 quarter

WEIGHTS (AVOIRDUPOIS)

437½ grains*/16 drams	= 1 ounce
7,000 grains*/16 ounces	= 1 pound
14 pounds	= 1 stone
28 pounds	= 1 quarter
112 pounds/4 quarters	= 1 hundredweight
20 hundredweights	= 1 ton

* The grain is the same whether it is avoirdupois, troy or apothecaries' weight.

MISCELLANOUS MEASURES

Bag of cement = 112 lb. = 1¼ cu.ft.
Barony of land = 4,000 acres

beef	= 200 lb.
butter	= 224 lb.
herring	= 500 herrings
potatoes	= 200 lb.

Billion = a million millions in U.K. and Germany
a thousand millions in U.S.A. and France
Bolt of canvas = 42 yards
Bottle of wine or spirits = 26 2/3 fluid ounces. A bottle of whisky

produces in England 32 singles, or tots; in Scotland, 26 singles.

Bushel of barley   = 56 lb.

        flour   = 56 lb.

        maize   = 60 lb.

        oats   = 42 lb.

        rye   = 60 lb.

        wheat   = 63 lb.

Carat = 3 grains

Cartload = 45 cu. ft.

Chaldron = 4½ quarters

Cental = 100 lb.

Clove of cheese = 8 lb.

Chest of tea = 84 lb.

Coil of rope = 112 fathoms

Coomb = 4 bushels

Digit = 0.91 inches

Ell, English   = 45 inches

   Scottish   = 37.06 inches

Gill, Imperial   = ¼ pint

  North and West England = ½ pints

Jeroboam = 4 bottles

Knot = 1.15 m.p.h.

Last = 10 quarters

Load of bricks   = 500

       flour   = 240 lb.

       hay and straw = 36 trusses

Magnum = 2 bottles

Noggin = ¼ pint

Peck of flour = 14 lb.

Pint, Imperial   = 0.125 gallon

   Scottish   = 0.376   ”

   Glasgow   = 0.5   ”

Pottle = 2 quarts

Puncheon of beer   = 72 gallons

        brandy = 120 gallons

        wine   = 84 gallons

Quintal = 100 kg.   = 220 lb.

Ream of writing paper = 20 quires = 480 sheets

Rehoboam = 6 bottles

Roll of butter   = 24 ounces
Sack of barley   = 224 lb.
       coals   = 224 lb.
       flour   = 280 lb.
       oats   = 168 lb.
       potatoes   = 168 lb.
       wheat   = 252 lb.
Stack of timber   = 108 cu. ft.
Stone of cheese, U.K.   = 16 lb.
       Scotland   = 24 lb.
Strike = 2 bushels
Truss of hay, old   = 56 lb.
       hay, new (till 1 Sept.) = 60 lb.
       straw   = 36 lb.
Wey (or Load) = 5 quarters
Windle of wheat = 220 lb.
Yard of land = 30 acres
1 gallon of milk = 10.3 lb.
1 ton of barley produces approximately 105 proof gallons of whisky.
100 average sized cigarettes contain about 3½ oz. of tobacco
1000   ”   ”   ”   ”   ”   2.2 lb. ”   ”
1000 medium size cigars   ”   ”   8.8 lb. ”   ”
1 cu. ft. of water = 6¼ gallons = 62½ lb.
1 inch of rainfall = 22,622 gallons per acre = 101 tons.
The circumference of a circle is 3.14 times its diameter.

SPEED

	Miles per hour
Antelope	55–60
Cheetah	70
Emu	40
Hare	45
Horse	44
Man	24 (running, during 100yds.)
Pigeon	67
Rabbit	35
Swift	200
Woman	20 (running)

	Feet per hour
Snail	1.916
Worm	10.5

2 miles per hour = about 3 feet per second

CONCRETE MIX
FOR FLOORS, PAVEMENTS, WALLS, PITS, STEPS AND PATHS
1 bucket Portland Cement (loose), 2 buckets sand (damp), 3 buckets coards aggregate (not larger than ¾") mixed together with ½ to ¾ of a bucket of water.

CROP YIELDS
For great Britain the ten-year average, 1941-1950, was, per acre: wheat, 19.5 cwt.; barley, 18.2 cwt.; oats, 16.8 cwt.; meadow hay, 19.8 cwt.; clover, lucerne and seeds hay, 28.4 cwt.; potatoes, 7 tons; mangolds, 20 tons; turnips and swedes, 14.6 tons; sugar beet (washed and topped), 9.5 tons.

LIVESTOCK
PUBERTY AND BREEDING AGE
The age at which puberty is reached is roughly:

Bitch	7 to 10 months
Cat	8 to 12 months
Ewe	8 to 12 months
Gilt (Pig)	4 to 5 months
Goat	8 to 12 months
Heifer	12 to 18 months
Mare	12 to 24 months

The age at which breeding starts is roughly:

Gilts	7 to 9 months
Heifers	18 months
Mares	in their third year

The seasons at which Oestrum Periods ("heat") occur are: *Mare*—February to July; *Goat*—autumn; *Ewe*—autumn; *Cow*, *Sow*, *Ass*, *Bitch* and *Cat*— all the year round.

PERIOD OF GESTATION AND INCUBATION

Days:	Shortest period	Usual period	Longest period
Ass	365	380	391
Bitch	55	60	68
Cat	48	50	56
Cow	240	283	321
Duck	28	30	32
Elephant	—	600	—
Ewe	146	151	161
Ferret	—	45	—
Giraffe	—	430	—
Goat	150	156	163
Guineapig	62	64	66
Hen	19	21	24
Mare	322	340	419
Pigeon	16	18	20
Rabbit	20	28	35
Sow	109	115	143
Turkey	24	26	30
Woman	252	266	280

FOR THE TRAVELLER ABROAD
KILOMETRE

A quick way of converting kilometres into miles (8 km. = 5 m.) is to divide by two and add a quarter of the result. *Example*: 100 km. = 50 + 12½ = 62½ miles. Or, rougher but readier, bring the number of kilometres up to the nearest ten, knock off the nought, and multiply by 6. Example: call 67 km. 70, and then multiply 7 by 6 = 42 miles.

LITRES

When buying petrol remember that 10 litres make 2.2 gallons. When buying oil (or milk) use the following table:

Litres	Pints
1	1¾
2	3½
3	5

Litres	*Pints*
4	7

METRES

If you are tempted by lengths of material in the market place, remember that a metre is a little longer than a yard. You can afford to ignore the difference till you get up to 5 yards, for which the equivalent is 4½ metres. If you want 6 yards, buy 5½ metres. The width of material is 39 inches instead of 36. There are 1094 yards in a kilometre.

KILOGRAMS

When buying by weight remember that a kilogram is 2¹/₅ lbs. (1016 kilograms is a ton). Half a kilo is called a livre and for all practical purposes can be regarded as the equivalent of a lb. In France some commodities will be marked at so much a 100 grs. (grammes), in Italy at so much an etto. This is a trifle less than ¼ lb.

CENTIGRADE AND FAHRENHEIT

For cold spells, heat waves, or illness:

°*Centigrade*	°*Fahrenheit*	
–10	14	(or 18 degrees of frost)
–5	23	(or 9 degrees of frost)
0	32	
5	41	
10	10	
15	59	
20	68	
25	77	
30	86	
35	95	
37	98.6	
38	100.4	
39	102.2	
40	104	

To convert °Fahrenheit to °Centigrade: subtract 32, multiply by 5, and divide by 9.

CONCLUSION

Be patient with your companions, O travellers. Remember that the donkey with whom you travel may be Apuleius. Therefore lead him into rose-gardens and keep him from low company.

PERPETUAL KALENDAR
TO FIND THE WEEK DAY OF ANY DATE IN
THE CHRISTIAN ERA

Add together the following numbers:

1. The number of the year.
2. The quotient (omitting fractions) after dividing the number of the year by 4.
3.★ Six times the number of completed centuries.
4.★ The quotient (omitting fractions) after dividing the number of completed centuries by 4.
5. The Index number of the month from Table I.
6. The number of the day of the month.

Then divide the total by 7: the remainder will give the day of the week according to Table II.

★ For dates expressed in Old Style (in Great Britain before 14th September, 1752, in France before 20th December, 1582) omit steps 3 and 4 and simply add 5 in all cases.

TABLE I				TABLE II	
Month	Index No.	Month	Index No.	Remainder	Day of Week
January	0	May	1	1	Sunday
January (in leap year)	6	June	4	2	Monday
		July	6	3	Tuesday
February	3	August	2		
February (in leap year)	2	September	5	4	Wednesday
		October	0	5	Thursday
March	3	November	3	6	Friday
April	6	December	5	0	Saturday

NOTE. A year is leap in OLD STYLE if its number is exactly divisible by 4. In NEW STYLE it is leap if its number is divisible by 4, unless its number ends in 00, in which case it is only leap if the preceding figures form a number divisible by 4 exactly (e.g. 1600 and 2000 are leap years; 1800 and 1900 are common years).

EXAMPLE. What was the day of the week on 9th July, 1930?

1.	Number of the year	1930
2.	Quotient after division by 4	482
3.	Number of completed centuries is 19. 6x19	114
4.	Quotient after dividing 19 by 4	4
5.	Index No. for July (from Table I)	6
6.	Day of the month	9

Total	7)	2545
Divide by 7		363
Remainder		4

From Table II the day of the week is Wednesday.

TO FIND THE DATE OF EASTER SUNDAY IN ANY YEAR OF THE CHRISTIAN ERA

Divide the number of the year by 4 and call the remainder a

Divide the number of the year by 7 and call the remainder b

Divide the number of the year by 19 and call the remainder c

Divide $19c+P$ by 30 and call the remainder d

Divide $2a+4b+6d+Q$ by 7 and call the remainder e

where P and Q are quantities to be determined by the method given below.

Then $d + e$ is equal to the number of days that Easter Sunday falls after March 22nd.

Thus if $d + e$ is equal to less than 9 Easter Day is March (22 + d + e)th, and if $d + e$ is greater than 9 Easter Day is April $(d + e - 9)$th.

SPECIAL CASES:

(1) If d + e = 35, Easter Day falls on April 19th (*not* on April 26th).

(2) If d + e = 34, and if also d = 28 and c is less than 10, Easter Day falls on April 18th (*not* on April 25th).

DETERMINATION OF P AND Q:

For OLD STYLE these are constants: P = 15, Q = 6.

For NEW STYLE they are constant for a century at a time.

Thus for 1700-1799: P = 23, Q = 3.
Thus for 1800-1899: P = 23, Q = 4.
Thus for 1900-1999: P = 24, Q = 5.
Thus for 2000-2099: P = 24, Q = 5.

To determine P and Q for any given century:

Call the hundreds' figure of the year	K
Divide K by 4 and call the quotient (excluding fractions)	L
Divide K − 17 by 25 and call the quotient (excluding fractions)	M
Divide K − M by 3 and call the quotient (excluding fractions)	N
Divide 15+K − L − N by 30 and the remainder will be	P
Divide 4+K − L by 7 and the remainder will be	Q

N.B.—Until the year 4200, M = O.

EXAMPLES:

On what day did Easter fall in 1930?

(For 1900-1999, P = 24, Q = 5.)

Remainder after dividing 1930 by 4	a = 2
Remainder after dividing 1930 by 7	b = 5
Remainder after dividing 1930 by 19	c = 11

Then 19 x 11 + 24 = 233.

Remainder after dividing 233 by 30   d = 23

Then 2 x 2 + 4 x 5 + 6 x 23 + 5 = 167.

Remainder after dividing 167 by 7   e = 6

Then d + e = 23 + 6 = 29.

Therefore Easter Sunday is April (29 − 9), i.e. April 20th.

Find P and Q for the hundred years 1900-1999.

Hundreds' figure	K = 19
Quotient after dividing 19 by 4	L = 4
(19 − 17 = 2) Quotient after dividing 2 by 25	M = 0
(19 − 0 = 19) Quotient after dividing 19 by 3	N = 6

Then $15 + 19 - 4 - 6 = 24$ and $4 + 19 - 4 = 19$.

Remainder after dividing 24 by 30	P = 24
Remainder after dividing 19 by 7	Q = 5

GAMES

If you can't volley, wear velvet socks.
S. Potter.

"Play!"
Any Umpire.

Life's too short for Chess.
Henry James Byron.

The player on the other side is hidden from us.
We know that his play is always fair, just,
and patient.
Thomas Henry Huxley.

I cannot play alone.
Felicia Dorothy Hemans.

Sport that wrinkled Care derides,
And Laughter holding both his sides.
Milton.

Games

'If you can't volley, wear velvet socks'

OUTDOOR ACTIVE GAMES

MAN-HUNT

This is strenuous and any number can join in. It is more exciting than a paper chase, and does not litter the country with paper.

First mark out an agreed area, say six miles by one, on the map, limited by recognisable natural features, outside which the men must not go, with your starting point on one end line and a suitable pub, as your objective, in the middle of the other end line. The hunters set off first and the two men a quarter of an hour later. The hunters may not blockade the starting point nor the objective but should stretch a cordon across the area and ambush likely points in the attempt to stop the men from passing through.

You have lunch at your objective and man-hunt home. It is unsuitable for crowded suburban areas.

FRENCH AND ENGLISH

or

PRISONERS' BASE

This game cannot be played without a suitable lawn.

Two well-matched sides are picked up or arranged, one half of the lawn being the camp or territory of the As, the other of the Bs. A given number of treasures (old shoes, red handkerchiefs and so on) are spaced along the base line of each camp, and the aim of the game is to seize the enemy's treasure. Yet if you are caught on the enemy's ground you are a prisoner and have to join the treasure on the base line until you are rescued, i.e. touched, by one of your side. Once a treasure or a rescued

139

prisoner is in your bag (and each sortie across the enemy lines can only achieve *one* prize) you can make the return journey to your own territory unmolested. Players usually make their own subsidiary rules as the game (after all it *is* only a game) progresses. But where there are young it is better to allow the charge across the base line of the enemy camp to bring immunity and not the actual picking-up of a treasure or touching a prisoner; this can then be done at leisure while gaining breath and applying the dock leaves. N.B. It can spoil the fun if each side places a grown-up with a sadistic streak as "goalie" guarding the treasure, for it paralyses the free movement of the game.

ROUNDERS

This *is* a good game, in spite of the quarrels which it engenders amongst those who do not study the observations following:

If a batsman's hit is caught, he only, and not the whole side, is out, unless a contrary convention has been made. (If you want to speed up the game, make such a convention.) Otherwise, a side is out only if, for any reason, there is none of the batting side home to bat. Further, a member of the batting side is out if he is touched by a ball, thrown or in the hand, when not on the base.

A player who is out may be redeemed by his side on payment of one rounder, if the side is in credit—otherwise as soon as a rounder is scored. This privilege cannot be postponed until it is proved that there is a tactical necessity for the redemption (i.e. the emergency of the lack of batsmen to keep the side going, all others being on bases). A player on a base may feint to go to another base and retire to his former; but he must regain this before he is touched.

The Bowler may feint and, instead of bowling, throw to a fielder; but if the ball leaves his hand, it counts as one of the three throws out of which one must be a "good" ball to the Batsman.

A "good" ball is a slow ball between shoulder and knee of Batsman, outside his body to the offside, and within one yard of his body. If the Bowler delivers three "bad" balls, the penalty is a Rounder to the other side. There should, if possible, be a Referee who would decide on good and bad balls, and all other points. If a batsman fails to hit any of three good balls, he is out.

A hit behind the batsman is not a "good" hit; it counts as a Good Ball not taken.

A Player on a base may run for a "bad" ball, or for a "good" ball not run for by the Batsman.

All running between bases is stopped by the bowler bouncing the ball. The runner must go unmolested to his nearest base. Players on the batting side must *never* run inside the bases, whatever these may be—trees, walking-sticks, hats, or coats. In the latter cases, bases should not be stood upon. As anything may be used for bases, so also with the tools of the game; but a tennis-ball, and the handle of a walking-stick, are not only the best in themselves, but are generally available.

"SMALL" CRICKET

This is called "Small" Cricket, as opposed to the Greater Cricket as played at Lord's, because, though there must be rules which are adhered to, these rules in a house-party—especially where there are Women and Children—must be considerably modified if everybody is to enjoy the game. It is to be remembered that in games on which no Championship depends, it is far more important that they shall be good fun than that one side or t'other shall win—an automatic certainty, in any case. Nothing is more dull for a youthful or feminine member of the team than to be certain that it will be bowled first ball and spend the remainder of the day entirely by itself in a remote corner of the ground, waiting to field a ball that never comes. It is advocated, therefore, that

A. All bowlers should be given a chance in turn by the Captain, and Overs should consist of 9 balls instead of 6.

B. Good bowlers in bowling to the Small Fry should
bowling should be the rule in Small Cricket.

C. Good Batsmen will *never* remember that very long hits, continually repeated, are a nuisance, and can ruin the game; before the game starts, therefore, Captains should consult and firmly fix certain boundaries, according to the nature of the ground. Such boundaries would penalize long hits; a hit into the cornfield or the pig-stye might count 6; but it should, at the same time, be "out".

D. Where the players are few and small, first-bounce catches should be "out". L.B.W. should also be strictly enforced; this is essential, because our more womanly women still grossly exploit their skirts.

E. Where the players are small and few, and fielders scarce, both sides should field. Any players fielding against their own side should remember that it is far more necessary to field well than that their side should win.

F. A tennis-ball is the best sort of ball for this game. A cricket-stump is the best bat. But anything can be made to serve, as also for wickets.

G. Captains should be all-powerful, unless you have an Umpire; but an Umpire is no use unless you trust him.

SMALL HOCKEY

Small Hockey is played as Ordinary Hockey; with a solid rubber ball if possible, and walking-sticks; but no freak sticks, cut specially for the purpose. Both sides of the stick may be used. Some "bunting" therefore will be unavoidable; but it should be reduced to a minimum.

In Small Hockey there is no offside, and there is no circle. A goal may be shot anywhere beyond the half-way line. For "Behind", instead of a Bully, there is a free hit for the goal from the "Go" line; but after a goal is shot, there is always a new centre bully.

Captains, as in Small Cricket, should be all-powerful, and should see strict enforcement of Stick Rule; sticks must *not* be raised above the shoulder, or the Hockey-Ground becomes a sacrificial altar to (and of) Brains and Beauty. Shoulder-height varies in all, however; therefore, if our team happens to include Carnera or Charlie Chaplin, we must take our chances.

Any number of players on a side; in proportioning his field afterwards, all the Captain has to remember is that there should be five times as many Forwards as there are Goal-Keepers.

HUMAN POLO

The biggest men are the ponies, and the girls or lighter weights mount them pick-a-back, hold on with one hand and use walking-sticks to drive a tennis-ball through goals at opposite ends of a lawn or tennis-court. Holding opponents with the hands is not allowed, nor kicking (of man or ball), but bumping, boring and hooking sticks are all part of the game. A player may remount; but may not play from the ground.

FLAT-RACING

Ponies similarly mounted race thirty yards on hands and knees; after which apply iodine to the kneecaps. Jockeys may not remount or touch the earth with their feet.

Wheelbarrow races and *Three-legged races* need no description; we give them a passing recommendation.
Relay races are amusing, particularly if each team contains a very small child, who cannot be relied on to keep to the course.

TIERCE

Or Twos-and-Threes. One player is "He", the others stand in a fairly wide circle in pairs, one in front of the other; but in one group there are three. The Behind Man in this group begins to run, and "He" has to try to catch him before or touch him before he slips into the circle and stands in front of any other pair. The moment he does so the Behind Man of that pair has to run and take his chance of being caught, as there must never be more than two people in a group. If "He" touches his prey before it saves itself by joining a new group, "He" instantly places himself in safety before one of the pairs, and the player just caught becomes "He", and chases the Third Man on the outside of the circle.

THE ROOF GAME

is played by two persons with a discarded tennis ball and a sloping roof. The ideal roof is 60 feet long, slopes at an angle of 110°, ends 8 feet from the ground and has a perfectly clear space in front of it. Each player in turn serves one ball from any position in this run-way and at any speed. The receiver must catch the ball before it touches the ground. If he does so, neither scores; if he fails, the server scores one point. In either event the service passes. The receiver scores one point if the server fails to reach the roof or throws the ball over the roof or so that it falls beyond the roof

143

at the ends. In the latter event he must fetch it, as well as lose a point. A game is five points, or nine for the very strenuous. Feinting is not allowed, but a disguise of direction by looking the other way is permitted. There should be no delay between receiving and serving. Given the right roof it is a great game, almost as sweaty as Squash.

A chimney is a hazard: a ball may be served against it with such force as frequently to elude the receiver; but if the server misses it he risks the penalties for throwing over the roof. This game can be played as a foursome.

WATER GAMES

Les Joûtes, or *Tilting*, between champions in boats is played by French fishermen, and is dangerous to life and limb.

The lances should be long stout bamboos, and for safety well padded at the ends, with a mop-head sewn up in canvas. The champions stand upright in the extreme stern of the boats and should wear wooden or cork breast-plates from the chin to well below the fork. Rudders should be unshipped before beginning.

Water Polo need not be played according to elaborate rules, but there must be no tackling an opponent who has not got the ball, and care should be taken not to kick one's opponent in a vital spot. It can be played with a football or any other ball or with a tenni-quoit rubber ring, but if the ball is small players must pass when tackled and not fight their way through.

Racing on rubber animals is amusing, but there are few jockeys skilled enough to complete a course of twenty yards, even in still water.

Kissing at the bottom of the sea is a strange experience and not likely to be spotted by the guardians of our morals. The lovers should stand about ten yards apart up to their necks, empty their lungs, and crawl towards each other along the bottom with their eyes open.

QUIETER OUTDOOR GAMES

GALLOWS

This is a game for two people—stranded in a pub in the rain or waiting on a deserted railway station. One of them writes a line of poetry with dashes representing letters and strokes between the words: he also draws a picture of a gallows (the old-fashioned kind). The other asks for various letters of the alphabet to be filled in in any one place where they occur, but if they don't occur at all then one of the six basic portions of his anatomy is suspended from the rope. His aim is to avoid being totally hanged before he has guessed the quotation.

THREE STEPS

This game was invented by Harry Farjeon.

The players scatter themselves about the lawn and its surroundings (but the kitchen garden should be out of bounds) each placing himself at a distance of at least three large paces from his nearest neighbour.

The Master of Ceremonies, with the name of each player on a separate slip in his hand, now goes round the lawn in his best hush-hush manner, passing a slip to each player. The name on the slip is that player's prey, to be caught with slow calculated cunning; but that player, or A., is, at the same time, someone else's prey.

When the distribution of slips has taken place the Master of Ceremonies reads out the names of the players one by one and *each in turn* takes three steps. Feints and dissimulation are of the essence of this game. A. catches his victim by touching him *without* falling over; B. is then out of the game and gives his slip to A. with the name of the player that A. is now after. When only two players are left in the game, each intent to catch the other first, the nicest judgments have to be made concerning very short or very long steps. N.B. The longest step must always be a *walking* step—no leaps and no drawing up of the foot and starting again. N.B. It tends to spoil the game, or anyway it is disappointing to the parties concerned, if, by the second or third round when a certain amount of handing-on of slips has taken place, two players turn out to be after each other. This can be avoided if the Master of Ceremonies distributes the names according to some secret order or sequence.

INDOOR ACTIVE GAMES

BALL GAME

You need a big barn, a football bladder and a badminton net. Two, three or four a side, according to the size of persons and barn. Scoring as in Squash, etc., i.e. only the serving side scores. The server punches the ball over the net, but he must not send it outside a prescribed area. (The area must vary according to your barn. In some cases the walls will fitly be included in the playing area, in others they will be "out".) The receiving side must punch back the ball, and a rally will, it is to be hoped, ensue. When the bladder is on your side of the net, any of your side may touch it once, and once only, before it is returned; and there may be a bounce on the floor (or against the wall, if that is "in" for your barn) between each player on your side. Thus a back will tap the bladder to his half, his half to a forward, who should be in position to deliver a massive shot over the net. There is, of course, no obligation that all one side should have a touch of the ball before it is returned. Only one hand may be used (except in the act of serving) and the ball must not be allowed to touch the body. Invented and developed (highly) by H.G. Wells.

TISHY-TOSHY

An early version of the game is said to have taught Bosanquet the googly. You need a table (rectangular, the largest possible) and a tennis-ball. Two players stand at opposite ends, and throw the ball to each other in turn; the Server may roll, bounce or full pitch the ball, but it must not drop off the sides of the table (only off the ends) and must only leave the table between imaginary parallel lines continuing the sides of the table. The Receiver may not put his hands over the table, or touch it with his hands or any part of his person. If he does so, or if he fails to catch the ball, the Server scores one point. If the Receiver catches the ball lawfully, neither scores. But the Receiver scores a point if the Server sends the ball off the sides of the table. Game is for any number of points agreed upon—say five. The very expert can make a rule to use one hand only, or to bar catches made against the body. Remember always that this is a game of skill, not of strength; and the ball must never be thrown at all fast.

146

FLOUNCE-FLORIN

Put a Florin in the middle of a shiny table. Four people stand one on each side of the table with a tennis-ball for each opposite pair and bounce the tennis-balls on the table, trying to knock off the coin by a direct hit. Each catches the ball of his partner opposite and tries to knock the coin off in his turn. The table *must* be very shiny.

The man who wins pockets the coin and the others have to put up the new stake. Originating with war-profiteers (but which war?) the game is *now* usually played with pence or half-pence, but keeps its extravagant name.

UP-JENKYNS!

Orders can only be legally obeyed when given by one of the Captains; and if the team which is hiding the Sixpence obeys any other order, it loses. The "In" team, which is hiding the coin, must put up its hands the instant the opposing Captain calls "Up-Jenkyns!" but he ought to allow them at least five seconds before he calls. He can keep their hands in the air as long as he likes, for examination purposes; the "Down" calls are "Down-Jenkyns" (hands can be put down as players please); "Smashums!" (hands must be crashed down on the table); "Crawlers!" (hands placed quietly on the table, and fingers quietly undone till the hands lie flat); "Open Windows" (hands must lie on the table with all the fingers, but not the thumbs, apart); and "Lobster-Pots" (fingertips only to rest on the table, and fingers to be held at an angle to the palm). In lifting the hands, only the Captain's order must be obeyed; but he should allow free and fair consultation to his own side first. Scores can be played for, by the number of separate "wins", or the show of hands on the table when the Sixpence is discovered. *Before* the game starts, all rings and spurs to be removed. *After* the game, let the provider of the sixpence see that he gets it back!

SLAP-PENNY

A racing game reminiscent of Up-Jenkyns. Two captains pick up sides which sit facing each other. Each side is armed with a shillingsworth of coppers, which are put on a table at the side of the two end men. At a signal the end men have to start sending off the pennies down the line to the other end, one after the other and as fast as possible. When all the pennies have got to the other end of the line they are sent back again. All hands have to be held perfectly flat and each penny slapped in turn from one palm to the next (never to the next but one). Dropped pennies must be replaced on the flat of the palm of the hand which did the slapping which caused the dropping, and the coins must pass in the sequence in which they are started. That side wins (did you guess it?) which gets all its pennies to the end of its line (or, better, back to the starting point) first.

BROCK

is an improved version of Hide and Seek in a dark house. The Brock (or Badger) is "He" and hides, and the rest have to venture out and draw him from his den, avoiding being captured while doing so, and get safe home again.

SARDINES

This may also be played in the dark; *con amore*. Only one player hides, all the others seek; the first to find him hides with him, the next to find *them* squashes in alongside. And so on till everybody but one solitary Seeker is hiding in the same spot.

THE ANIMAL AND STICK GAME

Two sides face to face. Each Captain has a stick. A member of one side calls the name of any animal, bird, fish or insect, beginning with A, and his Captain instantly begins to count 10 aloud (not *too* fast), thumping the floor with his stick at each count. Before he reaches 10, some member of the opposing side must retaliate with another creature beginning with A, on which the second Captain begins to count and thump, while the first side thinks of a new beast. Captains are allowed to call like the rest; but if two members of a side call out different names together, the opposing side may instantly bag the second name given. When one team wins, because the other has run out of A's, it may choose a member of the losing team and add him to their number. The second bout begins with B, and the game continues through the alphabet, until all of one side has been absorbed by the other. No penalty is incurred for Fake Names of animals, and if, when stumped for an N, you *can* bring off "Nicaragua" unchallenged, you may; but on the whole these should not be indulged in too often, and, once disproved, the Opposing Captain takes up the count where the bluff interrupted it.

This game can also be played more quietly with pencils and paper.

CHARADES

are too well-known to be described—but do you *bring in* the syllable or merely *suggest* it? and if you *suggest* it, are you vocal or dumb? And do you ransack the dressing-up cupboard or merely the pegs in the hall?

QUIETER INDOOR GAMES

FAMOUS PEOPLE ON PAPER

You have two or three minutes for writing as many Famous People, or Flowers or Things in the Room, or whatever you like, beginning with a certain letter, and you read them out in turn and score marks; if ten people are playing, nobody scores for a name everybody has thought of, but if nine people out of ten have it you each score one, and if eight people out of ten, they each score two, and so on. Bluffing with invented people is allowed, but only if the bluff is not challenged. A certain amount of feeling is generated if anyone persists in trying to put over St. Tradescantia for example.

HANGING

One member of the company is picked out and told that he is deemed guilty of murder and will be hanged at the end of five (or ten) minutes unless he can prove himself innocent. All the rest of the company are ~~sworn~~ ~~to~~ answer any question he puts to them. He questions them in turn, and is acquitted if he can find any contradiction or flat inconsistency in their story. The wildest improbabilities are allowable, and are to be encouraged, in their answers, but witnesses cannot abrogate the laws of nature, though they may play tricks with artificial human ones. E.g. You may make the criminal travel by a non-existent train, but if you make him arrive at his destination before he started, he is acquitted.

SUGGESTIONS

One member of the company says a word (usually a noun) and the man sitting next him says any word suggested by the first. After a round or two you begin to unwind the chain of suggestions, backwards. Anyone who makes a slip or gets stuck loses a life, and anyone who loses two or three lives, as agreed on, is dead. At the end you see who's left alive.

BOOK REVIEWS

is better for a round or two. It's played like Consequences but first you invent the Title of a Book—say "Crimson Nights"—turn down, and pass on; on the paper you receive you write a sub-title, say, "Or 366 Ways of Cooking Lentils"; round three is the Author's name, real or imaginary; round four a brief extract from the book, poetry or prose; round five another extract (for contrast); six, extract from a review of the book; seven, name of Journal the review comes from; eight, extract from another review (contrast again!); nine, and last, name of Journal.

REDUCED ANECDOTES

makes a variation. Each player writes some anecdote, or incident, in 80 words, and passes it on; he cuts down the anecdote he receives to 40 words, writing it out below the first one, leaving any sort of sense he can make without changing the order of the words or introducing any new ones; after the pass, this is reduced to 20, then to 10, finally to five. The anecdotes are passed once more, and the result read aloud, from top to bottom; or vice versa. Papers should be folded so that the players see only the lines they are to reduce.

THE WORD AND QUESTION GAME

Each player takes two slips of paper and writes a question on one and a word on the other. The slips are pooled and everyone draws a word and a question. (Or all may be given the same problem.) The object then is to write a poem, answering or treating of the question and introducing the word. The time-limit is a quarter of an hour. Here is an example by Sir Walter Raleigh:

Question: Who rang the bell?
Word: Life.

> Life rang the bell to call the people in;
> The play was played by Folly, Pride and Sin;
> Old Age, with fingers trembling and uncertain,
> Turned off the gas, and Death let down the curtain.

Maybe you won't write as good a morality as this, or any morality at all; but that doesn't invalidate the game.

BLINDFOLD COLLABORATION IN PROSE

Everyone writes down the beginning of a story occupying four lines and turns over the paper so that only the last line shows and passes it on. When the stories have come back to the writer of the first four lines, he writes the ending, and the stories are then read aloud.

Combination verses is played in the same way, but fixing a metre and rhyme scheme, and passing the papers round with the last line but one hidden.

PERSONAL ANALOGIES

You write the names of those present perpendicularly down your paper, and each in turn chooses a subject—a Colour, Food, Drink, Street, Material, etc.—which are written horizontally across the top. Then everybody sets to and writes against each person's name the nearest analogy he can think of in the different subjects. They're read out afterwards, and no one need explain *why* he thinks you are Scarlet or Putty-Coloured, or like Suet-Pudding or Pêche Melba, or Bond Street or the City Road. It's a good way of paying compliments *and* old scores.

QUALITIES

You make a list of qualities, good, bad and indifferent. There's one at the end of the "Week-End Book", ruled out ready to play on. The subject has to give himself marks for each quality and then pass the book on to the rest in turn to mark him. When all have finished with him, he would have to read out the verdicts and if you like, even work out his average for each quality. After all, he'll have his revenge later.

CATEGORIES

A four-letter word is chosen, let us say GNAT, and written in capitals downwards. Each player then provides a "category"—English musicians, Roman emperors, hot-house flowers, beverages (*G*rappa, *N*escafé, *A*sti, *T*okay), anything—and each player has to write down four of each category beginning with the initial letter provided. Easy, perhaps, but no one ever obtains full marks. Naturally the category each player gives is one in which he himself will shine—at least he will have all four filled in *there*... A time limit of course.

TELEGRAMS

Each player writes a given twelve-letter word downwards in capitals on a slip of paper—let us suggest CHIMNEYPIECE. A subject is set, a recipient (known to everyone) is selected, and a telegram has to be drafted, the words beginning with the initial letters provided. The theme of the telegram can be a public one (e.g. *C*hurchill *H*as *I*nfluenza *M*alenkov *N*euralgia *E*den *Y*ellowfever *P*lease *I*nform *E*isenhower (signed) *C*onference *E*xecutive). The first two and last two letters *may* be used to designate recipient and sender. Among a family or group of friends the private telegram gives better results—sent to an absent aunt, a distraught publisher or an expected guest telling something of the circumstances that await him. A time limit must be set.

THREE-ADJECTIVE PORTRAITS

Each player writes the name of the present company, excluding himself, along the top of a sizeable piece of paper. He then, within a prescribed time limit, writes three adjectives to describe each person—bold broad strokes like a charcoal sketch, instantly suggestive and significant (adjectives of character rather than of appearance). When the time is up each player in turn reads his list and the others guess to which person the adjectives refer. At the end each player adds up his total of correct guesses and the one with the highest score wins.

DRAWING CLUMPS

Two equally-matched sides go into separate rooms, each supplied either with blackboard, duster and chalk, or plenty of paper and a pencil. A Master of Ceremonies stands at a point equidistant from the two rooms armed with an already-carefully-prepared list of objects or drawable abstractions. This is a team race. At the word "Go" each side sends its youngest to the middle-man who whispers a word such as "milk" or "earth" and this has to be conveyed by drawing (no sound must be uttered) to the rest of the side who never for one moment stop guessing at what the shapes suggest. When the correct word has been hit on the next member of the team dashes from the room to get *his* word from the middle-man, and so on through the team.

By the time it is the turn of the older members concepts such as "emigration" or "depression" can be given, while teenagers can usually cope with "the last straw" or "Savonarola". No cheating allowed: only the exact word as given by the Master of Ceremonies, not one that approximates to it, must be accepted by the drawer however desperate and frustrated he feels, and he must remember that if one approach to his subject fails to get results, he must try another—e.g. if the word is "patience" and a monument has proved ineffectual, he must see if he is more successful with cards. He must never stop drawing—trying new angles of approach—just as the guessers must never stop guessing.

ACTING CLUMPS

Two evenly-balanced teams go into separate rooms. A. team prepares written slips of paper for each member (considered individually) of B. team, and *vice versa*. The writing on the slips is a word or phrase capable of being acted or anyway conveyed to the rest of the team by means of actions *only*—no props. For the young, advertisements ("prevents that sinking feeling"),

in the Cathedral are, for example, gifts—though the latter tends to be indistinguishable from *Death comes for the Archbishop*); a degree more difficult would be *The Odyssey, Measure for Measure, Brideshead Revisited*. For the older or more practised members of the team quite arbitrary phrases such as "a late night" or "worth his salt" serve.

Now, when the slips have been carefully prepared both teams congregate in one room so that all can share the fun. They sit

153

opposite each other and the slips are distributed and, of course, kept *strictly secret* by the recipients. Each member of A. team has now to act his word or phrase in turn to his own side, while B. team, all-knowing, looks on; and, as in Drawing Clumps, A. team never ceases to guess. When these guesses are warm the actor encourages the guessers with come–hither gestures, when cold he repudiates them with go–hence ones. No word whatever must be spoken by the actor, though different lines of approach can, naturally, be attempted. Then it is the turn of B. team, while the A.s watch benignly.

If the phrase on the slip of paper has one key or actable or give-away word, that can be acted first—in this manner: the victim—for he is no less—shows how many words his "phrase" is by holding up the same number of fingers, and again on his fingers he shows which word—the 2nd or 5th or whatever—he is going to act first, as being the most revealing. Further aids: if the phrase is a book–title he indicates that it is so by scrutinising the palms of his hands, if a play by striking a dramatic pose, if a film by turning an imaginary handle at eye-level.

ALIBI

A variant is Alibi. Two people are accused of being involved in a murder at a given time and place. They plan their watertight alibi in another room and are called, singly, into court. The rest of the company, in this case prosecuting, fire questions at the defendants in turn and if their alibi does not tally they are guilty. N.B. They are not allowed to "forget" what they were wearing or whether it was raining or what the bill came to.

A word about "going out of the room". It is inevitable that in some of these games two people, or a side, have to leave the comfortable room with a fire to hatch their plots elsewhere, hence it is desirable to have another centre of warmth and refreshment so that the "outs" are as cosy as the "ins".

RUSSIAN SLEDGES

We all write down the same list of a dozen of the dearest friends we have in common. Each of us then imagines himself crossing the steppes of Russia with all of them in a sledge pursued by packs of hungry wolves, and has to throw them out one by one.

Whom do you throw out first, whom next? You have to decide this, and number the names on the list accordingly, in the order in which you would throw out your friends to be torn in pieces. Needless to say you may not throw yourself out. ... The game provides valuable statistics, for all the marks we have given each person are added up afterwards. The man who gets the fewest is, of course, the least popular of our friends. When one list is exhausted you can start on another dozen, and after that make a composite list of the top six of each list. ...

HUMAN SACRIFICES

is a variant impossible amongst normally sensitive persons. We propitiate a vengeful deity by sacrificing one after another of the company in turn. A slip of paper with all our names is silently handed round and each of us makes a cross against the name of the man or woman he would sacrifice first. Whoever has most crosses against his name after the first round is sent out of the room. Then the paper goes round again for the survivors to mark again. When only two people are left in the room they call out the one whom they regard as the less worthy to survive.

WHO AM I?

The Scorer first writes the names of lots of *very* Famous People, and Characters in Books, and Notorious Recent Criminals, and all that, on separate bits of paper, and has lots of pins, and a scoring-sheet with all the names of the other players. They line up before him, and he pins a name on each one's back and says Go! Your object is to find out who you are. You may rush up to anybody, make him look at your back, and fire off three questions to which the only answers are "Yes" and "No": Such as "Am I a Man?" "Am I a Myth? Am I a ———?" When your three questions are answered, you must answer three of his in return; then you part, and grab somebody else, carrying on your investigation from the information gained. You mustn't ever ask more than three questions from a chap at one go. When you know who you are you tell the Scorer; he replaces your old name with a new one, and scores a mark to you. The game stops when everybody's hoarse, or the Scorer runs out of names; and the one who has guessed himself oftenest wins.

WHO ARE THEY?

Two go outside and decide who they'll be, and return to hold a conversation in front of the others, always talking in character, but of course not mentioning their names. When they are guessed, two others go out. It's a very good opportunity for bringing nice people together who would have liked to meet, but can't: Hobbs and Medusa, or Dempsey and Little Nell.

SALTED ALMONDS

It's called that, because it takes place between two people who are supposed to meet at a dinner-table. Before they meet, A goes outside, and B is given three statements or remarks, invented by the audience, which he must engineer as naturally as possible into the dinner-table conversation: such as that he never *can* remember whether it's pronounced Bill Sykes or Bill Seeks; and that the best cure for aeroplane-sickness is equal parts of Fuller's Earth and Petroleum; and that the First Carpet-Slippers were worked by Lady Jane Grey for Roger Ascham. Then A comes in, the two sit side by side, and they begin to talk. A's job is to head off B's attempts to steer the conversation towards his statements, though A doesn't know what they are. The game ends when B makes his third statement.

THE TRAY-GAME

Someone fills a tray with twenty objects usual to any room—a pencil, handkerchief, book, nib, and what not. The tray is set down in the middle of the other players, who stare at it for twenty or thirty seconds only, when it is removed. The Tray-Filler (and Time-Keeper) then calls Go! and the players have two minutes in which to write down all they can remember. The longest list wins.

LOOKING AT YOUR FEET THROUGH THE WRONG END OF THE OPERA-GLASSES

while you try to walk, step by step, one foot put straight in front of the other, down a string laid on the floor.

RUMMY

which can be played by almost any number of players, using two packs. The dealer gives each player seven cards, and turns up one card, putting it beside the pack face upwards. The next player has the option of taking this exposed card, or the top card of the pack, before discarding one of his own. He is allowed, if he likes, to discard the one he has picked up. The discard is placed face upwards on top of the exposed cards, and the next player has the option of taking either that card or the next card of the "blind" pack: and so on, each playing in turn.

The object of the game is to reduce the "pippage" of your seven cards. An Ace counts as one, a two as two, a three as three, and so on up to ten; all court cards count as ten. When the sum of the values in your hand is down to ten or under, you are allowed, though not forced, to "rumble", which is usually done by tapping the underneath edge of the table. You may not rumble immediately after taking a card, but you must wait your next turn. In other words, when your turn comes, you may either rumble, or draw a card, but not both in one turn. At the rumble, each player's pippage is counted up, and the deal takes place again.

The system of reducing pippage is as follows:

1. Three or more of a kind, or three or more in sequence in the same suit count as 0. Thus three or four knaves, or 5, 6, 7 in Clubs, do not count against you.

2. The same card can serve only one purpose in reducing pippage, that is, either as part of a sequence, or as part of a collection, but not both.

3. Jokers may serve as any card of any suit. Either one or two may be included by agreement.

4. A flush (that is, a hand composed entirely of one suit) counts 0.

5. If you reduce your score to 0 by holding a straight flush (i.e. seven cards in sequence in the same suit) or seven of a kind, the whole score standing against you from previous rounds is wiped out.

When your debt account reaches 100 you are dead. The later

stages of the game usually become quicker and more exciting, the ultimate survivor, who is winner, taking the pool. The pool is sweetened after each hand by everyone except the winner of the hand.

If the packs should be exhausted before a rumble the discards are shuffled and re-dealt.

The skill in the game depends, obviously, on observing the cards that are discarded; thus, not preserving two kings in your hand if six have already been thrown away.

DOUBLE-HANDED BRIDGE

Thirteen cards are dealt to both players, and the top card of the twenty-six remaining in the pack is turned up. The non-dealer leads, and thirteen tricks are played for which no points are scored, the winner of the trick taking the top exposed card of the pack and the loser taking the card underneath, which remains unseen. The winner of the thirteenth trick has the call in the auction which follows, and thirteen tricks of serious bridge are played.

The game is an extremely good one except with people having prodigious memories. The tactics depend very largely on exhausting a suit by continually leading it when you suspect that your opponent is saving it up, and in disguising the fact that you are collecting a suit yourself.

GO

You play it with coffee and haricot beans, *ad lib.*, on a board, or piece of paper, ruled into squares, 19 by 21; the two players play one bean at a time, in turns, on any square they like; you want to enclose your opponent's bean in a diagonal square of your own like this:

Which entitles you to remove the enclosed bean. The player who controls the greatest area of the board, so that it is useless for his opponent to put down more beans, as they will only be encircled, wins.

There's only one essential rule, called KO. In a situation like *this*:

Haricot could play in the empty square A, and remove Coffee from B; but then, you see, Coffee could immediately play in B again, and remove Haricot from A; and so on, for ever. To prevent this, the Rule is that in this particular position the *first* encircler keeps his opponent's bean, and cannot have his own retaken in that grouping.

GO-BANG

is played on a chessboard with 12 coloured beans, or counters or Halma men each. You play in turns and the object is to get five of your own colour in a row, in any direction, straight or diagonal. It's a superior Noughts and Crosses. Four-handed *Six in a Row* played with 13 Halma men to each player, on a Halma board (16 by 16) is excellent. Four-handed *Four-in-a-row* is too tight and agonising a game.

The players have nine men apiece—beans, or anything to show a difference—and if you look at the illustration you'll see the sort of board it's played on. It has 24 bases which read horizontally and perpendicularly, form 16 lines of three bases each. Players begin by placing their men alternately on any base that is vacant, and the great object (it's a sort of glorified Noughts and Crosses) is to get three of your men in a line, either up and down or across. As soon as you succeed, you can "Pound" any one of your

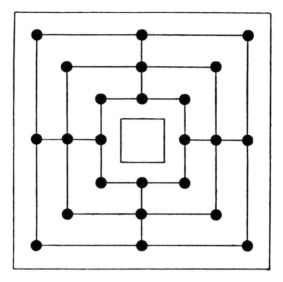

opponent's men, and remove it from the board. When the placing of the men on the board is completed (during which one or
more men may have been Pounded) you go on by moving in
turns from base to base; a man can only move to a base adjacent to his own, and then only if it is unoccupied by another man.
You can't take a man by moving on to his base, you can only take
a man when you get a line of three. In this way, one of the players is presently reduced to three men, and when that happens he
has the privilege of "hopping" from one base to another—that
is, any of his men can "hop" to *any* base he likes, so long as it is
vacant; but it need not be next the base he has just left. The player with more than three men must still go on moving in the old
way, until he wins or is reduced to three. The game ends when
one player has only two men left.

TRICKS

The following tricks may beguile the more vacuous moments of
the company:

GYMNASTIC FEATS

(1) Grasp a stiff stick about five foot long behind the back with the palms of the hands facing forwards. Pass stick over head. Lift right leg and put it round the right arm and through the stick. Without changing your grip pass the left hand over the head and back and step out of stick.

(2) Kneel down putting elbows to knees and palms flat on floor. Place pencil at finger-tips. Then clasp hands behind back and pick up pencil with teeth.

(3) Toe a line, go down on one hand and with the other place coin as far away as possible. Regain erect position in one movement, taking supporting hand cleanly off floor. The next man has to put another coin down further off and so on.

(4) Put a chair on its back, and grasping it by one of the legs on the ground, set it gently on its legs. Then weight the back of the chair with heavy books and repeat.

(5) Place a pin on right hand edge of the seat of a chair, sit down, and then without touching the floor crawl round the back of the chair and remove pin with the teeth.

To make a Cockyolly Bird. An old-fashioned night-gown is necessary. Put the legs through the arms, and the head through the neck, then have the bottom of the night-gown tied up as a tail. This fowl is more charming than it sounds.

MATCH TRICKS

(1) Tear off two book-matches and hold them parallel between index finger and thumb, exhibit them to the audience, pointing out that there is a printed inscription on one side of the matches and not the other.

Now turn them over swiftly, rolling them over fast and exhibit the plain surface on both sides.

(2) Strike a match and quickly stick its lately-exploded head into the largest side of the match-box so that the match stands upright, its head lightly buried in the box. Then place one match on the table parallel with the longest side of the box, about four inches in front of it. Rest another match on this at right angles to it, with the forward and tilted end aimed at the vertical match. Flick it, and you will bring down your target at the first shot.

(3)   THE HOLLYWOOD KISS

Take two matches, either book or ordinary wooden safeties. Make a slit in a safety match-box and in it stick one book match vertically, head up, as the lover. Lean the other match—the lady—against the lover so that her head is touching his and light her in the middle. It is an improvement to give the lady legs by slitting her lower end with a knife, but arms always seem to burn away to nothing.

ROUNDS AND SONGS

Everyone suddenly burst out singing.
Siegfried Sassoon.

Wednesday, 23 March (1763). I breakfasted with Lord Eglinton, who was very good to me. He said nobody liked me better than he did. He begun and taught me to sing catches, of which he was very fond. He gave me much encouragement, and said that there were not five people in the whole Catch Club who had a better ear than I have.
Boswell.

Come; and come strong,
To the conspiracy of our spacious song.
Richard Crashaw.

Rounds

'Everyone suddenly burst out singing'

O ABSALOM

Three voices.   *by Henry Lawes.*

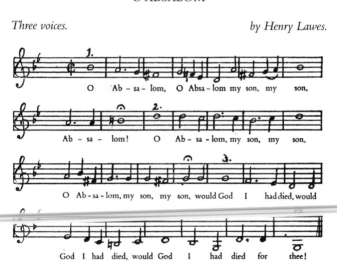

BOBBY SHAFTOE

Fairly quickly.

Bobby Shaftoe's tall and slim,
He's always dressed so neat and trim,
The lassies they all keek at him,
Bonny Bobby Shaftoe,
    Chorus.

Bobby Shaftoe's gett'n a bairn,
For to dangle on his airm,
On his airm and on his knee,
Bonny Bobby Shaftoe.

Final Chorus:
Bobby Shaftoe's been to sea,
Silver buckles on his knee,
He's come back and married me,
Bonny Bobby Shaftoe.
(And so on, *ad infinitum*, getting faster and faster.)

166

GOD SAVE THE KING

Six voices.

God save the King, long live the King.

May the King live, may the King live for

e — ver and e—ver. A — — men.

FRÈRE JACQUES

Not slowly.   *(Round for four voices.)*

Frè · re Jac · ques, Frè · re Jac · ques

Key G {| d :r | m :d | d :r | m :d ||

Dor - mez vous? Dor - mez vous?

{| m :f | s :— | m :f | s :— ||

Sonnez les ma - tin - es, Sonnez les ma - tin - es

{| s ,l :s .f | m :d | s ,l :s .f | m :d ||

Dig, din, don. Dig, din, don.

{| d :s, | d :— | d :s, | d :— ||

167

ONE MORE RIVER

In march time.

The animals came in three by three,
Vive la compagnie.
The elephant on the back of the flea,
Vive la compagnie.
One more river, etc.

The animals came in four by four, etc.

The camel, he got stuck in the door.

Some were dead and some were alive.

The monkey he was up to his tricks.

Some went to Hell, and some went to Heaven.

The worm was early, the bird was late.

Some had water and some had wine.

If you want any more you must sing it again.

BILLY BOY

Loud and with good rhythm.

Key E

Where have ye been all the day, Bil - ly Boy,
{l m:— :f ı s:-:s l f:-:mır:-:-l m:-:r ıd:-:}

Bil-ly Boy? Where have ye been all the day, me
{l r:-:t d:-:-l m:— :f ıs:-:s l fe:-:s ıl:-:s }

Bil - ly Boy . . . . I've been walk-ing all the
{l fe:-:s ır:-:-l:-:s:-:s l l:-:s ıl:-:t }

day . . with me charming Nan - cy Grey and me
{l d:-:t ıl:-:s l l:-:s ıf :m :r l d:-:t, 1,:-:s, }

Nancy kittled me fancy, Oh, me charming Billy Boy !
{l d:dım:r :d l s:-:s ıl:-:d' l m:-:d ır:-:tld:-:-:-ll

Can she cook a bit o'steak, Billy Boy, Billy Boy?
Can she cook a bit o'steak, me Billy Boy?
 She can cook a bit o'steak,
 Aye, and make a girdle cake.
  And me Nancy, etc.

Is she fit to be your wife, Billy Boy, Billy Boy?
Is she fit to be your wife, me Billy Boy?
 She's as fit to be my wife
 As the fork is to the knife.
  And me Nancy, etc.

Did she lie close unto thee, Billy Boy, Billy Boy?
Did she lie close unto thee, Billy Boy?
 Yes, she lay close unto me
 As the bark is to the tree.
  And me Nancy, etc.

169

SHE WAS POOR

With moral significance.

She was poor but she was honest, Victim of a
Key F {: s, .d | m :–ı .t, : r | d | t,. 1, :–ı .t, .r | s :–ı .f }

rich man's game, For she met the vil - lage
{| r .re | m :– ı s, .d | m :–ı .t, : r .d }

Squi–re, And she lost her mai-den name. It's the
{| t, .1, : t .r | s :–ı –.f : 1, .t, | d :–ı : s, .d }

same the whole world ov - er: It's the
{| m :–ı – .t : r .d | t, .1, :–ı : t, .r }

poor as gets the blame, It's the rich as has the
{| s :–ı –.f : r .re | m :–ı : s, .d | m :–ı .t, : r .d }

plea - sure. Aint it all a bleeding shame?
{| t, .1, :–ı : s .fe| f : –.m : 1, .t, | d :– ı ||

So she hastened up to London
For to hide her grief and pain;
There she met an army captain
And she lost her name again.

Chorus.

See him riding in his carriage
Past the gutter where she stands;
He has made a stylish marriage
While she wrings her ringless hands.

170

See him in the House of Commons
Passing laws to put down crime;
While the girl as he has ruined
Slinks away to hide her shame.

See him laugh at the theayter
In the front row with the best;
While the girl as he has ruined
Entertains a sordid guest.

In the little country village
Where her aged parents live,
Though they drink champagne she sends them
Yet they never can forgive.

MY MOTHER'S AN APPLE-PIE BAKER

With unction.

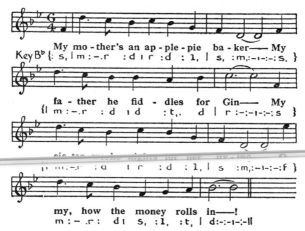

Key B♭ {: s, | m :-.r :d | r :d : l, | s, :m,:–:–:s, }

My mo - ther's an ap - ple - pie ba - ker—— My

{| m :-.r :d | d :t,. d | r :–:–:–:s }

fa - ther he fid - dles for Gin—— My

{| m :-.r :d | r :d : l, | s :m,:–:–:f }

{ m :- .r : d | s, :l, :t, | d:–:–:–:|| }

my, how the money rolls in——!

GREENSLEEVES

With a gentle swing.

If you intend thus to disdain,
It does the more enrapture me,
And even so I still remain
A lover in captivity.

Chorus.

Alas, my love, that you should own
A heart of wanton vanity,
So must I meditate alone
Upon your insincerity.

Chorus.

SHENANDOAH

Slowly, with great longing.

Oh Shenandoah, I love your daughter.
Oh Shenandoah, I love your daughter.

'Tis seven long years since last I see thee.
'Tis seven long years since last I see thee.

Oh Shenandoah, I took a notion
To sail across the stormy ocean.

Oh Shenandoah, I'm bound to leave you.
Oh Shenandoah, I'll not deceive you.

SWING LOW, SWEET CHARIOT

Intensely and rather slowly.

(Chorus.)

Swing low, sweet cha-ri ot, Coming for to carry me
{| m :d ı—:m | d :-.dı l,.s,:-| d .d :d ,d ım.s :s }

home. Swing low, sweet cha-ri-ot,
{| s :-ı-:-| l .s :mı— :s | d :-.dı l,.s,:- }

(Solo)

Coming for to carry me home. 1. I look'd over Jordan,
{| d .d :d ,d ım.m:r | d :—ı:m| s .d:-l, d :d }

What did I see, coming for to carry me home—? A
{| d .d :d l,.s,:-| d.d:d ,d ım.s,:s | s :-ı-: s }

band of angels coming after me——
{| l.s :m ım:d | d .d :d .dı l,.s,:- }

Coming for to carry me home.

Repeat chorus after second verse.
{| d .d :d ,dı m .m:r | d .;-ı-·—‖

174

STARSHINE AT NIGHT

The pride of the height, the clear firmament,
    the beauty of heaven, with his glorious shew.
                            Ecclesiasticus.

Night of South winds—night of the few
    large stars!
                            Walt Whitman.

I stood and stared; the sky was lit,
The sky was stars all over it,
I stood, I knew not why,
Without a wish, without a will,
I stood upon that silent hill
And stared into the sky until
My eyes were blind with stars and still
I stared into the sky.
                            Ralph Hodgson.

the pride of the height, the clear firmament:

Starshine at Night

ISTI MIRANT STELLA

the beauty of heaven, with his glorious show.

THE EARTH AND THE MOON

The Earth is grilled by the Sun like a joint on a spit. It returns round and round on its axis, one complete turn taking a time of 24 hours. It is this rotation of the Earth that causes the procession of night and day. It is daytime when we are turned towards the Sun and it is night when we are turned away from the Sun.

In addition to this spinning motion, the Earth also moves along a more or less circular path around the Sun. It takes a year to make a complete circuit of this path and it is this second motion that causes the seasons of the year. Our yearly trip around the Sun also causes the stars that we see in the night sky to change with the seasons. (See star maps on pages 182-189.)

The distance from the Sun to the Earth is about 93,000,000 miles, a vast distance compared with the size of the Earth itself, which is a mere 8,000 miles or so in diameter—or, what comes to the same thing, when viewed on an astronomical scale the Earth is a very tiny body.

We do not travel our yearly journey around the Sun alone. Always accompanying us is our faithful satellite, the Moon. The Moon is another very tiny body, about a quarter of the dimensions of the Earth. Although it is so small the Moon appears a notable object in the night sky because it is very near to us, a mere quarter of a million miles away. The Sun and the Moon appear to the eye to be of about the same size, but this is because the Sun is nearly four hundred times farther away.

In addition to sharing the Earth's motion around the Sun, the Moon possesses a motion of its own, one that takes it round and round the Earth. The Moon completes one circuit of this path in 27^1/$_3$ days, which is known as the lunar month. Now because of this monthly motion, the Moon sometimes lies on the sunward side of the Earth, and at other times it lies on the lee side. In the latter case we see the Moon in the night sky and in the former case we see it in the day time. During each lunar month there is a point at which the Moon lies in practically the same direction as the Sun. This is the time of new Moon. There is also a time, about a fortnight later, when the Moon lies in nearly the opposite direction from the Sun. This is the time of full Moon.

The Moon shines because it reflects sunlight, not because it emits light of its own. The well-known phases of the Moon are a property of the reflected sunlight. For a week before and after it is "new" the Moon is seen as a crescent. For a week before and after full Moon it is seen in its gibbous phases.

The Moon is dotted with largish dark nearly circular patches, patches that are 500 miles or so in diameter. These it is that produce the well-known "Man in the Moon" appearance. At one time they were thought to be oceans and were given rather fanciful names: *Mare Crisium*, the Sea of Crises; *Mare Tranquillitatis*, the Sea of Tranquillity; *Mare Humorum*, the Sea of Mists; and so on. But we know that they are not oceans for there is no water at all on the Moon. Future travellers to the Moon will have to take their drinks with them.

Being so near to us, the Moon is well situated for telescopic study. Indeed, astronomers can detect objects on the lunar surface that are no larger than St Paul's Cathedral. Photographs show that the whole surface is pitted with craters large and small. These are thought to be a product of the impact of chunks of material that once struck the Moon. They are the relics of an age-old celestial bombardment, a bombardment that was probably associated with the process in which the Moon itself was formed. The Earth must have suffered a similar, or even a greater, bombardment, but the terrestrial scars have long since disappeared through the erosive action of wind and water. As we have already remarked, there is no water on the Moon, and there is no atmosphere either. Because of this the Moon suffers another sort of bombardment, a bombardment of ultra-violet light and X-rays from the Sun, a bombardment against which we are protected by the shielding action of our atmosphere. This second bombardment must cause the surface rocks of the Moon to be powdered and it seems very likely that for this reason the lunar surface is very dusty.

The lack of an atmosphere produces extremes of temperature on the Moon. At midday on the lunar equator your blood would boil. At night time the temperature falls to about -250° F and you would be frozen solid. It seems that those people who wish to visit the Moon can be dubbed, appropriately from every point of view, lunatics.

THE PLANETS

Besides the Earth there eight other planets, five of which can be seen with the unaided eye. Like the Earth the other planets all move around the Sun and they also move along paths that are very nearly circular. Not only this, but the paths all lie in more or less the same plane; that is to say, the whole solar system can be fitted very nearly into one plane. This plane intersects the sky in a line—a line on which all the Planets and the Sun and the Moon lie. You can often see the Moon and two or three Planets in the night sky and indeed you will find that they do lie on a common line.

The four planets nearest the Sun are all small. They are made mainly of rock and iron, and in their order of distance from the Sun they are Mercury, Venus, the Earth and Mars.

MERCURY is the smallest of the planets, not very much larger than the Moon. Because it is so close to the Sun it can only be seen just after sunset or just before sunrise and even then it is a very fleeting object, as indeed its name implies. Yet if you are fortunate, and the conditions are just right, and you know just when and where to look, it is not difficult to see

There is no procession of night and day on Mercury; one half of the planet lies in perpetual day and the other half lies in perpetual night. If you want to consign someone to Hell, send him to Mercury. It doesn't matter whether you want the hot Hell of the Mediterranean and near-Eastern religions, or the cold Hell of the Nordic peoples, Mercury has got them both.

VENUS, the next planet, is practically a twin sister of the Earth, although as befits a sister she is a little smaller than the Earth.

Venus wraps herself perpetually in a mantle of white cloud. No one has ever seen through to the underlying surface of the planet. The nature of the clouds of Venus is an astronomical mystery. They do not seem to be made of water like the clouds of our own atmosphere.

MARS is the first planet beyond the Earth, and is reckoned the only planet except the Earth on which it might be possible for life to exist. From time to time greenish markings appear on Mars and it is a matter for speculation whether they arise from the growth of plants. Some astronomers think that they do.

The next four planets differ enormously from the four inner planets. They are much bigger and they are made of quite different materials. They seem to contain very little rock and iron but great quantities of water ammonia, methane and possibly neon, while Jupiter and Saturn, but not Uranus and Neptune, contain enormous quantities of hydrogen. These are all planets highly hostile to life.

JUPITER is the largest of all the planets and like both Venus and Mars it is a notable object when seen in the night sky. It has twelve satellites that move around it. SATURN, the next planet in order of size, has nine satellites and is, in addition, surrounded by a beautiful system of rings composed, it is thought, of fine particles of ice.

URANUS and NEPTUNE are considerably smaller than Saturn but are still very much larger than the Earth. Because of their great distance from the Sun, they cannot be seen with the unaided eye. Beyond them lies the last planet of the solar system, the little Pluto. PLUTO is not a member of the family of great planets. It is small like the four inner ones. Indeed it is thought by some astronomers to be no more than a satellite that at one time succeeded in escaping from the influence of Neptune.

When seen through a telescope the two largest planets, Jupiter and Saturn, are easily the most striking. They show wonderful variations of colour. Jupiter is rich in reds and browns with an occasional olive green. Saturn has a brilliant yellowish zone near the equator and darkish caps of a greenish hue at its poles. Uranus shows red, orange and green tints, but Uranus is too far away and appears too small to be really impressive even when seen in a large telescope. Neptune also is too small to be really noteworthy. It appears as a small green object, rather like a little shrunken apple.

Of the four inner planets Venus appears a dazzling white, Mars derives its name from its pronouncedly red colour, while we can only guess at what the Earth must look like. Probably the Earth is the jewel of the solar system with an amazing variety of colour: white from the clouds; light green from growing crops; darker greens from the forests; reds, browns and yellows from the deserts; the flashing white of the polar ice caps, and the sombre dark tones of the oceans, except perhaps where here and there a brilliant flash of sunlight happens to be reflected from the surface of the water. When seen from afar off, the delicate rich colouring of the Earth must be in a truly strange contrast with the dull sterile surface of the Moon.

To get an idea of relative sizes in the solar system, imagine the Sun to be the size of a football. Then Mercury would be a speck of dust some 15 yards away from the Sun, Venus would be another speck 25 yards away; the Earth 35 yards away, Mars 55 yards away; Jupiter would be a little pea about 190 yards away; Saturn 350 yards; Uranus about 700 yards; Neptune over 1,000 yards; and Pluto very nearly a mile. There is plenty of space inside the solar system.

THE CONSTELLATIONS

We lie inside a vast aggregate of stars. Most of them are so far away that you can't see them at all with the naked eye. It is only the very nearest of the stars that show up at all notably. There is nothing special about the way that they are distributed over the sky. This was not understood by the astrologers of the ancient world, who sought to relate the stars to human experience. Attempts were made to associate groups of stars with animals and people. The stars in one patch of the sky became Draco, the dragon; another became Leo, the lion; Pisces, the fish; Ursa Major, the great bear; Orion, the hunter; Andromeda, after the heroine of ancient legend; and other such picturesque names. These imaginary associations became known as the constellations. They are still retained as appellations in modern astronomy in spite of their complete lack of physical significance, because it is often convenient to have a rough and ready way of referring to various parts of the sky.

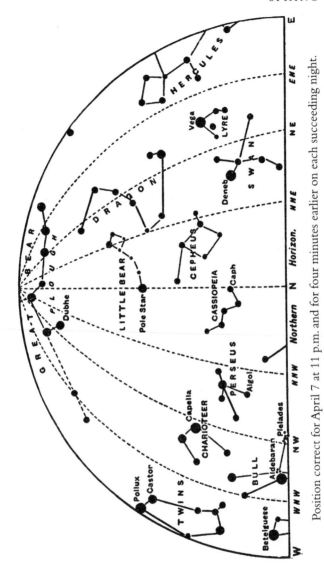

Position correct for April 7 at 11 p.m. and for four minutes earlier on each succeeding night.

182

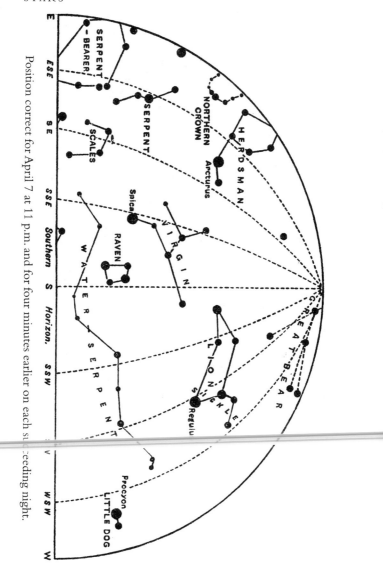

Position correct for April 7 at 11 p.m. and for four minutes earlier on each succeeding night.

183

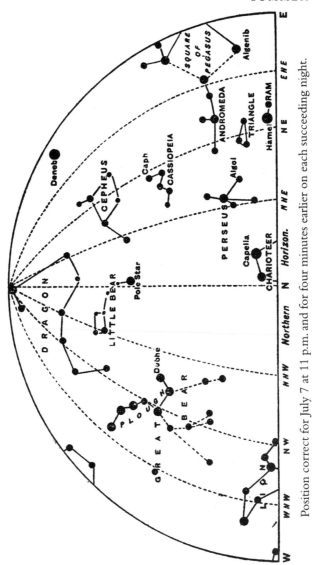

Position correct for July 7 at 11 p.m. and for four minutes earlier on each succeeding night.

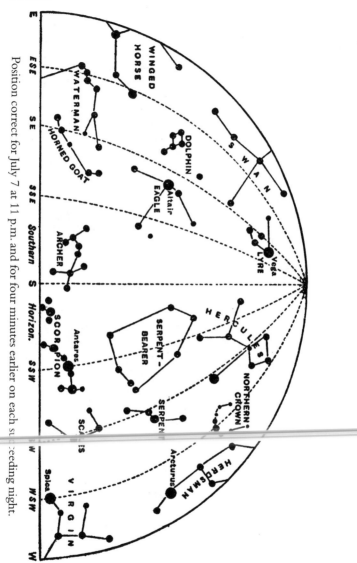

Position correct for July 7 at 11 p.m. and for four minutes earlier on each succeeding night.

185

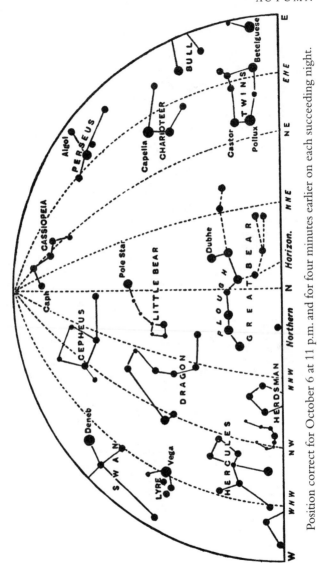

Position correct for October 6 at 11 p.m. and for four minutes earlier on each succeeding night.

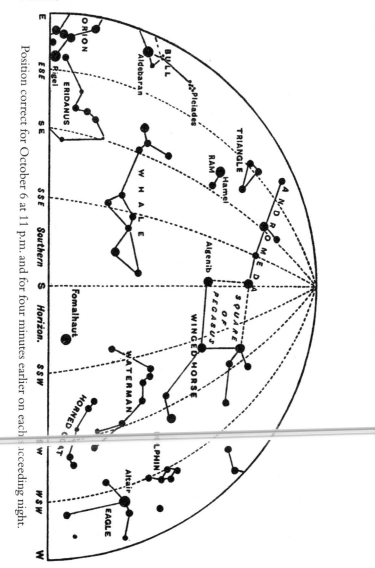

Position correct for October 6 at 11 p.m. and for four minutes earlier on each succeeding night.

187

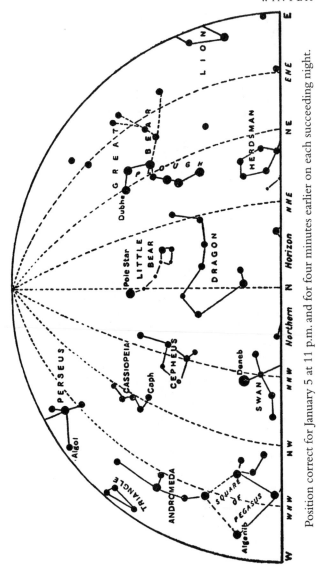

Position correct for January 5 at 11 p.m. and for four minutes earlier on each succeeding night.

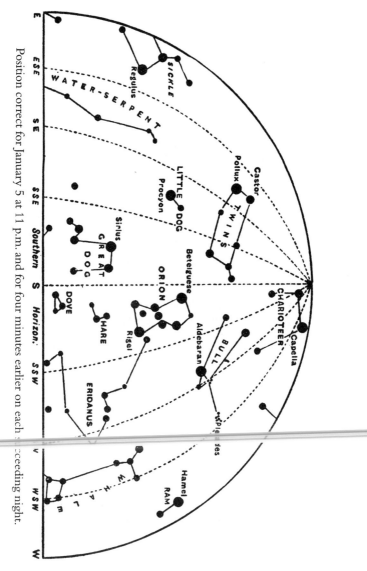

Position correct for January 5 at 11 p.m. and for four minutes earlier on each succeeding night.

189

NIGHT SKY IN SPRING
(*See* Map, pp. 182, 183)

At this time of year URSA MAJOR or the Plough or the Great Bear or the Dipper or Charles's Wain (or the Waggon, as the Babylonians called this constellation) shines right overhead. The arrangement of its seven bright stars suggests the shape of a ploughshare, and the countryman knows the minute one close to the central of the three which form its handle, as "Jack by the middle horse." The two stars which bind the Great Bear on its north-western side are the "Pointers" to STELLA POLARIS, the Pole Star, which forms the nether tip of URSA MINOR's tail. Though the Persians said of this, the most constant among the stars and the pivot of their whole population, that "it held all the constellations by the hand", it is, to our eyes, the least impressive among its fellows.

To the south-east of the Great Bear lies the constellation of BOÖTES, the "Keeper of the Bear", whose glory is ARCTURUS, the seventh brightest star in all the sky. The glittering semi-circle to the east of Arcturus is CORONA BOREALIS—the Northern Crown, and another brilliance to the west of Arcturus and south-west of the Great Bear is REGULUS, the southernmost luminary of the constellation of LEO. Yet another star of the first magnitude is VEGA, the fourth brightest in the heavens, gleaming blue in the constellation of LYRA and almost directly east of the Pole Star. South of the Great Bear, beyond Leo, is the constellation VIRGO, conspicuous only for the star SPICA, while LIBRA, a little to the east, lacks any dominant stars. Not so subdued are CASTOR AND POLLUX, the Gemini or Heavenly Twins of a religion far older than the Greek, gleaming to the west of the Great Bear. Beyond the Twins to the south-west is CANIS MINOR, containing PROCYON as its pride, the eighth brightest among the stars. Other constellations visible near the north-eastern and western horizons are in the order named— CYGNUS, ANDROMEDA, CASSIOPEIA—the great W stretched world-beyond-worlds across the sky—PERSEUS, AURIGA and TAURUS. The Milky Way, low in the heavens, is at its dimmest in the spring.

THE SUMMER SKY
(*See* Map, pp. 184, 185)

VEGA is the guiding star in the summer sky and shines almost directly overhead. But the splendour of the firmament in mid-year is the Milky Way, now flowing across the middle of the heavenly vault from north to south. The constellation of CYGNUS, a little to the north-east of Vega, marks the point where the starry river splits into two great streams. In the cleft of the northern stream is the constellation of AQUILA, dominated by ALTAIR, the eleventh brightest star. The course of the Milky Way flows on south-westward to the constellation of SCORPIO, near the horizon, with its sickle-shaped row of stars and ANTARES, glowing red, to form the eastern beacon. CASSIOPEIA lies in the north-eastern reach of the Milky Way between two stars of the first magnitude—CAPELLA in Auriga and DENEB in Cygnus—to the north and south of it. Nearer to the north-eastern horizon are PERSEUS and ANDROMEDA. ARCTURUS, being nearer to the zenith, is at its greatest brilliance in the summer sky. Between Lyra and the Corona Borealis, which have shifted their spring positions from E.N.E. to S.S.W., lies the constellation of HERCULES.

THE AUTUMN SKY
(*See* Map, pp. 186, 187)

The square constellation of PEGASUS, almost overhead, is a convenient landmark for observing the autumn sky. In its north-eastern corner is the Great Nebula of ANDROMEDA, just visible to the eye. By now the Milky Way has made an immense curve across the sky-world until it lies almost due west and east, with Cassiopeia at its central culmination a little to the north of the zenith. The most prominent stars of the autumn sky are Vega, Alpha Cygni or Deneb, and Capella, south-east of which are the PLEIADES. Below the Pleiades flames the great star ALDEBARAN, the eye of TAURUS the Bull. Now for the first time in the year the constellation of ORION, with SIRIUS, the brightest star in all heaven, comes into view low above the southern horizon.

THE WINTER SKY
(*See* Map, pp. 188, 189)

CAPELLA, the golden star in Auriga, is near the zenith of the winter sky and the Milky Way has swung round to its fourth quarterly position spanning the heavens from north to south and separating the Gemini, Procyon, Lyra and the Great and Little Bears from Canis Major, Orion, Taurus, Andromeda and Perseus.

The constellation of Taurus with its fiery red Aldebaran hangs from a branch of the V-shaped cluster of the HYADES (neighbours of the Pleiades), in which the brightest is ALCYONE, once thought to be the central star of the universe. ORION, with its jewelled belt, is the chiefest glory of the winter sky. Hanging in the south, a tremendous question mark thrown out upon so vast a canvas, this "burning rhetoric" across the heavens has stirred the awe of countless generations of watchers.

East of Orion is Canis Major, containing SIRIUS, the first heavenly light to draw the speculations of the human mind and fix the divisions of the calendar.

STARS, GALAXIES, AND THE UNIVERSE

The number of stars that you can separately distinguish with the unaided eye is surprisingly few, only two or three thousand. Yet with even a small telescope millions of stars can be seen and with a large telescope the number rises to many thousands of millions. The naked-eye stars are found all over the sky. In contrast, the great multitude of telescopic stars are confined to a special strip of the sky—they are found along the Milky Way. It is indeed just the combined light from a huge number of very faint stars—too faint to be seen separately by eye only, that makes the Milky Way appear as a bright band across the sky. Few sights are so impressive as this vast glowing arch seen on a clear moonless night. Unlike the conjuring trick that loses interest as soon as we know how it is done, the night sky actually gains in its impressive qualities (and perhaps even in its romantic qualities) from a knowledge of what it is that we are looking at. We are looking at nothing less than the stage on which the Universe acts out its play.

Some important settings of the stage can be guessed from a casual glance at the sky: for instance, that we live inside a disc-shaped collection of stars. Imagine two dinner plates placed rim to rim so as to enclose a lens-like space between them and imagine that in this space there are a hundred thousand million stars, one of them being our Sun. Then you will have some idea of what the Milky Way is and of why the great majority of stars are found in the band of the Milky Way. When we look at the Milky Way we are looking along the dinner plates; when we look at parts of the sky distant from the Milky Way we are looking outside and away from the plates. To make this a little clearer think of a plate covered by grains of rice and suppose that you are a tiny microcosm attached to one of the grains—as we are attached to the Sun. Then if you look along the plate you will see a multitude of rice, but if you look away from the plate you will see only a few neighbouring grains. This is just the situation with the stars. The ones that we see outside the Milky Way are close neighbours: that is why so many of them seem very bright, because they are comparatively close to us. But when we look along the Milky Way we see a multitude of stars, appearing faint for the most part because they are very much farther away.

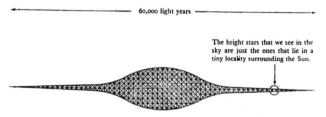

◄─────────── 60,000 light years ───────────►

The bright stars that we see in the sky are just the ones that lie in a tiny locality surrounding the Sun.

A schematic representation of our Galaxy seen on edge. The shaded area is the space between our dinner plates. It contains about 100,000,000,000 stars.

A few words now about distances. Astronomical distances are so vast that it is inconvenient to measure them in miles. Instead the length of the path travelled by light in a year may be used as a distance indicator. Thus it takes light about 60,000 years to travel right across the Milky Way. In each second of time light travels 186,000 miles, so that in 60,000 years the length of its path becomes about 400,000,000,000,000,000 miles. This is the size that our dinner plates must have.

193

The Milky Way is usually referred to as our Galaxy, or as *the* Galaxy. The Sun is one of a hundred thousand million stars that make up the Galaxy. Together with its attendant planets (the Earth being one of them) it lies far out from the centre, almost near the edge of the Galaxy. It moves around the centre along a roughly circular path, much as the Earth moves along a roughly circular path around the Sun itself. But whereas the Earth takes only a year to move around the Sun, the Sun (plus planets) takes some 200 million years to move around the centre of the Galaxy. Since the Sun was born about 4,000 million years ago it has done only about 20 trips around the Galaxy. In contrast, since the Earth was born it has done some 3,000 million trips around the Sun. Recently important differences have been discovered between the stars in the central regions of the Galaxy and stars like the Sun that lie away out from the centre. The latter are called Type I stars and the former Type II stars. The great majority of the naked-eye stars are Type I stars, as indeed are most of the stars of the Milky Way that you can distinguish with binoculars or with a small telescope. It needs a large telescope to pick up the vast number of Type II stars located in the central regions of the Galaxy.

As the common run of stars go, the Sun is quite a bright specimen. But it is not by any means the most outstanding member of the stellar company. With increasing rarity, stars are found ten thousand, a hundred thousand, times brighter than the Sun, and the brightest star known is about a million times more luminous than the Sun. Such giants (as they are called) all belong to the Type I group. They are all exceptionally young stars, in some cases no more than a few million years old. In contrast, the Type II stars are all old stars, perhaps some 5 or 6 thousand million years old.

Gas is required to make stars. Stars originate as condensations within great gas clouds that lie along the band of the Milky Way. Since young stars are ones that have condensed recently, it is clear that young stars will be found only in the vicinity of gas clouds, and since most of the gas of the Galaxy is confined to its outer parts—little gas is present in the central regions—this explains why the very bright giants are always situated in the outer regions, never in the centre of the Galaxy. It also explains why only old stars are to be found near the centre.

A notable cloud of gas in which star formation is apparently going on at the present time can just be detected with the naked eye. It appears as a slight fuzziness in the "sword" of Orion. The gas of this cloud is heated by stars inside it and is thereby set aglow. It is this glow that you see.

Recent observational work on the formation of stars inside gas clouds like the Orion cloud makes it seem likely that the Type I stars are not born singly, one at a time, but in groups. Showers of several hundred stars are formed simultaneously. For the most part the showers are self-dispersive. That is to say, the stars of a particular shower usually spread out from the region of their origin and separate away from each other. But there are exceptions to the general rule.

Occasionally a shower of stars stays together as a cluster instead of dispersing. The Pleiades, a well-known and notable group that you can easily see for yourself, is one such cluster. These remarks apply to the Type I stars. Since the Type II stars are old stars, born long ago, it is not possible to determine the conditions of their birth quite so readily. But it seems likely that the Type II stars also originated in showers—not in showers of a few hundreds at a time, however, but in showers of many thousands of millions at a time. The Type II stars must have been born in a truly gigantic star-making cataclysm.

The degree of compression required to produce a star is very great indeed. A cloud such as the one in Orion probably averages about 1,000 atoms to a cubic centimetre. The material of the Sun averages rather more than 1,000,000,000,000,000,000,000,000 atoms to the cubic centimetre. Evidently then an enormous condensation of gas must take place in the process of star formation. We require a cloud that is initially very large, perhaps some 10,000,000,000,000 miles in diameter, to shrink down to a diameter of about a million miles, the density within the cloud rising meanwhile to an enormous degree.

Not only does the density rise during the process of star formation but the temperature inside the shrinking cloud rises very considerably too. Eventually temperatures in excess of ten million degrees are attained. A crucially important process is then set up. In the central regions of the cloud the hydrogen of the original gas begins to be very slowly changed into helium.

Energy is released by this conversion. Ultimately when the internal temperature has risen high enough, the energy production becomes sufficient to balance the energy that constantly streams out of the cloud and which is radiated away into space from its surface. When this stage of balance is reached the shrinkage of the cloud stops and the birth of the star is complete.

The conversion of hydrogen into helium takes place by nuclear reactions. A star is a gigantic nuclear reactor. Nuclear energy is indeed a cornerstone in the structure of the Universe.

It may be wondered what happens inside a star once all the hydrogen of the inner regions has become converted into helium. While this is a problem that scarcely concerns the Sun—since the Sun has not yet by any means exhausted its inner hydrogen—it is a matter that does concern some stars, particularly stars of great intrinsic brightness, the giants. What happens is that exhaustion of hydrogen leads to a further shrinkage of the innermost parts of the star. This further shrinkage leads to increasing temperatures that eventually become high enough for nuclear energy to be generated from the hitherto inert helium. The helium then becomes largely converted into carbon, oxygen and neon. This happens at a temperature of about a hundred million degrees.

Once the helium becomes exhausted there is a further shrinkage phase that again leads to rising temperatures, causing carbon, oxygen and neon to be changed into sodium, magnesium, aluminium, silicon, phosphorus, sulphur, chlorine, argon, potassium and calcium. This happens at temperatures between five hundred million and two thousand million degrees. At still higher temperatures the material changes mainly into iron, but appreciable quantities of chromium, manganese, cobalt, nickel, copper and zinc are also produced. Deep inside the stars the dreams of the alchemists are completely realised.

When temperatures above five thousand million degrees arise, stars explode with unprecedented violence—the explosion of one star being equivalent to the simultaneous explosion of some 1,000,000,000,000,000,000,000,000 hydrogen bombs. The explosions are generated by an instability that develops in the nuclear reactions. Such exploding stars are observed to happen. They are called supernovae.

It is now generally believed that hydrogen is the only primaeval material and that all other elements are produced by nuclear transmutations inside these very hot stars, stars that distribute their contents into space by gigantic supernova explosions. Apparently the iron of the cutlery that we feed ourselves with was once cooked in a star to temperatures of thousands of million degrees. So was the material of the Earth and much of the materials of our own bodies.

We have referred to our Galaxy as a vast plate-shaped aggregate of stars. It was at one time thought that the Galaxy lies alone in space with nothing outside it. This old view is now known to be utterly wrong. Space is populated with other similar great aggregates of stars. With large modern telescopes more than 100,000,000 of these "galaxies" can be detected. For the most part the galaxies are grouped in clusters. Some clusters are small, containing only two or three main members, while other clusters contain upwards of a thousand large galaxies. Our Galaxy belongs to a small cluster, the so-called "Local" Group. The Local Group contains two monsters. One is our Galaxy and the other is a galaxy that can be seen by the naked eye, if you know just where to look for it, in the constellation of Andromeda. It shows up as a fairly extensive faint blur of light—faint because it is at the enormous distance of 1,500,000 light years (1 light year = 5,880,000,000,000 miles) away from us. Even so it lies within the Local Group.

The largest modern telescopes can detect galaxies out to a fantastic distance of some 2,000,000,000 light years. The outcome of a telescopic survey of a truly gigantic region of space is easily described—the contents of one bit of space are very like the contents of another bit. The galaxies that inhabit our particular neighbourhood are very similar to the galaxies that populate the depths of space.

Just as stars are condensations that form within the gas clouds within a galaxy, so the galaxies themselves, and the clusters of galaxies, seem as if they must be condensations that formed within a supergalactic cloud. And since the galaxies are spread through space it seems that the supergalactic cloud from which they formed must also have occupied all space. It must have been (or must still be!) a veritable universal cloud.

To explain how such a universal cloud came into existence is perhaps the most difficult problem in astronomy. Some scientists believe that the whole Universe "began" about 5 thousand million years ago, and that the universal cloud came into existence at the moment of the origin of the Universe itself. Other scientists reject such a "beginning" of the Universe. They believe that matter is originating in space all the time—that the universal cloud is constantly being augmented by new matter.

At first sight this latter idea might seem open to the objection that as time goes on space would become more and more crowded with material. This would certainly be the case if the Universe were static, but it is known from astronomical observations that the Universe is not static. The distances between the clusters of galaxies (but not the distances within a cluster) are constantly increasing in a uniform sort of way. That is to say, the speed with which two clusters separate is in direct ratio to the distance between them.

Now if matter were not originating continuously in space this expansion of the Universe would lead to space becoming less and less occupied with matter. Thus we have the following situation: the continuous origin of matter tends to fill space while the expansion tends to empty it. Might it not be that one effect just balances the other? According to the theories that have recently been developed such an exact balancing does indeed take place. Nor does this turn out to be a fortuitous circumstance but a deep-rooted consequence arising from the expansion being caused by the origin of matter. Expansion must keep step with the rate of origin—if by some magic the rate of origin were doubled the rate of expansion would also have to double. In short, the origin of matter apparently forces the Universe to expand at just such a rate that the average density of the material in space remains constant.

This conclusion carries with it an interesting philosophical implication; for if the average density of matter does not change with time, the large-scale features of the Universe will also remain unaltered. This does not mean that individual galaxies will not change—they will. It means that an observer at a random point in space who happened to sleep—not like Rip Van Winkle for a mere twenty years, but for, let us say, ten thousand million years—would not notice much change when he awoke. He would certainly notice changes in the nearby galaxies but he would find it difficult to detect much change in the aspects of comparatively distant galaxies.

The philosophical upshot is that, if the bulk features of the Universe have always been the same as they are now, the necessity for supposing that the Universe came into being at a definite epoch in the past disappears. There is no reason to suppose that the Universe as a whole ever had an origin. An individual aggregation of matter, whether a galaxy or a star or a man must have a definite origin, but we need no longer suppose that there was once a time before which the Universe did not exist and after which it did. Time does not lie outside the Universe.

ARCHITECTURE

Architectooralooral.

Dickens.

When we build, let us think that we build for ever.
Ruskin.

They dreamt not of a perishable home
Who thus could build.

Wordsworth.

What is a church?—our honest sexton tells,
'Tis a tall building with a tower and bells.

Crabbe.

Nor till the hours of light return
All we have built do we discern.

Matthew Arnold.

Architecture

'Architectooralooral'

KEY: *a* and *b* 15th-century hand-axes; *c* small paring-knife; *d* stonesetter's trowel (15th cent.); *e* carpenter's gouge; *f* fine chisel for wood; *g* moulding-template; *h* Cotswold tile-pick; *i* Cotswold tiler's hammer; *j* Cotswold tiler's pegging-knife; *k* Cotswold waller's hand-hammer; *l* Elm mallet; *m* hammer for use with cup-headed carving-chisel; *n* cup-headed chisel; *o* punch, to reduce stone in a series of parallel furrows; *p* claw-tool, used in sequence to the punch; *q* pitching-tool, for coarsely reducing surface of stone.

The kinds of building one happens upon most often in country walks, and on week-end visits, are farms and manor houses and parish churches, with an occasional ruined Abbey or Great House by way of grandeur and diversity. For this reason the first place in these short notes will be given to the more modest kinds of architecture. These have a special fascination in that, being built by local contractors of local material, they vary in character with every district, for example, the brick or timber houses and flint churches of the Eastern Counties, where stone was an expensive luxury imported by water-carriage from a distance, and by contrast the Cotswolds where almost every kind of building is in stone. Mention of the Cotswolds brings in another interesting aspect of country building: the filtering down into the country of new architectural fashions from London and the big towns, so that one can often find charming simplified variations of smart London architectural features in the attempts of

203

the local builders to keep up-to-date. The Cotswold builders, from among whom came most of the great contractors who executed the masonry of St Paul's Cathedral, showed the effect of this training under the eye of Sir Christopher Wren in the astonishingly accomplished series of early Georgian houses to be found in almost all the villages of that district. Other local styles are the extravagant timber work of Tudor and Stuart times in Lancashire and Cheshire and the Welsh Border counties, the timber in combination with tile and brick of Surrey, Sussex and Kent, the splendid Georgian brickwork of Buckinghamshire with its extraordinarily high proportion of darker burnt bricks, and the luscious golden stone work of the Ham Hill quarries which is to be found all over Dorset and South Somerset, and, finally, the work of all the good stone-building counties stretching diagonally across England from Somerset, through the Cotswolds, Oxfordshire, Northants, Rutland to Lincolnshire. In all these local styles the determining factor is in the main the materials used in construction, though political and economic conditions appear in some places as the Peel towers of the Scottish border, where defence was a primary consideration, or the Oast houses of Kent.

The Georgian architecture of America, called by its owners colonial, though it continued long after the War of Independence, comes intermediate between a regional or local school and a small national school such as that of Ireland or Scotland. There is good Georgian brick building in America, but the most remarkable feature of this group to English eyes is the weather-boarded work. This is found in England, in Surrey especially (there are good examples in Dorking), but in America houses of a size and dignity that would have demanded stone or stucco in England were carried out in weather-boarding. (The "Cape Cod House", rather in favour in America for a week-ending style, resembles the simpler and sturdier form of Georgian cottage. Its charms are rather those of atmosphere than architecture.) The great majority of old farm-houses are either Tudor or Stuart, that is, late mediaeval, for the Middle Ages lingered on in the country till the eighteenth century almost, or what we may call classical, that is, Georgian and early nineteenth century. The typical late mediaeval house is as illustrated overleaf.

The part between the Porch and the Upper end chambers (sometimes called Parlour and Solar above) was in the earliest examples, that is before Edward IV (1550 about), all one room open from the ground to the roof—the "baronial" hall in fact—but in the second half of the sixteenth century a floor was often inserted in older houses, providing a big upstairs sitting-room in the roof part of the old hall, and leaving the hall itself as rather a low-ceilinged, unimposing room below. This making of a big sitting-room upstairs was the origin of the grand staircase in larger houses: in the Middle Ages proper staircases are rarely of much importance. This division of the hall into two storeys is the only important change in medium-sized house design from Plantagenet times down to Cromwell. Various details do alter, however, and can serve as closer indications of date. The barge-boards on gables, for example:

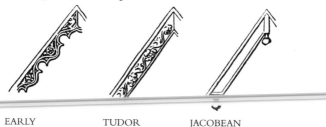

EARLY   TUDOR   JACOBEAN

Windows, too, are a good rough guide to date (*see illustration overleaf*).

Most of these examples have been taken from timber-built houses, but the main forms are the same all over the country. The Great Houses of Mediaeval and Tudor times follow the same general plan, but in these cases the Upper and Lower end chambers

205

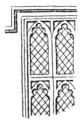  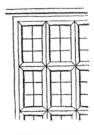

TUDOR I   TUDOR II   LATE TUDOR

have grown into long wings which are returned to form a court like those of the Colleges of Oxford and Cambridge. Often a second court was formed in front of the house proper out of ranges of farm buildings. These courts were entered through gate-houses over which were sets of rooms, in some cases important enough to be a little annexe to the house.

Simpler examples of gate-houses had a timber top storey on a brick or stone gate.

 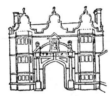 

But in Tudor times brick gate-houses with octagonal turrets became popular. They were bright with gilding and diaper patterns, and generally picturesque, and there is a smack of knightly chivalry about them that pleased an age of realistic politicians playing at romance. This taste for pageantry, colouring and a flavour of chivalry in architecture is the first "art" fashion that can be recognised in England. Beside the fondness for gate-houses and turrets and gay colouring, all symptoms of this first fashionable taste, there are the Tudor chimneys, of which a few examples below.

206

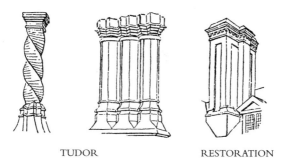

TUDOR   RESTORATION

In the later sixteenth century the "chivalrous" taste is seen rapidly giving place to a "classical", not real classic in the sense of Roman archaeologists or even true Italian Renaissance, but a sort of barbarised version of the Italian derived from copybooks printed and engraved in Belgium or Germany. In grand houses the decorative work was often actually done by Flemish and German workmen. Below are instances of typical Flemish ornament in English buildings.

This thoroughly over-decorated Flemish type of architecture was the last word in fashion at the time of Shakespeare, but as the seventeenth century proceeded the influence of Holland began to supersede that of Belgium and a bolder, rather less rich and

less over-ripe manner began to prevail. The type of gable shown is found chiefly in the South-East of England, and is definitely Dutch in origin. It is a sort of halfway house between the pure barbarity of James I architecture and the complete Classicism that came in with the Restoration.

The Restoration and William-and-Mary to Queen Anne type of country house is rightly celebrated for the way in which it is able to combine classical restraint with geniality. The typical house of the time takes this form:

The roof and chimneys are marked features of the design, and a sure indication of this period is the heavy ornamental cornice and wide-spreading eaves. The ornament to doors is bold and rich.

As the Classic movement became more and more rigid, large

roofs came to be considered barbarous (that is, not Italian) and this type of house became fashionable during the reigns of George I and II. The roof is hidden behind a parapet. (See below.) Window frames in Classic houses vary considerably and there is even more variety and freedom of invention shown in the country than in London, where the tyranny of the Italian masters was strong.

The earliest form of Classic window—it is rare to find it unaltered—retains the mullion (vertical post) and transom (horizontal crosspiece), relics of the great Tudor windows, but the window opening has taken on its classic shape.

When sash windows were introduced—the first recorded is in the sixteen-eighties—many of these early Classic windows were adapted and lost their mullion and transom. The early Georgian sash windows have very thick glazing bars, and are

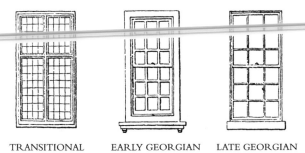

TRANSITIONAL   EARLY GEORGIAN   LATE GEORGIAN

often placed flush with the surrounding brickwork. As the eighteenth century went on, however, the tendency was to make the glazing bars more and more thin and elegant, and by the time of George III (1790) they began to assume the thickness we are accustomed to. Many delightful varieties of window were made by local firms during the eighteenth century, as the "Siamese Twin" and the Venetian.

The latter became fashionable with London architects after the return of Lord Burlington (after whom Burlington House is named) from his Italian tour in George I's time, but they do not appear much in country districts till the seventeen thirties and forties. All these types of window are often to be seen inserted into earlier buildings. There is hardly space here to do more than mention the extraordinary variety of types of bow-window, often richly decorated, and of ornamental doorways. It is often possible to recognise the work of one local firm in the windows and doors of a district.

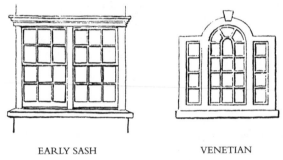

EARLY SASH   VENETIAN

Toward the end of the eighteenth century and in the first quarter of the nineteenth (Regency and George IV), a new type of country house appears.

It is long and low and has a roof of very flat pitch and very far-overhanging eaves. The roof is very often of slate. It is generally severely plain as regards stonework—when it is of brick it is often stuccoed and painted—and the chief ornamental feature often takes the form of a balcony or verandah or porch—sometimes all three—of cast-iron treillage of geometrical design. These are the counterparts of the houses in Bloomsbury

and Phillimore Terrace in London. Cheltenham and Brighton were largely built in this style, and there are many charming examples in South Devon. It prevails in the older seaside resorts such as Sidmouth, which came into fashion after George III was ordered sea bathing for his health. There are a great many pleasant country rectories built in this style.

Of the great houses of the Georgian period the most striking feature is the pillared portico. The earlier Georgian mansions tend to be designed on the scheme of a big four-square central block connected by low passage wings often with arcades or columns to wing pavilions.

In the latter part of the eighteenth century the wings and the connecting arcades tend to disappear, leaving nothing but a grand square box. The Portico, however, remains the symbol of grandeur to the end. A curious by-product of the "Great House" architecture of the Regency and George IV periods is to be found in the gamekeepers' cottages and lodges of the time.

211

They are the result of the theory of "picturesque beauty" or "sketchable bits" that prevailed at that time. Remembering how our great aunts were taught to sketch, and forgetting the works of Gainsborough and Constable, we are apt to scoff at the Picturesque Theory. But our own crazy pavements hardly establish our right to do so. These lodges and cottages anticipate the Babel of styles which characterizes the reign of Queen Victoria.

Most people's interest in church architecture, and on country holidays it is generally parish churches that are met with, is confined to spotting the date. But again, spotting the local building character and assessing the good purpose to which it has been put is a considerable improvement on the merely chronological game. Of course, church architecture takes us back so far in time, to the twelfth and eleventh centuries even, with their echoes of the arts of the heroic age of the Vikings and the early Christian East, that the question of dates so romantically remote overwhelms all other interest: moreover, these survivals from such very early times are hardly plentiful enough for comparison to establish local building schools. Date spotting is best done by mouldings:

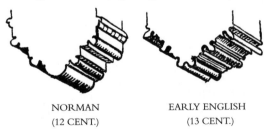

NORMAN
(12 CENT.)

EARLY ENGLISH
(13 CENT.)

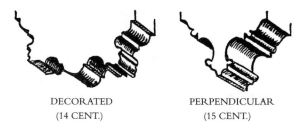

DECORATED
(14 CENT.)

PERPENDICULAR
(15 CENT.)

or less safely by windows:

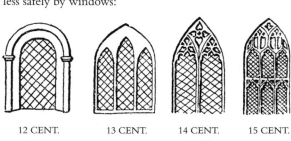

12 CENT.   13 CENT.   14 CENT.   15 CENT.

Windows are not so safe because they were often altered to give more light and more room for a display of stained glass, and one often finds windows of the last phase (called in the guide-books Perpendicular or Perp.) inserted in earlier buildings. There are, of course, plenty of other indications of date, for example, the character of the ornament, changing from the primitive barbaric splendour of the twelfth century through gradual stages of refinement to the immensely varied, slightly sentimental, naturalistic ornament of the end of the thirteenth and beginning of the fourteenth centuries, and finally to the standardised decorations of the last phase with its frequent use of heraldry and endlessly repeated angels. In the earlier phases of Mediaeval architecture experts can date by mouldings to within very few years, but in this last phase, which had begun to establish itself by about 1375, one can hardly be certain without external evidence to within 50 or even 100 years. But it is in this phase that we can see the local varieties of church building most clearly, for in the period 1350-1550 England enjoyed such an unparalleled commercial prosperity that parish churches were rebuilt and

213

done up all over the country, very often, as in Somerset, the Cotswolds and East Anglia, to mention only three outstanding cases, on the proceeds of the woollen industry. The money for all this rebuilding came from the parishioners themselves, and was therefore spent on the naves of the churches or on the western towers, parts of the church fabric for which the parish as a whole was responsible, as against the chancel, which was often appropriated with the living to some richly endowed institution, monastic or other. The institution, having many such livings appropriated to it, regarded the care of the chancel of any one of its parish churches merely as a business liability and did not care to spend more money on it than was absolutely necessary, hence chancels were often patched up from generation to generation, and often contain the oldest surviving parts of the church. The picture of Lavenham Church makes this point very clearly. The chancel with its old-fashioned high-pointed roof can be seen standing out among the flat roofs of the later parts of the building, the nave to the west of it, and the private chapels of rich parishioners on each side of it. In this matter of roofs the flatter pitch gradually tended to supersede the steeper, probably because it was found that the lead sheets were inclined to sag with the heat on a high-pitch roof. Often one can see the line of the older high-pitch roof quite clearly marked on the face of a tower.

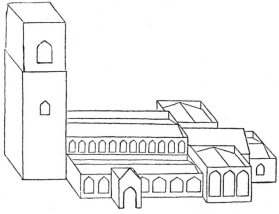

ISOMETRIC VIEW OF LAVENHAM CHURCH

The churches we have mentioned so far have western towers. The true cross plan, with a central tower, is to be found at all dates, but is more popular in earlier times, and is related to the Abbey church plan of the great period of monastic building— the twelfth century. Abbey ruins are chiefly of interest to those who week-end in Yorkshire, where there are a number of celebrated examples. For date-spotting the rules are the same with Abbeys as with parish churches, except that one should rely on mouldings rather than on window forms, as windows are apt to be altered to meet the increasing desire for more light. On the whole Abbey buildings tend to belong to the earlier periods, for men gradually began to prefer to rebuild their own parish church as something more individual to themselves instead of leaving their money to be swallowed up in the already vast endowments of a monastery. Unless there are special circumstances, a disastrous fire, or a sudden access of wealth from unexpected sources, to occasion the rebuilding of an Abbey church, the later monastic buildings are inclined to be of a domestic character, a gate-house as often as not. While speaking of Abbey ruins and gate-houses, a word should be said of castles. The earliest form often met with has a keep which in some cases is filled up with living-rooms, and even a chapel, but the more usual form relies on its immensely strong outer walls and towers. Within these was a house for the lord, planned like the ordinary mediaeval house we have illustrated, and there may be, as often as not, a strong tower on a mound as a place of last resort in time of siege.

Church furniture, stalls, screens, fonts and so forth, are a special sideline; not to mention sculptured tombs. Most surviving church woodwork is either fifteenth or sixteenth century or Victorian imitation, the latter unhappily predominating. But it is always exciting to find odd bits of James or Charles I or Georgian church furniture. It has often been said that this kind of woodwork, the three-decker pulpits and the high-panelled pews, is too domestic and not churchy enough. This is an accident of survival. More church woodwork has survived from the Middle Ages than domestic, and more domestic Jacobean and Georgian than ecclesiastical. In both cases the style was the same for houses and churches. It was not till last century that a special style became associated with religion and nothing else.

ABOUT PUBS

Next to the house and (if he is devout, a hypocrite or an anti-quarian) the church, the English week-ender goes more often into the pub than into any other kind of building. It is therefore worth his while to notice pub architecture and the deeply rooted traditions it possesses; the more so because these are rapidly being confused, and are even in danger of being exterminated, by the modernisation schemes of well-meaning brewers, by losses due to age and obsolescence and by changes in social habits—such as, for instance, the introduction into pubs of women, the juke-box and the television set.

THE INTERIOR OF THE COUNTRY PUB
REFLECTS ITS ORIGINS IN THE
FARMHOUSE KITCHEN

A STONE-BUILT PUB:
TUDOR WITH LATER ADDITIONS

A WAYSIDE PUB: EARLY VICTORIAN IN
PLAIN BRICK AND TILE

A VILLAGE PUB IN ROMANTIC VICTORIAN
GOTHIC STYLE

Do not let these words suggest, however, that the devotee of pub architecture should look back to past times in the belief that the good old ways are always the most desirable. In that direction lies the cult of the phony-antique, a disease to which the pub has always been specially prone. Who does not know plenty of "olde hostelries" crammed with improbable black oak beams, hung with horse-brasses and lit through leaded, bottle-glass windows, installed by brewers and landlords who imagine that to have been visited by Elizabeth Tudor or described by Charles Dickens (or to look as if they might have been one or the other—or even both) are the only attributes a successful pub requires?

A pub, on the contrary, has a vital social function which it can perform only if it keeps up with the times. The sense in which it must also remain true to tradition is that—inside at any rate—it must conserve those qualities that have always made people feel at home in pubs. Although for obvious reasons these are more likely to be found in old, mellowed pubs than in new, they have nothing to do with the survival or imitation of period styles. They can equally well be evoked by modern means and materials—

so long as the main objectives are not lost sight of. These are: warmth and cheerfulness and a sense of seclusion, to which should be added a capacity to lift people a little out of themselves.

Warmth and cheerfulness are chiefly given by the colours used—especially those of grained and polished woods—and by low varnished ceilings; also by the glitter of glasses and bottles, which at the same time helps to create the required effect of heightened reality. Seclusion is given by the subdivision of the interior into smallish rooms, and of these into bays and screened-off corners, which besides enabling crowds to separate into groups, creates a sense of something intriguing round the corner—a surprising number of pubs, it will be noticed, have L-shaped rooms.

Such are the traditional ingredients of the sympathetic pub interior, ancient and modern. Yet how much havoc has been wrought—and still is—on charming, homely pubs all over the country by the introduction, in their place, in the name of modernisation, of cold, hard "easy-to-clean" materials like stainless steel and plastics, of cream paint and scumbled plaster and tasteful lounge furniture, and above all by the growing practice of merging the small, separate bars into one, to crowd in more people at peak hours or to placate the licensing magistrates' passion for supervision? The conversion of a sequence of cosy bars into one cheerless public hall has been further encouraged by the arrival of television. The traditional means by which the proper pub atmosphere is achieved—rich colours, sympathetic materials and intricacy of plan—can best be studied, of course, in the town pub, where the woodwork is elaborated into the form of mahogany curlicues, where the colours of the paintwork are supplemented by red velvet upholstery, and the glitter of bottles and glasses by multiple mirrors in which every movement is reflected and engraved glass screens that enhance, by partly disclosing, the mystery of what lies next door. But this gin-palace style of interior decoration, though it has influenced pubs everywhere, is a thing of its own which belongs strictly to the era when the town pub was changing its character from that of a house where drink was consumed at leisure to that of a shop where it was sold over the counter in an atmosphere of somewhat hectic sociability.

The village or country pub retains a more relaxed domestic character; indeed the arrangement of its various rooms still reflects the way it gradually evolved out of the ale-house kitchen in which it had its beginnings. This was simply the kitchen of a roadside cottage or farmhouse in which the owner sold refreshments to passers-by. It had its brew-house at the back, across the yard, but as time went on a corner of the kitchen was screened off to hold an evening's supply of beer and save repeated journeys outside. This was the origin of the tap-room, which later became a servery and was eventually provided with a serving-counter or bar, the name *tap-room* being transferred to the public room as a whole—which afterwards happened to the name *bar*. Meanwhile as the kitchen became crowded, the landlord had begun to invite favoured callers—the gentry or his own special cronies—into his private parlour, which itself was taken over in due course as part of the pub, the landlord retreating to some inner sanctum. Arrangements were then made to serve this parlour direct, usually by transferring the servery to a more central part of the house, and it became the bar-parlour. Later the landlord's inner parlour was invaded in turn and became the private bar, and his living-quarters were confined to the upper floor.

So evolved the sequence of rooms that make up the pub as we know it, served in part from a bar (which in the town pub grew into a wide shop-counter, a feature that did not appear in the country pub till well into the nineteenth century) and in part through hatches from the service area. The interior of the town pub is dominated by the bar and its elaborate bar-furniture (or "wagon", as the range of shelving behind it is called); not so the country pub, were the word parlour is not a misnomer and the main public bar often still retains the style of furniture—scrubbed tables, high-backed settles and seats built into the wide fireplace—that it has inherited from the farmhouse kitchen.

The story of the exterior is much the same. Country and village pubs differ but little architecturally from cottages and farmhouses of their period and locality: Jacobean, Georgian or Victorian; brick, stone or plaster. The best examples, however, are distinguished from their domestic prototypes by a kind of unconscious heightening of every effect: gables are more pointed,

A GEORGIAN MARKET-TOWN PUB, WITH
CHARACTERISTIC LARGE BAY-WINDOW

ODDITY OF CHARACTER AND PROPORTION
IS FOUND IN MANY PUBS

barge-boards more elaborately carved, bay-windows (a speciality of pubs) more pronounced. Oddity of any kind is emphasised, giving the building a subtly uninhibited flavour, so that whether it be a hedgerow ale-house, the house where farmers gather on market-day, the social centre of the village or a remote inn catering for the casual wayfarer or the seasonal fisherman, it does not require the hanging sign, the seats outside the door or the brewer's house-mark on the wall to proclaim its purpose.

ON FOOD AND DRINK

It snewed in his hous of mete and drinke.

Chaucer.

And cooks recorded frames of mind
In sad and subtle chops.

G.K. Chesterton.

I told him…that we ate when we were not
hungry, and drank without the provocation
of thirst.

Swift.

It snewéd in his hous of mete and drinke

On Food & Drink

The faculty the Stomach has of communicating the impressions made by the various substances that are put into it, is such, that it seems more like a nervous expansion from the Brain than a mere receptacle for Food.

Dr Waterhouse's
Lecture on Health, 1823.

NOTABLE AND AMUSING FOOD

Week-end cookery should be either very quick, a good meal produced in half an hour, or very slow, put on before you go out. However witty the talk, however shady the garden, however original the cottage and its furnishings, it won't be by these things alone that your week-ends will be judged for repetition, but also by the food you offer.

Serve unusual dishes that will be remembered and spoken of. Settle on a speciality and learn it up, be it the art of devilling, of making pancakes, of serving hors-d'oeuvres, or of compounding a salad. Get an unusual, not a humdrum, cookery book and practise a few dishes between week-ends. Never let any dish be dull. Your guests eat with their eyes as well as with their palates and noses.

Week-end food can be divided into four parts: food which you take out with you ready to eat; food which you cook out-of-doors; dishes which, prepared before setting out, are left to cook slowly in readiness for your return; and dishes which can be prepared very rapidly when you come home.

PICNIC FOOD: READY TO EAT

Although sandwiches are often the mainstay of a picnic there are many ways of ringing the changes. Take screw-topped jars filled with cold kedgeree, fish mousse, or soused herrings. A jar filled with potato salad will go well with any kind of cold meat, poultry or game which can be taken tinned or previously home-cooked and carved, wrapped in greaseproof paper and put in a container. (Flat hinge-lidded "sandwich" tins can be bought very cheaply and are ideal for this purpose.) Or take tins of tunny fish, goose pâté, sardines; or stuffed eggs, with the halves put together again and wrapped in lettuce leaves to keep them moist. If you are a good pastry hand, pastry cases filled with savoury mixtures are well worth the extra effort. Cold omelettes are an excellent picnic dish. Salami and other ready-to-eat sausages, a choice of cheeses and fruit in addition to the main dish make it certain that there will be enough for even the most epicurean and the hungriest.

A green salad can travel in its own bowl if it is washed and dried in advance. The dressing must be in a separate jar. If the weather is hot, pack cos lettuces in a tin with a very little water. The lettuce will remain crisp and a jar of butter and a small plastic bottle of milk placed between the leaves will stay cool and fresh. Unbuttered French rolls, French bread, water biscuits or crisp-breads can then be taken in addition or as an alternative to thin brown bread and butter, which should be wrapped in a damp cloth.

For sandwiches themselves, bread is easier to cut and digest if it is a day old—much nicer if it is new. If rolls are preferred they must be fresh, or they can be crisped by sprinkling them with water and heating them for a few minutes on a baking sheet in a very hot oven. Finger out the soft middles, so that you have two empty "boats" for your filling. You might also consider using brioches, poppy-seed rolls and scones instead of bread; and malt and raisin bread make good sweet sandwiches.

Prepare the butter in advance by creaming it with a perforated spoon in a warm bowl. Half a cup (a quarter pound) of creamed butter will spread a 2lb loaf (about 45 slices). Mustard, horseradish cream, vegetable extract, mayonnaise, curry sauce, chopped chives or parsley can be added to the butter according to the filling.

Use a palette knife for spreading, butter the inner sides of both slices of the bread, and when filling sandwiches with meat remember that several plies of thin shavings are far, far better than thick slices. Remember that if you are using fat meat the butter should be reduced or eliminated. Salted meat and fish fillings are improved by a drop of lemon juice (a drop means a drop, no more), chopped pickles or capers. To keep sandwiches fresh wrap them in aluminium foil, or failing that, in waxed or greaseproof paper.

To make a Sandwich Loaf cut off the ends of a French loaf, scoop out the crumb, brush the inside with melted butter, and pack with any fairly solid sandwich mixture. Alternatively, stuff a number of rolls in the same way, one for each member of the party.

SANDWICH FILLINGS

Cream cheese and grated walnuts or chopped olives or, creamed with paprika, with sliced tomatoes.

Flaked fish mixed with a thick shrimp sauce.

Finely-chopped cooked liver and crisp bacon.

Tunny fish with lemon juice, grated onion and parsley.

Kipper fillets with mustard butter (if the fillets are marinated instead of cooked they make an excellent substitute for costly smoked salmon).

Chopped egg with chutney or "Gentleman's Relish" or Worcester sauce.

Eggs fried in oil (oil being the only cooked fat that is nice cold) until the yolks are almost hard.

Minced ham and anchovy.

Peanut butter and grated onion, or chopped olives or chopped

Flaked buckling with lemon juice and plenty of pepper.

Minced corned beef and mustard butter.

Chopped crisp bacon and peanut butter.

Sardines and tomato sauce; or sardines mashed to a paste with an equal quantity of sieved egg yolk seasoned with salt, cayenne pepper, a drop of lemon juice and moistened with olive oil.

English Cheddar, Cheshire or cottage cheese with slivers of green peppers or chopped tinned pimiento.

Any kind of cold meat, game or poultry—and try mixing thin shavings of different kinds of meat.

Chopped dates, cheese and nuts.

Honey and fresh mint.

Honey and banana (with lemon juice added).

Devonshire cream and strawberry jam.

MEALS COOKED OUT-OF-DOORS

The Barbecue is a means of cooking meat on a spit or grid over direct heat, with or without a special highly seasoned sauce. The trick is to get a red-hot, almost smokeless fire, lay the meat on the grid and grill it, turning when necessary. Steaks, chops or sausages can be cooked in this way; or you can make Shish Kebabs, one of each of the following being arranged on long skewers, one for each member of the party: loin of lamb in inch-thick cubes, chipolata sausages, small mushrooms, squares of onion, small pieces of bacon, a bay leaf and quarters of tomato or slices of red pepper. These ingredients are improved if they are taken to the picnic covered with a pile of chopped raw onion. Lay the loaded skewers on the grid for about ten minutes; turn them over and cook for another ten minutes.

If a frying pan is available, and there are not more than four people in the party, Minute steak is your best bet, the thin steaks being fried for one minute on each side in a mixture of butter and Worcester sauce. Bananas baked in their skins are a delicious substitute for green vegetables.

Stews and soups can be re-heated over a picnic fire if you have a solid grid over the fire or a suitable pot with a clamp-on lid.

Frankfurters and toasted marshmallows are the easiest of all picnic food. The only cooking implements needed are long skewers or forks or strong green twigs.

THE OYSTER BAKE

If you have a sea-shore, seaweed, a piece of sail cloth, oysters, and hours to spare you can make a Memorable Meal (but notice that this is a neutral term).

The sea-shore is the natural place for the oyster bake. Begin the preparations several hours before the time set for the meal and make a circle of flat stones 2 to 4 feet in diameter and in this circle build a hot fire of wood. When this has burned for two to three hours, rake out the fire and on the bed of ashes arrange a layer of fresh seaweed, and then your oysters in their shells, potatoes in their skins or corn on the cob. Cover with a thick layer of seaweed and then with a piece of sailcloth, fastening down the edges with stones. Leave for two to three hours and then rake out the food.

THE DUCK AND THE HARE

If you are camping, and tomorrow's meal has to be thought of as well as today's, then be sure to have in sequence a hare and a duck. Today's hare, jugged, will have (you must see that it has) a quantity of thick gravy left over. In this gravy simmer your cut-up duck on the next day. You will have, simply and inexpensively, a Canard Rouennais that the Tour d'Argent itself would be proud of.

ADVICE TO THOSE WHO ATTEMPT TO SUPPLEMENT
THEIR DIET FROM NATURE'S LARDER

FRESHWATER FISH: Trout and salmon should be eaten as soon as possible after being caught, as they are then at their best.

If the other freshwater fish you catch must be eaten, they should be soaked for at least 12 hours in brine. This removes both the slime and the taste of mud. Even carp or tench can in this way be made palatable.

MUSHROOMS AND TOADSTOOLS: Ordinary mushrooms are white on top, with a skin which peels readily, and have pinkish or chocolate gills underneath, according to age. They grow in grass.

PUFFBALLS are round and white, such as here, when young, they are excellent fried. They also grow in grass.

PARASOLLE mushrooms are white with brown flecks on top and with white gills. They are light and elegant in appearance, and grow in grass. Round the stem is a ring or band like the similar band frequently found on the shafts of umbrellas.

There is a BOLETUS TOADSTOOL found in woods which is excellent. It is dark brown on top, like a bun, and white and spongy underneath.

There is another boletus, yellow underneath, which it is also safe to eat.

ALL MUSHROOMS AND TOADSTOOLS are dangerous if they are not eaten fresh; therefore reject all botanist's specimens.

DON'T cook and attempt to eat YOUNG BRACKEN SHOOTS because the Japanese do. What suits the hardy races of the extreme East may not suit you.

DON'T cook YOUNG NETTLES as a substitute for spinach. It is a stringy one.

DON'T eat BOILED RHUBARB LEAVES. This practice caused a large number of deaths during the war.

DON'T take PLOVERS' EGGS from a nest containing four. It is unkind to the parent birds, and at least two of the four will be addled.

DON'T cook things in clay.

N.B. – MICE IN HONEY should be imported from China, not prepared at home.

DISHES TO COME HOME TO

Dishes to come home to are either prepared the day before and re-heated, or are dishes which have been cooking slowly while you were out. Dishes which are improved by having been made the day before are: Curry, Hungarian Goulash, Chicken Paprika, Oxtail with haricot beans, Irish Stew, Lancashire Hot-pot, Baked Beans, Mushrooms in Sour Cream, Red Cabbage with chestnuts, and Veal Matelote.

BAKED BEANS

Empty two large tins of baked beans into a large fireproof dish. Stir in two tablespoonfuls of treacle, 1 small onion, 1 teaspoonful of made mustard, a pinch of soda bicarbonate. Lay 6 slices of streaky bacon on top and cook in a very slow oven for 2 hours. When ready to eat, reheat and place under grill to crisp the bacon.

MUSHROOMS IN SOUR CREAM

Wash one pound of mushrooms, and cut a sliver off the end of the stems, but do not peel. Then slice each mushroom down through the stalk. Heat three tablespoonfuls of butter in a frying pan, add a thin layer of mushrooms, being careful not to overcrowd them or to stir them roughly (this lets the juice escape). When they are delicately brown, remove them and do another layer, adding more butter if necessary. When the last layer has been removed from the pan, mix two tablespoonfuls of flour with the remaining fat and cook, stirring continuously; then add one-and-a-half cups of milk to make a smooth sauce. Put the mushrooms back into this sauce, add half-a-cup of sour cream (a little yoghourt mixed with cream and allowed to stand will make an excellent sour cream), salt and freshly-ground pepper to taste. Cook over a low flame for about 5 minutes. This can be stored for days in the refrigerator, and can be used in a number of ways. It can be served plain on toast, or as a sauce over gently fried slices of ham on buttered toast. It also makes an excellent casserole.

For the casserole, open a tin of lobster, crab, or boned chicken, or take shelled prawns or shrimps, or bits of left-over fowl of any sort, and arrange them, together with one hard-boiled egg for each person, sliced lengthwise, in a shallow oven-dish. Cover with mushrooms in sour cream and heat in a moderate oven.

RED CABBAGE WITH CHESTNUTS

Melt an ounce of fat, preferably dripping, in a heavy saucepan. Add about a pound of shredded red cabbage, a large onion, sliced, 1 large apple, sliced, 2 tablespoonfuls of stock (or water), 1 tablespoonful of wine vinegar (or red wine), 1 heaped dessertspoonful of brown sugar, 2 teaspoonfuls of salt, and several turns of the pepper mill. Cover with a tightly fitting lid and cook gently for about 40 minutes, shaking the pan occasionally to prevent sticking.

The chestnuts are cooked separately, and added to the cabbage when it is re-heated. Cut crosses in the end of each chestnut, then cook them for 15 to 20 minutes in boiling water. Take them out of the water one at a time and remove their skins with a sharp knife while they are still very hot. Just before serving the cabbage, sauté the chestnuts in butter and surround the dish of cabbage with them.

VEAL MATELOTE

Cut 2 lbs of stewing veal into small cubes, removing the bones. Brown these gently in pork or chicken fat, and then put them into a saucepan. Fry in the same fat 6 sliced onions and about 6 diced carrots. When they are gently browned add them to the meat. Then fry a quarter pound of mushrooms in the same fat, and put them aside (or use a tin of mushrooms baked in butter). Add 1½ ozs of flour to the frying pan and cook it slowly with the fat, adding gradually ½ pint of boiling water and ½ pint of red wine. Boil this for 10 minutes, stirring continuously, and pour over the meat and vegetables. Season with salt and several turns of the pepper mill, add a little thyme and 1 bay leaf, and simmer for 1½ hours, putting the mushrooms in for the last half hour. Serve with shell-shaped pasta.

CHICKEN IN WINE

Cut a young tender chicken in serving pieces, rub with salt and pepper and roll in flour. Brown in butter, and add 10 small onions or shallots and 8 slices of bacon, diced. Cover and cook for 15 minutes. Now add a tin of mushrooms, a glass of wine, ½ bay leaf, ½ teaspoon minced parsley and ¼ teaspoon each of thyme and marjoram, salt and pepper. Cook for a further 30 minutes.

RISOTTO MILANESE

Clean one large cupful of Patna rice by rubbing in a tea cloth— no, don't wash in water—then fry in 2 tablespoonfuls of butter with 2 finely chopped onions for 5 minutes. Add 1 pint of chicken bouillon, boiling, 4 tablespoonfuls wine, 2 tablespoonfuls tomato puree, a pinch of saffron, salt and pepper. Cook covered for 20 minutes; then mix in 2 tablespoonfuls of butter and serve with plenty of grated cheese.

ROASTS

Of all week-end dishes the easiest to prepare is the roast, especially if you have one of the new covered self-basting roasting pans. Very little advance preparation is needed, and there is nothing to do while it cooks in the oven beyond occasional basting if you use an ordinary roasting pan.

For a change from the usual mint sauce, lamb is delicious when larded, sparingly, with slivers of garlic (not more than one clove of garlic for a leg or shoulder of lamb) before roasting. Pan-roasted potatoes cut lengthways or potatoes baked in their jackets are the obvious accompaniment.

Carrots can also be cooked at the same time in the oven and take about 45 minutes to cook if sliced very fine lengthwise (this brings out the best flavour). Put them in a covered casserole with a good lump of butter and about ½ cup of water and salt and pepper to taste.

Incidentally, any batter or dough (whether it be for Yorkshire pudding or scones) should be mixed in advance. If it has no leavening it can be completely mixed and ready to put in the oven or frying pan. If it is made with leavening (other than yeast which does not take to this treatment) the dry and wet ingredients can be mixed and the two bowlfuls combined when wanted. The important thing to remember is that baking powder and soda bicarbonate must stay dry until you are ready to cook them.

QUICK DISHES
TO MAKE AT HOME-COMING

GRILLS

Of all forms of cookery that allow you to get a meal ready after you come in and before your guests' appetites ruin their tempers, grilling or frying is the best: cutlets, chops, steaks, lambs' kidneys or fish. Meat should first be placed very close to the heat to seal the juice, then moved to a cooler spot (or the gas turned lower) and cooked four minutes or so on each side, according to thickness. Salt only when on the dish.

Food is given an unusual taste before grilling by being marinated, that is, steeped in a mixture of oil and vinegar to which herbs have been added. Steep for some hours.

Well-grilled steak dished with watercress and potatoes fried in deep fat is excellent. But next time try putting on top of your

with a spoon, season with pepper, and work in parsley chopped as finely as may be, or anchovy pulp: pounded anchovies and sieved capers.

OMELETTES

The secret of making the best omelettes is to withdraw the white of one egg for every six eggs used, and not to beat the eggs but to mix them gently. Omelettes containing minced ham, potatoes, pimientos, mushrooms, spinach are easy to improvise, and the "Spanish" omelette, which contains a mixture of vegetables (onion is a "must") and a little chopped ham, makes a delicious change. This omelette is left flat; not folded over.

SCRAMBLED EGGS

With mushrooms and/or kidneys which have just been fried in butter.

HOT SANDWICHES

Cut bread slices, butter them and fill with one or a mixture of these fillings: bacon, tomato and cheese; chopped onion, egg and red pepper; cream cheese, watercress and salad dressing; cinnamon powder in ham paste; bacon, lettuce and mayonnaise; chopped apple with nut and lettuce. These sandwiches may be either buttered all over the outside or dipped in a batter made by stirring one beaten egg into half a pint of milk. They are then fried until they are a golden colour on both sides.

SAVOURY PANCAKES

The day before you plan to eat this dish (1) Cook a large finnan haddock in milk and, removing skin and bone, flake the fish. (Keep the stock, skin and bones to make an excellent soup for another meal.) (2) Make a batter with 4 ozs flour, 2 eggs, 1 table-spoonful of olive oil and ½ pint of milk. Keep it in a cool place—in the refrigerator if you have one. The pancakes will be the thinner.

The following day when you come home, melt 1 oz butter, stir in the fish, add pepper and 2 oz cream. Fry the pancakes, keeping them very thin. Stuff and serve very hot.

A good filling can also be made with the remains of a goulash or pieces of left-over game or poultry mixed with some Mushrooms in Sour Cream (see p. 230) or any other thick and savoury sauce.

CORNED BEEF HASH

Grate 3 onions and add to the contents of a tin of corned beef with ½ lb of diced cooked potatoes (held over from the previous day), some Worcester sauce and horseradish sauce. Heat some butter in a frying pan and put in the hash mixture. When heated through, turn out in the shape of a flat cake into a fireproof dish. Brown under the grill and serve with tomato sauce.

CONSOMMÉ WITH POACHED EGG

Take 2 pints of consommé and bring to the boil. Slice 2 French rolls, butter the rounds, then brown in the oven. Poach 4 eggs in the boiling consommé, removing each one when cooked to a soup tureen in which you have already placed the French rolls. Pour the soup gently over and serve with grated cheese.

VEAL WITH MUSHROOMS

Take 4 veal cutlets, white and tender; trim them and fry in butter. When they are brown, put them in the oven to continue cooking, and pour stock over the meat, repeating at intervals until the veal is well cooked. Remove the cutlets to a hot dish, brown a little flour in butter and add to the gravy in the dish. Allow this to thicken over a low heat, stirring all the time; then add a tin of mushrooms and a large glass of sherry and heat again. Pour the sauce over the veal and serve hot.

EGGS IN RAMEKINS

Butter some ramekin dishes and two-thirds fill with flaked salmon or smoked haddock and cooked rice. Break an egg into each, season and stand in a covered pan of boiling water until the eggs are set. Add a teaspoonful of cream to each with salt and pepper and drop of Tabasco sauce. Put under the grill for a minute or two before serving.

SALADS

Green salads may be made of many plants other than lettuce. Chicory, dandelion leaves, sorrel and white cabbage, for instance. They should be perfectly clean and perfectly dry. For drying, use a wire basket, whirling it at arm's length—out-of-doors. The best dressing for green salads is French dressing which can be made in large quantities and stored in a jar in a refrigerator for weeks. When it is needed all you have to do is to shake the jar thoroughly. A good recipe is 4 ozs olive oil, 2 ozs *white wine* vinegar, 1 dessertspoonful of sugar, 1 teaspoonful salt, ½ tea-spoonful dry mustard, ten or more twists of the pepper grinder, and a garlic clove which should be removed once the dressing has been very thoroughly shaken and tasted. An alternative is to rub the salad bowl with half a clove of garlic.

Waldorf salad is made of equal parts of raw cooking apple and raw celery, sliced, disposed on a bed of lettuce, liberally garnished with half-walnuts, and dressed with mayonnaise. Orange and lettuce; grapefruit and lettuce; shrimp and lettuce; watercress and creamed cheese with nuts, are quite as easy to mix as lettuce and beetroot, and much more fun.

Try Huile d'Arachides instead of olive oil. It is a great deal cheaper and very nearly as good for salad dressings and for cooking. For cooking it is infinitely better than lard or margarine and for some dishes part oil, part butter makes an excellent mixture. (Beef, pork or poultry dripping is always good to use for frying or roasting, but never use mutton dripping.)

A passable mayonnaise can be made by adding oil and a little cream to a reputable bottled mayonnaise. (Heinz is the best.)

TINNED AND PACKAGED FOODS

Use tinned foods, but disguise them. No one should ever suspect that they are tinned. All tinned foods are improved by additions during the heating up. (Never follow the directions on the tin for heating up; it takes longer than applying direct heat to the contents; all but the most agile burn their fingers and spot their clothes when opening a heated tin.)

SOUP

Remember that Campbell's and Heinz's Tomato soups are not the only good tinned soups. There are also creams of mushroom, of asparagus, of pea, of chicken, of onion and (if you are lucky enough to find it) Shippam's excellent hare soup. Tinned soups may be made more interesting as well as disguised as to origin, which has its own advantage, by mixing cream of chicken and cream of mushroom; cream of chicken and cream of onion; cream of pea and cream of chicken—and others as fancy dictates.

There are also three good brands of packet soups: Knorr

(onion and pea are admirable but some others are too glutinous); Batchelor's (particularly the chicken noodle); and Maggi.

Clear soups are improved by a tablespoonful of sherry or white wine. Likewise tomato and spinach soups are improved by the addition of a little thick cream just before serving; celery and cauliflower soup are improved by the addition of an egg beaten in a cup of milk (this is true of most cream soups). Use the water in which vegetables have been cooked to vary and extend tinned soups. And do not forget the virtues of grated parmesan with any clear soup.

FISH

If you are not eating it cold, tinned fish should be wrapped in buttered paper and heated in a covered frying-pan; or cooked in crumbs and cheese; or served with a good lemon or anchovy sauce; or poached in white wine or broth and served with shrimps, mixed gherkins, chipped olives, minced onion or anchovy paste.

MEAT

To re-cook tinned meat place it on a bed of finely shredded vegetables, top with fried minced onion, pour gravy over, bring to the boil, then simmer, adding herbs, currant jelly, or a touch of lemon. Spiced sausages renew the youth of a tinned stew to be served on a bed of rice or macaroni.

VEGETABLES AND FRUIT

Tinned sweet corn should be heated with additional butter, salt, pepper and sugar. Tinned peas should be drained, washed very thoroughly and treated like sweet corn, with the addition of a sprig of mint. I don't use processed ones, and don't use those bright with artificial colouring and over-flavoured with mint essence. Tinned spinach, blanch or purée; celery and, for those who have donkey-tastes, tinned carrots (which are delicious sliced very thinly and sautéd in butter) are useful stand-bys. Avoid cut-up asparagus and artichoke hearts. Both are expensive, and neither are worth eating.

Frozen vegetables, and fruit, are quick and easy, and, though not as good as fresh ones, they are far better than most tinned

237

ones, and allow you to have out-of-season foods at a reasonable price. But don't keep them once they are defrosted—and remember that even a refrigerator is not cold enough to prevent them defrosting.

QUICK SWEETS

The French fashion of fruit and cake served after the cheese may well replace elaborate puddings. But if you are drinking wine and serving pudding, again follow the French fashion and serve the cheese before the pudding and your wine will not be sour on the palate.

Fresh fruit alone with some white wine and sugar, or with junket, is an ideal sweet. Failing that, have a plentiful stock of tinned fruits, to serve as they are or in jelly form. Buy packets of jellies in preference to gelatin by the ounce, even though their flavours are usually unpleasant; they are surer in use and you can superimpose a real fruit flavour by adding fruit juice instead of water. For fruit jelly, add berries or any fruit cut in slices. For a sponge jelly, whisk white of egg into the jelly just before it begins to set. For a wine jelly: 1 packet of lemon jelly, a wine glass of orange juice, a wine glass of sherry (or Marsala, or Madeira) and boiling water to make a total of 1 pint of liquid.

When Sir Thomas B., that wise and gracious man—he has the best collection of Hocks in England and the best private collection of Dürer prints in Europe—was, very young, at his first party, leaning against the wall, nervously fingering his tie, there came to him an obviously assured Man-of-the-World. "Your first party? I thought so. I am going to tell you something which will stand you in good stead for the whole of your life. If they serve wine-jelly, and they probably will, help yourself to the knobs. They always make the damn things upside down and all the wine runs into the knobs."

Tinned cherries, muscats, green figs, loganberries are as nice as peaches, pineapple, and pears and less hackneyed. Don't buy the most expensive form of peaches: the cheaper kinds are packed riper. Don't buy pineapple chunks. Only sliced pineapple eliminates the wood-like core of the fruit. Hawaiian brands are the best.

ZAMBAGLIONE

This is a memorable sweet. For four helpings: 4 eggs, 4 table-spoons sugar, 8 tablespoons Marsala, ¼ teaspoon vanilla essence. Combine all ingredients in the top of a double boiler, place over hot water and beat constantly until frothy, smooth and thick. Remember that a Zambaglione boiled is a Zambaglione spoiled, but do not be disheartened if it separates: it does not look as nice, and it should not be so—but it will still taste delicious. When it is thick, empty into warmed glasses (to be eaten hot) or turn it into a dish and go on beating it until it is cold.

PRESERVED GINGER

(or DATES with their stones taken out) with whipped cream.

APPLE FLUFF

Beat 2 tablespoonfuls of castor sugar into 1 stiffly beaten egg white and fold into a small tinful of apple sauce with ¼ tea-spoonful of nutmeg, a few drops of lemon juice and a little grated lemon rind. Top with whipped cream.

JAMAICA JUNKET

Add 1 tablespoonful of treacle, instead of the usual sugar, to a pint of warm milk, and make the junket as usual. When set, cover the junket with 2 tablespoonfuls of Jamaica rum. Serve with cream.

MELON WITH LIQUEUR

Remove the top of a ripe melon, scoop out the seeds and pour in a glass of any favourite liqueur or white vermouth. Chill for several hours.

HONEYED PINEAPPLE

Fry slices of fresh or tinned pineapple with honey over a very low heat. A little Marsala can be added before serving.

RASPBERRIES IN WINE

Use fresh raspberries, or if they are not in season, defrost a packet of frozen raspberries slowly. Add a glassful of red wine.

APPLE MUESLI

Grate an unpeeled apple for each person, stir in 1 heaped table-spoonful rolled oats to each apple and add enough cream or top milk to make a moist mixture. Add any of the following: soaked sultanas, chopped dates, grated nuts, chopped ginger. Serve in individual glasses.

BANANA WHIP

Mash two bananas for each person. Add the juice and grated rind of ½ lemon for each 4 bananas, and sugar to taste. It is fine and unrich like this. But you can also mix it with an equal quantity of cream. (The lemon makes a Jamaica taste like a Canary.)

MERINGUES

The shells can be made in advance and kept for several days. Serve with whipped cream, or chestnut purée and whipped cream.

BAKED EGG CUSTARD WITH CARAMEL SAUCE

The custard can be made in advance and the sauce keeps almost indefinitely. For the custard, take 6 eggs, beat them slightly, add ½ cup of sugar and ¼ teaspoon of salt. Heat 1 pint of milk and pour it gradually on to the eggs and sugar, stirring all the time. Strain the mixture into a greased dish and stand this in a baking pan with hot water halfway up the sides of the dish, and bake in a moderate oven (350°) until firm (when an inserted knife comes out clean). While baking you must take care that the water around the moulds does not boil or the custard will whey.

To make *Caramel Sauce* take 1 lb of lump sugar. Put 9 lumps in a heavy pan and burn them. Add 2 tablespoonfuls of boiling water, the rest of the sugar and another 2 tablespoonfuls of hot water and let it boil until it thickens. This will take about half-an-hour but there will be enough sauce for several custards. Store in a screw-top jar. Do not place in the refrigerator. This sauce is also delicious served with junket.

COFFEE

Coffee, as used on the Continent, serves the double purpose of an agreeable tonic and an exhilarating beverage, without the unpleasant effects of wine.

Coffee, as drunk in England, debilitates the Stomach, and produces a slight nausea. In Italy it is made strong from the best Coffee, and is poured out hot and transparent.

In England it is usually made from bad Coffee, served out tepid and muddy, and drowned in a deluge of water, and sometimes deserves the title given it in "the Petition against Coffee", 4to, 1674, page 4, 'a base, black, thick, nasty, bitter, stinking Puddle Water'.

from *The Cook's Oracle* by
William Kitchiner, M.D. 1838.

But coffee need not be "Puddle water". There is no difficulty in making good, strong, aromatic, stimulating coffee. How is it done?

First, remember a few basic facts about coffee. There are oils in the coffee bean and they provide the aroma and flavour. They are partly released in the roasting and more so in the grinding. They are volatile. Therefore, freshly roasted beans, ground just before use, will make the best coffee. Use vacuum-packed coffee as a stand-by only: you pay for the pack and you lose much of the aroma. (If it has chicory in it, it is not to be tolerated even as a stand-by. It is said that when Bismarck was in a Paris hotel he ordered the waiter to bring him six cups of an infusion of chicory. Six were brought and he ordered a dozen. They were brought and he ordered two dozen. The waiter came back trembling with only twenty-three cups: "Alas, Excellency, there is no more chicory." "Ah," said Bismarck, "now bring me a cup of coffee.")

Coffee beans stored in an air-tight container should keep 10 to 14 days; ground coffee from 2 days (if finely ground) to 4 days (if medium or coarsely ground). The days are reckoned from the date of roasting or grinding, *not* the day of purchase. Therefore, the grocer who gets a delivery once a week or once a fortnight may not be much use to you. If you can, grind your beans shortly before you use them. It is not arduous and it is well worth the trouble. Electric grinders are now available, and many of the

241

hand-operated coffee-mills are efficient; or perhaps you are lucky enough to have a Kenwood Liquidiser: this will deal with coffee beans as promptly as it will pulverise vegetables and fruit.

Next, what coffee should you buy? Go to a good coffee merchant, tell him what coffee-making appliance you use and take a small quantity of the blend and roast he recommends. (As coffee is nowadays sold in the form of blends only, there is no point in asking for one particular kind—Santos, Costa Rica, etc.). If what your merchant has sold you is not to your liking, try another blend, or another roast, or another merchant; and don't despair: there is a blend and a roast for every palate. Here is, however, a tip which we can give you. If you have had a cup of coffee which you particularly enjoyed, it will in all probability have been made from a blend which was highly roasted (commonly called continental roast) and which contained a fair quantity of mocha.

There are many methods of coffee-making, and there is a confusing choice of coffee-making appliances in the shops. The least good, and perhaps the most generally used, is the so-called percolator which is so made that water circulates through the coffee continuously at boiling point, thus stewing and spoiling the coffee. If you use one of these pots, do consider buying one of the simple Italian coffee-makers which range in price from half-a-guinea for the smallest *Napolitana* to several guineas for the larger sizes of the *Vesuviana*, *Columbia* and other makes. They are very economical in use; they are quick—and they are virtually unbreakable.

But if you want your week-end guests to exclaim after dinner "this indeed is different, this is cream of coffee, nay elixir of coffee ... liqueur of coffee", then you must buy the small domestic *Espresso* machine. And by this we mean the one true Espresso machine called *Gaggia* and not the many other machines, admirable though some of them are, to which their manufacturers have chosen to attach the label "Expresso" (with an "x", not "Espresso"). The Gaggia is interesting to handle, it looks good, but it is without doubt expensive. If you cannot afford one now and if you really care for superlative coffee, start saving immediately. You will not regret it. And meantime practise your palate at the Espresso bars.

DRINK

For hard drinkers, whisky, gin and the vermouths; for soft drinkers, tea, coffee and ginger-beer are the standard refreshments supplied at the village pub. But imagination and bold experiment can break this monotony with many happy improvisations.

"Ginandit" is the weary walker's counsel of despair. Any enterprising week-end pub, or cottage, will possess ingredients from which one or other of the following may be compounded:

COCKTAILS

EAST INDIAN: Equal parts of French vermouth and sherry, with a dash of orange bitters.

WEST INDIAN: Two parts rum to one part fresh lime or lemon juice, with some sugar dissolved in it, or failing this, "Kia-ora" lemon crush (not squash) or Rose's lime juice.

HAWAIIAN: Four parts gin, two parts orange juice and one part curaçao (or any other of the orange liqueurs).

SIDE-CAR: Equal parts of fresh lemon juice (no alternative), cointreau (or one of the orange liqueurs) and brandy.

SATAN'S WHISKER (*straight*): Of Italian vermouth, French vermouth, gin and orange juice, two parts each; of Grand Marnier one part; orange bitters.

Ditto (*curled*): For the Grand Marnier substitute an equal quantity of orange curaçao.

JOHN WOOD: Italian vermouth, four parts; Irish whisky and lemon juice, two parts each; Kummel, one part; Angostura bitters.

MR. GUTTON'S GIN BLIND (*to be drunk with discretion*): Six parts gin, three parts curaçao, two parts brandy and a dash of orange bitters.

NOTE ON THE USE OF BITTERS: When cocktails are mixed in bulk, any bitters should be introduced in the proportion of one half to one teaspoonful per pint. In more intimate drinking, delicacy of flavour and economy of material are secured by rinsing each glass with bitters, which are then returned to the bottle, while the glass is filled with a mixture from which bitters have been omitted. If possible, ALL COCKTAILS should stand on ice for at least half an hour before shaking and taking. If you cannot wait so long, you must adulterate your mixture with ice. A large jug, and an egg whisk (or even a fork) efficiently replace the shaker. The glasses should be as cold as possible before the cocktail is poured out.

ICED DRINKS

GINGER-BEER: (*a*) with gin and lemon or lime juice, preferably fresh but, if need be, bottled; (*b*) (for sweet-tooths) with cointreau and orange juice. (There is no bottled substitute for orange juice, but the orange Crushes taste much better than the old Squashes—though they don't keep as well.)

Strong, cold black COFFEE with a wineglassful of brandy to a quart and some ice.

For people who can bear to be seen drinking it: Equal parts of GIN and CRÈME DE MENTHE, with plenty of cracked ice.

JOHN COLLINS: The juice of two oranges and one lemon with an equal measure of gin, some soda water and ice.

BAVARIAN CUP: Mix a small wineglassful of cherry brandy (or plain brandy) with a bottle of white wine, and add crushed strawberries and ice *ad lib*.

CIDER CUP: Three large bottles of sparkling cider, a pint of old Marsala, a little sugar, a lot of lemon rind, two bottles of soda water and maraschino or brandy.

RAJAH'S PEG: A claret glass of old brandy in a pint of dry champagne.

MINT JULEP: Pack a tumbler as tightly as possible with alternate layers of finely cracked ice and sprigs of mint, freshly picked and bruised; fill the interstices with whisky (rye if available, otherwise Irish or, if need be, Scotch). This tastes as good as it smells. It is drunk by degrees, as it melts, and through a straw.

CASSIS (blackcurrant syrup made in France) is obtainable in Soho, and when mixed with French vermouth, soda-water and ice, makes a delicious "soft" drink. If you can afford the veritable liqueur Cassis, it is not "soft". If you cannot shop in Soho, Ribena is a good alternative to Cassis syrup.

COLD TEA should be made as follows: Steep the leaves in *cold water* (the same proportion as you use when boiling) for 12 hours and then strain.

HOT DRINKS

TEA with rum, lemon juice and a shaving of lemon peel.

MULLED CLARET (1) *For Boys*: Warm (but do not boil) the wine with nutmeg, cinnamon, cloves, sugar and lemon rind. (2) *For Men*: Ditto, adding dry port one part to six of claret. (3) *For Heroes*: As for boys, adding one part port to three parts claret and as much old brandy as you think the company can stand.

RUM PUNCH: one part rum, one part whisky and two parts (or a trifle less) water, heated with sugar, cinnamon, nutmeg, cloves and dried orange and lemon peel.

HANDY PUNCH: to two bottles of whisky and one of rum, add an equal quantity of water. Heat these with a little nutmeg and cinnamon, the juice of two lemons and sugar to taste. When it is very hot, set it alight with a red-hot poker and, after a moment's admiration, blow out the flames.

REDCURRANT TEA is a good hot "soft" drink. It is made by pouring boiling water on plenty of redcurrant jelly and adding a squeeze of lemon juice. Blackcurrant jam will make BLACK-CURRANT TEA.

FOR THE WEEK-END STORE CUPBOARD

Salt, black pepper (*ground and corns*), mustard
Curry powder (*Indian*)
Paprika
Garlic salt
Onion salt
White or Red Wine Vinegar
Anchovy Sauce
Italian tomato purée and sugo (*they can be bought in Soho and in special shops*)

Chestnut purée

Rennet

Garlic

Spices and Herbs (*as good a collection as you can make; these can rarely be bought in the country and it is very annoying to have to change the menu for the want of one of them*)

Gentleman's Relish (*this can be used as a ready-made anchovy-butter*)

Tinned and packeted soups and bouillon cubes

Pimiento (small tins)

Olives

Liver pâté (*Danish*)

Tinned Mushrooms baked in butter

Sardines in varieties

Anchovies

Tunny fish

Parmesan cheese

Tinned sweet corn

Frankfurter sausages

Corned beef

Rice

Packets of long Italian spaghetti and other Italian pasta

Packets of Jelly

Tinned Fruit

Orange Crush

Lemon Squash

FOOD AND DRINK

WHY has our poetry eschewed
The rapture and response of food?
What hymns are sung, what praises said
For home-made miracles of bread?
Since what we love has always found
Expression in enduring sound,
Music and verse should be competing
To match the transient joy of eating.
There should be present in our songs
As many tastes as there are tongues;
There should be humbly celebrated

ON FOOD AND DRINK

One passion that is never sated.
Let us begin it with the first
Distinction of a conscious thirst
When the collusion of the vine
Uplifted water into wine.
Let us give thanks before we turn
To other things of less concern
For all the poetry of the table:
Clams that parade their silent fable
Lobsters that have a rock for stable
Red-faced tomatoes ample as
A countryman's full-bosomed lass;
Plain-spoken turnips; honest beets;
The carnal gusto of red meats;
The insipidity of lamb;
The wood-fire pungence of smoked ham;
Young veal that's smooth as natural silk;
The lavish motherliness of milk;
Parsley and lemon-butter that add
Spring sweetness unto river shad;
Thin flakes of halibut and cod,
Pickerel, flounder, snapper, scrod,
And every fish whose veins may be
Charged with the secrets of the sea;
Sweet-sour carp, beloved by Jews;
Pot-luck simplicity of stews;
Crabs, juiciest of Nature's jokes;
The deep reserve of artichokes;
Mushrooms, whose taste is texture, loath
To tell of their mysterious growth;
The rich, the warm, the comfort glowing in
A baked potato's crackled skin;
The morning promise, hailed by man,
Of bacon crisping in the pan;
The sage compound of *Hasenpfeffer*
With dumplings born of flour and zephyr;
Spinach whose spirit is the soil;
Anchovies glorified in oil;
The slow-gold nectar maples yield;

Pale honey tasting of the field
Where every clover is Hymettus;
The cooling sanity of lettuce
And every other herbal green
Whose touch is calm, whose heart is clean;
Succulent bean-sprouts, bamboo-shoots;
The sapid catalogue of fruits:
Plebeian apple, caustic grape,
Quinces that have no gift for shape,
Dull plums that mind their own affairs,
Incurably bland and blunted pears,
Fantastic passion-fruit, frank lemons,
With acid tongues as sharp as women's,
Exotic loquats, sly persimmons,
White currants, amber-fleshed sultanas,
(Miniature and sweetened mannas)
Expansive peaches, suave bananas,
Oranges ripening in crates,
Tight-bodied figs, sun-wrinkled dates,
Melons that have their own vagaries;
The bright astringency of berries;
Crepe-satin luxury of cream;
Wedding-cake that fulfils the dream;
Pepper, whose satire stings and cuts;
Raw liberality of nuts;
Sauces of complex mysteries;
Proverbial parsnips; muscular cheese;
Innocent eggs that scorn disguises;
Languid molasses; burning spices
In kitchen-oracles to Isis;
Thick sauerkraut's fat-bellied savour;
Anything with a chocolate flavour;
Large generosity of pies;
Hot puddings bursting to surprise;
The smug monotony of rice;
Raisins that doze in cinnamon buns;
Kentucky biscuits, Scottish scones;
Falstaffian tarts that mock the chaste
Rose-elegance of almond-paste;

Venison steaks that smack of cloisters;
Goose-liver for the soul that roisters;
Reticent prawn; Lucullan oysters;
Sausages, fragrant link on link;
The vast ambrosias of drink:
Tea, that domestic mandarin;
Bucolic cider; loose-lipped gin;
Coffee, extract of common sense,
Purgative of the night's pretense;
Cocoa's prim nursery; the male
Companionship of crusty ale;
Cognac as oily as a ferret;
The faintly iron thrust of claret;
Episcopal port, aged and austere;
Rebellious must of grape; the clear,
Bluff confraternity of beer—

All these are good, all are a part
Of man's imperative needs that start
Not in the palate but the heart.
Thus fat and fibre, root and leaf
Become quick fuel and slow grief.
These, through the chemistry of blood,
Sustain his hungering manhood,
Fulfilling passion, ripening pain,
Steel in his bone, fire at his brain…
So until man abjures the meats
Terrestrial and impermanent sweets,
Growing beyond the things he eats,
Let us be thankful for the good
Beauty and bounty of food,

Let us join chiming vowel with vowel
To rhapsodize fish, flesh and fowl,
And let us thank God in our songs
There are as many tastes as tongues.

                                    Louis Untermeyer.

FIRST AID

Some of your hurts you have cured,
 And the sharpest you still have survived,
But what torments of grief you endured
 From evils which never arrived!

Emerson.

'Tis his great happiness that he is distempered, thereby to have an opportunity of experiencing the efficacy and sweetness of the remedies which you have so judiciously propounded. I approve 'em all.

Congreve.

First Aid

Some of your hurts you have cured,
And the sharpest you still have survived,
But what torments of grief you endured
From evils which never arrived ! '

Now we give you Physic and other Remedies for certain Accidents, Sicknesses and Infirmities which may trouble your week-ends. But should any of the graver mishaps befall you of which we treat hereafter, remember that our advices must be used only to allay the harm and to beguile the time while your Physician is delayed. Remember also that the drugs are essential drugs, to be used rarely and compounded with discretion. For, though our simples be culled from venerable masters and our compounds be furnished worthily and though your apothecary be scrupulous to the last minim, yet these alone shall not avail to save you. According to the nature of your mishap, and your diligence in following these prescriptions, they may save your life, render your misfortune more tolerable, cancel it, or prevent it.

THE PRUDENT WAYFARER may equip himself against sundry common emergencies with the following armamentarium.

BANDAGES, ABSORBANT WOOL, ADHESIVE PLASTER, SAFETY PINS, and packets containing STERILE GAUZE and sterile LINT, a small quantity; and of various remedies hereafter described, according to his carrying capacity and his apprehensions.

ACETIC ACID: vinegar slightly diluted with water. Neutralises alkalines.

BICARBONATE OF SODA SOLUTION: one teaspoonful to half a pint of water. Neutralises acids.

EMETICS: (1) Salt and water: two tablespoons in a tumbler of lukewarm water. Or (2) Mustard and water: two teaspoonfuls in a tumbler of water.

FOMENTATION: a dressing which is applied hot and damp. The moisture is retained by placing a piece of oiled silk or grease-proof paper immediately over the dressing. The heat is retained by placing a piece of cotton wool over the oiled silk or paper, and the whole is kept in place with a bandage.

SALINE SOLUTION: NORMAL: dissolve one teaspoonful of sale in a punt of water.

SALINE SOLUTION: QUADRUPLE: dissolve four teaspoonfuls of salt in a pint of water.

TOURNIQUET: can be improvised by tying a scarf or large hand-kerchief around the limb, between the injury and the heart. A stick should be tied in the knot, and twisted until the tourniquet is really tight. It should then be fixed in such a way that it cannot become loose. The patient must have a large letter T marked on his forehead, and the time at which the tourniquet was applied. The tourniquet must be loosened for a few moments every fifteen minutes. A tourniquet is better not placed on bare skin.

AGAINST STINGS AND BITES

If stung by a bee, remove the sting by pressing the hole at the handle end of a small key over the puncture. The sting of a bee is acid, therefore neutralise this by the application of bicarbonate of soda solution (see above).

If stung by a wasp, the wasp does not leave its sting in its victim. Its sting is alkaline, therefore neutralise with acetic acid (see p. 254).

If the sting is on the tongue, avert the grave mischance of asphyxiation from the swelling, by applying inside the mouth an ice bag, or, lacking this, cold water or dilute ammonia; and hot, well wrung out foments to the surface of the neck. But the physician has remedies that are more effective than these.

To take away the Stinging of Nettles use the above application; but, where there is Dock nearby, apply of this a bruised leaf to the area of stinging and chant the following Cantrap:

> Out Nettle, in Dock:
> Dock shall have a new smock.

To search for Harvesters, dig in the skin with a needle first heated in a candle flame; and afterwards cleanse the spot with iodine.

To search for Fleas, be seated on a white and woolly blanket, for this most readily entangles and makes visible your enemy. But some hold that to clap an open bottle of chloroform or a wet cake of soap upon the spot attacked is better.

HARM BY VENOMOUS SNAKES

Against the Harm by Venomous Snakes take measures to prevent the poison from diffusing itself through the system generally and to destroy what is already in the wound. To achieve the former object a tourniquet may be improvised by tying a handkerchief loosely round the limb between the wound and the heart, placing a short stick in the ring bandage thus formed and twisting this until the limb is tightly compressed. Now withdraw the venom locally by sucking the wound. (This proceeding is dangerous only in that it creates a reputation for courage and presence of mind which is difficult to maintain except in the rare advent of another case of snake bite. It is, however, quite unnecessary to swallow the venom and one may go far to undo the unfortunate impression of heroism by using an antiseptic mouthwash at the earliest possible moment.) It is good to encourage bleeding by bathing the fang apertures with warm water and to extend the wounds down to the subcutaneous tissues with a clean, sharp knife.

If the means be available, apply crystals of potassium permanganate or a strong carbolic acid solution to the wound. Give also, to counteract the severe shock, good doses of whisky or brandy, repeated several times if necessary. Some people prefer sal volatile in doses of a teaspoonful to a wine glass of water. No one knows the reason for this.

BURNINGS AND SCALDINGS

Burnings and Scaldings by Fire and Water and Corrosive Substances may, when slight, be treated by pouring over them ordinary Salad Oil, or a mixture of Olive (or Linseed) Oil and Lime Water in equal parts, and then covering with a dressing of lint soaked in oil. Remember that it is necessary to exclude air from the burn as quickly as possible, to administer stimulants, and on no account to break a blister. Severe burns must not be touched by the untutored hand.

BLISTERS

The popular Indulgence of Biting off Blood Blisters is strongly to be deprecated. The proper treatment is to sterilise the skin that covers them with an antiseptic and then to evacuate the blood with a needle which has previously been reddened in a flame.

Prevent blisters on the feet by (1) bathing the feet with methylated spirit and then dusting them with talcum powder daily for several weeks before a walking week-end; (2) wearing woollen socks, soaped at toe and heel, and ball of foot. If after these precautions blisters nevertheless occur treat by (1) swabbing the blister with methylated spirit; (2) pricking the blister in two places with a needle sterilised by being held in a candle or match flame; (3) pressing the fluid out of the blister; (4) applying an Elastoplast dressing. Do not remove the loose skin as this acts as an additional dressing.

TO STAUNCH BLOOD

To Staunch Blood that oozes gently or that flows in a continuous stream of dark purple, it is sufficient to apply a pad of lint on which Iodine has been poured and then to fix this by means of a handkerchief, scarf or bandage. But when the blood is scarlet and issues from the limb in a series of jets, you must act with coolness and promptitude. Press the thumb or forefinger tightly to the wound, while another improvises a tourniquet, which must be bound to the thigh or upper arm between the bleeding point and the heart. The only modification of the already described tourniquet (vide *Venomous Snakes*) is that now there is included within the folds of the handkerchief a smooth pebble which presses directly upon the artery when the tourniquet has been fixed in position. When the bleeding has been arrested it is good to cleanse the wound and apply a simple Iodine dressing. Unless collapse has occurred it is forbidden to administer stimulants until the Surgeon has taken measures to prevent recurrence of bleeding.

EPISTAXIS (NOSE-BLEED)

When the Nose bleeds do not bow the head over a basin, or you will very soon need another. Sit with the head slightly thrown back and apply Cold Water Compresses to the root of the nose, the face and between the shoulder blades. It is good in moderately severe cases to inhale the Vapour of Turpentine or a Snuff of powdered Alum. Where these methods fail or are not available, it is an emergency measure to plug into the nostrils long, narrow strips of gauze, packing these as far back as possible and continuing until the whole nasal cavity is filled.

SYNCOPE

When Syncope (fainting) is imminent, let the sufferer clasp his head between his knees and the crisis may pass. Should unconsciousness supervene, keep the head low, loosen the clothing and hold to the nose smelling salts or burnt feathers. It is pleasant and fitting that the patient celebrate the first moment when he is able to stand upright by partaking of a fluid ounce of brandy or whisky. Sal volatile should not be withheld on grounds of principle.

PERIPALPEBRAL ECCHYMOSIS

Peripalpebral Ecchymosis (black eye). First counteract the swelling and discoloration of this and every other manner of bruise by gently dabbing with Witch Hazel. Then apply with a moderately tight bandage a compress made of cotton wool or lint steeped in cold water. To any unbroken surface, except near the eye, the application of a pad soaked in lead lotion (from the Chemist) is useful. When bruised all over and feeling shaken but not faint there is much relief in a hot bath.

FOREIGN BODIES IN EYE

There are three methods of removal. (1) Grasp the lashes of the upper lid and pull it down over the lower lashes, leave go, and allow the inside of the upper lid to be swept by the lower lashes as it returns to position. (2) Bathe the eye with like warm normal saline (see p. 254), using an eye bath. (When bathing the eyes it is safer to use a different eye bath for each eye to avoid spreading possible infection.) (3) Stand behind the patient, tilt his head back against your chest, and, holding the affected eye open with your first and second fingers, irrigate the eye by pouring normal saline (see p. 254) from a jug across the eye, from the inner corner to the outer. (Use the hand on the same side as the patient's injured eye to hold the eye open, otherwise his nose gets in the way.) The eye may now be sore, so put in a drop of castor oil. This must not be more than six months old or it will smart. Do not fear you have failed in your quest if it prove very small. The patient's description of its size as maybe less than a plover's though surely more than a pigeon's egg is usually not correct.

FOREIGN BODIES IN NOSE

To eject a foreign body from the nose stimulate sneezing with pepper or a paper spill.

FOREIGN BODIES IN EAR

A foreign body in the ear does not constitute an emergency and is not remedied by the introduction of other foreign bodies such as bare bodkins or syringes. It is in such matters as this that the Art of the Physician and Surgeon still avails.

FISH HOOK

If a fish hook should become embedded in a fleshy part of the anatomy, push the hook further on, so that the embedded end, that with the barb, protrudes through the skin. Cut off the barb and withdraw the hook, back the way that it went in. Cover the wound with a clean dry dressing. Later, apply a quadruple saline fomentation (See p. 254). The dressing should be changed every four hours except at night.

AFTER EXPOSURE

After Exposure to Wind and Rain it is good to seek the *Abortion of Nasal Catarrh*.

TO REMEDY THE TOOTHACHE

Whisky or brandy held in the mouth may alleviate the pain.

SEA-SICKNESS

On Becoming Indifferent to the Fate of your Ship, pack the ears firmly with gauze until the pressure on the tympanic membrane can be felt. It is best to lie on the right side with the knees drawn up to the abdomen.

OF SUN-BATHING

ARSENIC, like sunshine, is good for the blood; but to partake of an ounce or two, on the ground that "one cannot have too much of a good thing", would be folly. Folly likewise (though not lethal) is it to expose the whole body, pale and unprepared, for hours at a time to the hot sun. Those who do so may expect a red and peeling skin, headache, exhaustion and sickness of the stomach. To savour the pleasures of the sun-bath and rise from it refreshed and vigorous, with a smooth and daily deepening tan, first inure yourself to the rays as follows: the first day, modestly uncover only the feet and ankles and bathe them in the sun for three periods of five minutes each, allowing an interval of ___ ___ between them. Then turn the body and expose the equivalent area on the dorsal surface for three similar periods. The second day, uncover to the knees and bathe the whole area for five minutes; then cover down to the ankles and continue to bathe the area that has already been exposed on the previous day for another five minutes; making thus ten minutes in all. The third day, bathe up to the hips for five minutes, up to the knees for ten minutes, and up to the ankles for fifteen minutes. The fourth day, bathe up to the navel for five minutes, up to the hips for ten minutes, up to the knees for fifteen minutes, and up to the ankles for twenty minutes. The fifth day, bathe up to the shoulders for five minutes, up to the navel for ten minutes, up to the hips for fifteen minutes, up to the knees for twenty minutes, and up to the ankles for twenty-five minutes. The sixth day, make these times, ten, fifteen, twenty, twenty-five and thirty minutes respectively; and on the seventh day increase them by yet another increment of five minutes each. Each day you should bathe for three periods with intervals of ten minutes between them, and then repeat the whole process on the dorsal surface of the body.

Those who are habituate, as well as those in training, should bear in mind the following beneficial rules: If after sunbathing you experience vertigo, fatigue, or great excitement, you have done too much and must expose a smaller area and for a shorter period on the next occasion. Keep the head covered with a wide-brimmed hat and the eyes protected with dark-rimmed glasses. Prefer the morning or late afternoon to noontide when heat-bearing waves preponderate and choose a place in shelter from the winds; but do not attempt to take a sun-bath under glass, for it is opaque to the more potent rays. Beware of sunbathing when you are exhausted from exercise (or any other cause) and during the hour that follows the midday meal. If you are debilitated or have the slightest suspicion of Tubercle you must not sunbathe except under the special guidance of a physician.

Those who sunbathe for a cosmetic rather than for a therapeutic purpose will anoint themselves with olive oil.

TO SOOTHE THE FACE

To soothe the Face tormented by the Sun and Wind, apply calamine lotion.

To withstand the Pigmentation of Freckles, wash in Sour Milk or in Buttermilk. This should be dabbed on the face with cotton wool twice each day.

SUNSTROKE

Upon such as are Overcome by the Sun, cold water should be dashed, especially over the head, neck and chest. Apply frequently to the forehead cloths wrung out of iced water; and ice itself is very good.

SPRAINS

Before treating a Sprain of the Ankle or any other Joint remember that there may be a grave injury present; a dislocation or even fracture of one of the component bones of the joint. But as emergency measures (having transported the victim home, with the limb in the position that gives greatest ease) remove the clothing, put the patient on a couch and, under the guidance of his sensations, rest the limb on cushions, preferably in such a way that it is well elevated. Now try the application of cold compresses; or, if these fail to relieve pain, of hot fomentations, which should be tightly bandaged over the joint. It is good, if pain is excessive, to apply a teaspoonful of laudanum to the fomentation.

Treat Tennis Elbow and Jumper's Sprain by massaging the injured part and applying a firm bandage. Bathing alternately with hot and cold water is soothing and beneficial.

TO STAY THE HICQUET

To stay the Hicquet drink water backwards. This art consists in applying the lips to the far side of the glass and bending forward the head and body till drinking becomes possible. As a prophylactic measure it should be practised secretly.

Another method is to sip slowly a glass of water with both ears and nostrils stopped. A few drops of essence of peppermint on sugar are very effective in the case of such patients as cannot take water.

RELIEF OF THE WINDY SPASMS

For the Immediate Relief of the Windy Spasms take on sugar Oil of Cajuput, five minims; or of Sp. Ætheris Composita thirty minims, repeated every fifteen minutes if necessary.

POISONED FOOD

After Partaking of Poisoned Food it is correct to send for a doctor. (It is good to inform him of the purpose for which he is needed.) Preserve for the doctor's examination all vomited matter and excreta and all suspect food, etc. Meanwhile provoke vomition by titillating the back of the throat with a finger or by administering, every five minutes until successful, any of the following emetics:

261

Salt: a tablespoonful to a tumbler of water.

Mustard: a teaspoonful to a tumbler of water; or Ipecacuanha wine, a teaspoonful.

Meanwhile the patient should be put to bed, hot bottles and hot foments applied to the Abdomen and, if there are signs of collapse, brandy or other stimulants administered. Finally give an ounce of castor oil. These measures are good against Surfeits of Wholesome Meats and Drinks as well as other forms of food poisoning.

BEFORE HOBNAILING THE LIVER
Before Occasions devoted to Hobnailing the Liver it is recommended to take a half to one ounce of Olive Oil or to drink a glass of milk. The Parkinson Herbal states that "if one doe eate five or sixe bitter Almonds before he fall into drinking company, it will keepe him from being overtaken more than the rest."

THE MORNING AFTER
On the Morning After, comfort the cold and feeble brain by recalling the warning of Mayster Isaac Judæus who saith: "It is unpossyble for them that drinketh overmoche water in theyr youth to come to ye æge that God ordained them."

ANOTHER
Let no cautious weekender set forth without good stock of tobacco, for, in the words of an old ballad:

It helpeth digestion,
Of that there's no question
  The gout, and the toothache, it easeth:
Be it early, or late,
'Tis never out of date,
  He may safely take it that pleaseth.

Tobacco prevents
Infection by scents,
  That hurt the brain, and are heady;
An antidote is,
Before you're amisse,
  As well as an after remedy.

The cold it doth heat,
Cools them that do sweat,
   And them that are fat maketh lean:
The hungry doth feed,
And, if there be need,
   Spent spirits restoreth again.

Tobacco infused,
May safely be used,
   For purging, and killing of lice:
Not so much as the ashes,
But heals cuts and slashes,
   And that out of hand, in a trice.
Anon., 17th century.

Such are the ills that commonly befall those who walk abroad with their fellows to enjoy the pleasures of the country. Should you ail anything else then "all the Nation are already Physitians, … every one you meet, whether man or woman, will prescribe you a medicine for it." But take their medicine, like ours, with circumspection, Reader.

THE LAW AND HOW TO BREAK IT

Who to himself is law, no law doth need,
Offends no law, and is a king indeed.
George Chapman.

Never make a defence of apology before you
be accused.
Charles I.

I have no great regard for The Law.
Samuel Butler.

the Law & how you break it

Who to himself is law, no law doth need,
Offends no law, and is a king indeed.

The laws of England are of two kinds: public law and private law.

The PUBLIC LAWS are those which are enforced by the police and the public authorities, and to which the State attaches the sanction of fine or imprisonment, according to the nature of the offence. Such are the laws against theft of all kinds, against murder and breaches of the peace, against disorderly or unseemly conduct, and other offences which shall be nameless. A breach of public law is a crime and renders the offender liable for prosecution. These are the laws with which most people are most familiar.

The PRIVATE LAWS, on the other hand, are those which govern the rights of individuals *inter se*. These may be either rights common to all citizens, or rights arising between particular persons as the result of some agreement or contract. Private law in general may be roughly outlined as follows: First: that everyone has a right to preserve his property and person inviolate (note well that a footstep on his pasture may be as much a violation of the one as a blow on the nose is of the other); Second: that, if a binding agreement is made between two people and one breaks it, he must pay for whatever damage the other suffers. To explain what constitutes a binding agreement is a very long story, but two points may be mentioned in passing. First: except in certain special kinds of contract (e.g. trusts) a one-sided promise is not binding unless embodied in a deed, i.e. a document signed and sealed before witnesses. Except in the case of a deed there must always be a "consideration" in return for any undertaking. That is, an agreement between you and your neighbour, stipulating a certain course of conduct on the part of your neighbour, is not

267

binding unless there is a reciprocal provision, pledging you also to certain performances. Second: an agreement need not, except in certain particular cases, be in writing. It is, however, easier to prove the existence of such a contract if it is. To break a contract, trespass on someone's land, or run over him in a car is not a crime, nor will the Crown take action to prosecute a man who thus runs counter to his neighbour's rights; but the neighbour himself may sue the transgressor and exact payment to compensate him for his damages. It is also possible that a driver who is not careful as to the *manner* of his collision with foot passengers or other vehicles may incidentally violate some national or municipal traffic regulation and thus render himself liable to prosecution. Moreover, the result of such a collision sometimes leads to the prosecution of the more active party for manslaughter.

OF ARRESTING AND BEING ARRESTED

The policeman's powers of arrest are wide, and it is unwise to resist his attention, however inconvenient. But private persons also may arrest and, on some occasions, it is held by the law to be their duty to do so. If you wish to prosecute someone, go to the nearest magistrate or justice of the peace and lay your information. The offender will then receive a summons or be arrested, according to the nature of your story. If a serious crime has to your certain knowledge been committed, it may be held to be your duty to prosecute, and failure to do so may render you yourself liable for prosecution as an accessory after the fact. Anyone arrested without a warrant must be taken as soon as possible before a magistrate. If that is not possible within twenty-four hours, bail must be granted, unless the offence is very serious. Should this misfortune befall you, communicate with your friends, who may or may not be prepared to go bail for you.

OF HIGHWAYS

The term highway comprises all portions of land over which every subject of the Crown has a right to pass. The right of the public on a highway is a right of passing and repassing. Technically a member of the public can only justify *passing along* and not *being in* a highway. Carriages and other vehicles are lawfully in the highway for the purpose of passage only. A learned judge once said, "The king's highway is not to be used as a stableyard." Had he lived today he would certainly have opposed its use as a garage. A highway must be used reasonably and not for purposes for which it is not intended. "Reasonable" use is by wheeled traffic on the road and foot-passengers on the path. It is not reasonable but "excessive" use to drive a car along a footpath, but no ruling has yet decided that to walk even on the most crowded motor roads is "excessive". It is not permitted to obstruct the highway or footpath by pitching tents or by playing games; nor to annoy passengers by letting off fireworks or firearms. It is an offence to deposit filth or rubbish within fifteen feet of the centre of the road and to obstruct traffic by lecturing or preaching on any part of the highway or footpath.

OF ACCIDENTS

In traffic accidents motorists driving recklessly or at an excessive pace are responsible for any damage to pedestrians, but if the motorist is not reckless or his speed excessive and if the pedestrian walks carelessly among the traffic, then the pedestrian and not the motorist is guilty of the accident. When a road accident is caused by obstructions, such as a pile of stones or an uncovered drain-pipe, the person who placed the obstruction (or his employer) is liable for damages, provided that the injured person was sober and reasonably careful in his progress.

Whoever carries a pickaxe, a spiked stick, or other dangerous object along the road, is responsible for any damage that may ensue.

So also one is liable for damages who rides or drives an unmanageable horse along the road; or who leaves any horse unattended in the road; but if he can prove his ignorance of the intractable character of the horse, he may be held innocent of negligence.

In letting out a horse for riding or driving the owner of the horse implicitly guarantees the horse's roadworthiness, and he is therefore liable for any accidents or breakdowns while it is fairly and prudently used.

Any person who takes money for insecure seats or stands let to spectators at any race meeting, coronation or other public spectacle is liable for injuries caused by the collapse of his structures.

OF RAILWAYS

The purchase of the ticket does not guarantee the purchaser a seat in the train.

A timetable is not a guarantee that a train will run.

The guard can call upon anyone who is disorderly and causing annoyance to the passengers to leave the train, and, if necessary, remove him.

The much vexed question of window up or window down is not dealt with in the bye-laws or by Act of Parliament. In the event of a violent dispute the guard could direct one of the disputants to another compartment.

Each carriage is designed to hold a certain number of passengers. If there are more than this number, a passenger can call upon the guard to reduce the number; and there is a penalty for non-compliance. But this penalty is not paid to the man who lodges the complaint, who has no remedy against the company.

A railway company is responsible for damage or injury caused by sparks falling from its engines.

Those who want more information than is here provided should read the bye-laws of the railway company and the conditions subject to which tickets are issued.

OF COMMONS AND OTHER RIGHTS

Those stretches of uncultivated land which are known as commons are not, as is popularly supposed, common property; nor are they places where anyone is entitled to do as he pleases. The public are usually allowed almost unrestricted use of common land, but the common *rights* belong to local tenants and farmers, and extend to the grazing of cattle and such matters wherein the visiting public are not interested. There are certain rights held "by immemorial custom" which entitle the inhabitants of some villages to use particular wells or ponds or to dry their fishing-nets or to erect maypoles and dance about them or perform other rustic sports on certain pieces of land. To qualify as immemorial such customs must be continuously practised "for a time whereof the memory of man runneth not to the contrary", which for legal purposes was originally the reign of Richard I. Now, however, under certain Acts of

Parliament, 60 years is usually, and 30 years may be, sufficient. A right of way may be granted by the landowner or may be acquired by continuous undisputed use for twenty years. It may, however, be lost by disuse after an indefinite number of years. If a landlord place an obstruction where there is a right of way any person entitled to this right of way may remove the obstruction; for if all rightful users meekly acquiesce, then after twenty years the right of way is lost.

OF BEACHES

Another place often and wrongly considered public property is the seashore. The beach belongs to someone just as much as the land behind it—probably to the same person. Beach land property is bounded to seaward by high-water mark. Below that the land belongs to the Crown. Thus, unless there is a highway, the beach cannot be reached without trespassing. Even when high-water mark is lawfully reached, it is extremely doubtful whether the public have any *right* to bathe.

In many big watering-places it should be remembered that the foreshore is the property of the town council, who therefore have the right to make any rules they like as to the way people should dress, undress, or otherwise behave themselves before they are permitted to bathe.

OF BATHING

There is one crime which every bather who has forgotten (deliberately or by accident) his bathing costume is in danger of committing at one time or another, though he may not be so unfortunate as to get into trouble for it. Whatever openly outrages public decency and is injurious to public morals is a misdemeanour. That means your body, dear reader. Any public exposure of the naked person is an indictable nuisance, and it has been held that this is so when there is no exposure beyond what is necessarily incidental to bathing without a bathing suit. To constitute the offence it must be an exposure in a public place before more than one spectator, or in view of the public even though not in a public place. Week-enders should note that, although one person does not constitute the public, exposure before one person (and indeed any unsuitable conduct) in a public place may be an offence punishable under the Vagrancy Act.

FLOTSAM, JETSAM AND LIGAN

Goods which float on the sea after a shipwreck are called "flotsam"; but if they are thrown out to lighten the ship they are "jetsam", and if sunk, with a buoy attached, then "ligan". When it cannot be ascertained who is owner of such goods, then, if they are found in the sea, they belong to the finder. But all wrecks and wreckage cast ashore are in general the perquisites of the Crown, unless the owner of the land on which they are found has a legitimate "grant of wreck".

Week-enders (and other persons) who happen to find a corpse on the shore are obliged to notify the police within six hours. The reward for fulfilling this obligation is five shillings.

OF TREASURE TROVE AND OTHER LOST PROPERTY

Treasure trove is "any gold or silver, in coin, plate or bullion, found hidden". If the owner cannot be found the treasure belongs to the Crown and must be delivered up on pain of fine or imprisonment; but "the Crown" customarily rewards the finder by paying him the intrinsic value of his find in money. The coroner decides who is the finder.

All other lost property, if the owner cannot be found, belongs to the finder, who may, if it be subsequently stolen, bring an "action of trover" against the thief. But if a finder takes charge of property he is regarded as a depositary unless he can show that he has good grounds for believing that the owner has abandoned it. If, however, he takes it meaning to keep it and knowing or having reasonable grounds for believing that the owner can be found he will be guilty of larceny, which is stealing.

Any person who finds a new-born child must go before the Registrar within seven days and give such information as he has concerning the foundling.

OF MONEY AND KINDRED SUBJECTS

Where there is no agreement to the contrary, a debtor may be compelled to pay his debts in cash and a creditor may be compelled on pain of forfeiting his claim to accept such coin of the realm as his debtor chooses to offer; subject to the following limitations: copper coins are legal tender only up to the amount of one shilling and silver coins up to the amount of forty shillings. Foreign coins are not legal tender; but everyone has the right to call upon the Royal Mint to coin for him, free of charge, any gold of standard quality.

An I.O.U. is evidence of the existence of a debt and may be produced in support of a legal claim against the debtor. If it is dated, i.e. if it contains the words "to be paid on" such and such a date, it becomes a promissory note and must be stamped; otherwise it is valid without a stamp.

For loans under 40s. a pawnbroker may only charge a halfpenny a month for every two shillings or part of two shillings lent and a charge of one halfpenny on the making of the loan for each five shillings lent. For loans over 40s. and under £10, unless otherwise provided by special agreement, the rate of interest is limited to 20 per cent per annum. For loans over £10 no limit to the rate of interest is provided. Pledges which are not redeemed within twelve calendar months and seven days become the property of the pawnbroker. If a pawn ticket is lost, the owner of the pledge must produce evidence of his identity to a magistrate and obtain from him a form of declaration as evidence of his claim to the pledge. Failing this, the pawn-broker is obliged to deliver the pledge to anyone producing the pawn ticket. Obtaining a false declaration is equivalent to perjury.

OF NEIGHBOURS

Failing any evidence of ownership, the *hedges, walls or fences between adjoining properties* belong equally to the owners of both properties. But if one owner has habitually repaired the dividing structure this constitutes *prima facie* evidence that it belongs to him. When there is a ditch as well as a hedge or fence, the hedge is generally deemed to belong to the owner on whose side of the hedge there is no ditch.

The owner of *fruit trees* which overhang a neighbour's property has a right to any of his fruit which falls upon his neighbour's land, and if the neighbour refuses to give it to him he may (provided that he use no force and cause no damage) go upon his neighbour's land without permission and take it.

Roots and Branches penetrating or overhanging a neighbour's land may be cut by the owner of the land without notice to or permission from the owner of the tree.

OF TRESPASS TO LAND

Every invasion of private property is a trespass, whether the material damage be large, small or non-existent. No man has any right to go upon the land of another except by leave or licence, or where there is a right of way. And, when once the wrong has been done, any cutting of wood, picking of flowers, lighting of fires, or other Arcadian wantonness will but serve to increase the damages payable should the owner choose to enforce his rights by an action at law.

Now some free spirits, remembering how in their youth they treated themselves, at 6s.8d. a time, to the pleasure of walking across college lawns, may argue that a corresponding damage to a common meadow should cost them but as many pence as formerly they paid shillings to the college authorities. These, in a week-end mood of exuberant rejuvenation, may offer to buy from other landlords a sixpenny right of way. They forget that the costs of an action at law, should the landlord prove implacable, will fall upon the trespasser and will by far exceed sixpenny worth of common grass or even six and eightpence worth of cloistered and historic lawn.

Lest the weekender in the bonhomie of his heart protest that no landlord in his senses will bring an action for trespass unless considerable material damage has been done, we would remind him that all landowners are not in that enviable state of mind; and, furthermore, that a pugnacious landlord may lawfully resort to force in removing such trespassers as will not depart peaceably, sixpence or no sixpence. In doing so he may use as much force as is "reasonably necessary", and, if the trespasser feels that the reasonable limit has been overreached, he in turn (if he has been so foolish as to allow this development) can bring an action against the landowner for assault; and the Court will decide.

Most landowners are amenable to friendliness, argument or money, and it must be left to the genius of the trespasser to choose the right remedy. But there remains one type of landlord for whose injured proprietary instincts no balm can be found: like a powerful nation, he is filled with righteous wrath by the sight of another creature doing something which he is entitled to stop. Prestige must be maintained. Indemnities and apologies are demanded. In fact he should never be spoken to except from the other side of a five-barred gate. A slow but dignified retreat to the highway is the best course to pursue.

OF DOGS

The trespasser has no remedy for misfortunes which may befall him from the savagery of the landowner's animals, domestic or wild. But the righteous man is entitled to security from attack.

Any man who keeps a savage animal does so at his peril, and, if it escapes, he must answer for the damage that ensues. Therefore those who take panther cubs or baboons on weekend rambles do so at their own, as well as at their neighbour's risk. The law does not regard a dog as a savage animal until, by biting someone, the true nature of the animal is betrayed; for, until then, the owner is ignorant of its savage nature and will not be held responsible. Therefore, if you must be bitten, let it be by an animal that makes a habit of biting and not by a mere amateur. The owner of a dog cannot rely upon his dog's previous good record if cattle are bitten instead of human beings. There is a statute that makes the owner of a dog, however tame, liable for all damage to cattle.

OF CATS

The privilege of being presumed tame until shown to be otherwise (if a recent action at law may be taken as a precedent) is now extended to cats.

OF CATTLE

If you should chance to be gored or trampled by cattle in a private pasture, you have no remedy at law. But if the same mischance befalls you on the public highway then you may claim and, perhaps, receive some compensation from the owner of your assailant. But first you will have to prove that such an accident both could and should have been foreseen by the lawful guardians of the animal in question. If it was a bull you will have no difficulty in doing this, but if it was a cow of hitherto unblemished repute, whom the gods suddenly visited with madness, it may happen that your damages will go unsolaced by payment. You may, however, plead that the heat of the noonday sun, or the recent maternity and bereavement of the cow, or some other cause, gave its owner enough warning of impending danger to justify the jury in pronouncing him guilty of wantonly endangering the public safety. And the Court shall decide.

OF NOISE AND OTHER NUISANCES

Any object or occupation which causes noise, smell, dirt or any offence to the senses or health of the surrounding population, may be classified as a nuisance. If the damage is general it is a common nuisance and may be prosecuted by indictment. If it is damage to a particular person, he may bring an action against the offender or he may abate the nuisance himself; and if he goes upon another's land for this purpose (without doing unnecessary damage) it is not trespass.

The noise of children and piano-players is not actionable, unless it is nocturnal and continuous.

When a man has plied a noisy trade without contradiction for twenty years he acquires a prescriptive right to continue; so there should be no unnecessary delay in bringing an action against those who cause such nuisances.

Motor horns and other devices designed to give audible warning, may not be used for other purposes when the car is stationary.

It is not lawful for organ-grinders or other musicians to continue their performances in the streets of London, if any householder within earshot has requested them (for a sufficient reason) to desist.

OF PURIFYING THE PERSON

A magistrate has power to order the cleansing of persons infested with vermin. Any such person may voluntarily and gratuitously make use of the cleansing apparatus belonging to any local authority. To be relieved of parasites in this manner does not count as "relief" under the Poor Law.

OF GAME AND FISHING

All wild swans, whales and sturgeons belong to the King. Game, as defined in various statutes of William IV and Victoria, may not be hunted or killed on Sundays or on Christmas Day. But snipe, woodcock and wildfowl are not game within the meaning of the Acts. Nevertheless it would be rash to attempt to correlate the rarity of these birds in England with an anti-sabbatarian tendency during the last century. Game which is started, hunted and killed on one and the same property belongs to the owner of that property. But if it is started on one property and killed on another it belongs to the hunter, although he is liable for trespass to the owners of both properties.

Traps for rabbits or hares must be visited daily on pain of a fine not exceeding £5. Weekenders who have been moved by James Stephens's "The Snare", may find in this law a useful weapon against trappers.

Every British subject has the *right to fish* in British waters and in public navigable rivers. In non-navigable rivers, subject to specially vested rights, the fishing belongs to the riparian owners, each from his bank to mid-stream. *Crabs* measuring less than four and a half inches across the broadest part or carrying spawn, or having cast their shells, or *lobsters* measuring less than eight inches (outstretched) from beak to tail, may not be taken or sold, except for bait.

OF GAMBLING

The playing of cards, or dice, when practised honestly, innocently and for recreation, is not unlawful. There appear to be certain games which are unlawful in themselves though there is no record of anyone being punished for playing them.

These are "Ace of Hearts", "Faro", "Bassett", "Hazard", "Passage" and "Roly-poly".

The laws on the subject are really directed against persons who seek to make a business of gaming. The first of these, under Henry VIII, was aimed at encouraging the more patriotic sport of archery, which was held to be falling into disuse because of the undue popularity of other games.

It is unlawful to keep premises for the purpose of gaming,

although games played are not unlawful in themselves. Gaming in public places is also unlawful. A bar-room or a coffee-room or a railway carriage is a public place within the meaning of the Act.

But the playing of cards or dice when practised honestly, innocently and for recreation, is not illegal.

OF INNS

An Act of Parliament in the reign of James I describes as follows the nature and function of an Inn: "The ancient true and principal use of inns, alehouses and victuallying houses was for the receipt, relief and lodging of wayfaring people travelling from place to place and for such supply of the wants of such people as are not able by greater quantities to make their provision of victuals. ..." Unless an establishment lodges wayfaring people it is not an inn. All licensed houses are not inns. All inns are not licensed. An innkeeper can only refuse admission to *bona fide* travellers when the inn is full. But he is not obliged to allow a traveller to sleep in any living-room if all the bedrooms are occupied. An innkeeper is entitled to payment in advance and there is no liability for refusing admission unless a reasonable sum is tendered.

He is bound to supply what food and drink he can. The lateness of the hour is no ground for refusing admission unless the wayfarer is drunk or disorderly; or accompanied by (and inseparable from) a large dog; or is a chimney sweep in working clothes, or in general an object of distaste for other customers.

The wayfarer has no immediate means of enforcing his rights when admission is wrongfully refused. He may, if revengefully disposed, indict the innkeeper and cause him to lose his licence, but he is entitled to no compensation; and revenge is a poor consolation for a night spent without a bed. A person who orders a meal without having the means to pay for it does not by that action alone become guilty of obtaining goods by false pretences. He may, however, be held to be a debtor obtaining credit on false pretences. But as the penalty for this offence is one year's imprisonment it is not likely to be imposed upon him for the price of a meal.

An innkeeper cannot sue a bar-customer for the price of

drinks consumed consumed on the premises unless the debt amounts to twenty shillings or more.

Knowingly to let a room which was previously occupied by someone suffering from an infectious disease and which has not been adequately disinfected is an offence for which the innkeeper may be fined £20.

An innkeeper is responsible for a traveller's goods while in the inn. His liability is limited to £30, unless the loss is due to his wilful default or neglect, or if the goods have been given to him for safe custody.

A visitor staying at an inn at which he had booked rooms would not be a traveller, but a lodger, and would lose the benefit of this protection.

OF JOY-RIDES

To take and use a car belonging to another and afterwards abandon it is not theft, provided that the "borrower" can prove he had not the intention "permanently to deprive the owner thereof". But it is now an offence under the Road Traffic Act 1930.

OF MASQUERADES

To go about by night with the face disguised, blackened or masked and having the intent to enter any building, is sufficient to make a person guilty of a misdemeanour. Therefore, since it is difficult to establish the innocence of one's intentions, it is imprudent to be found in such a situation. If one disguises himself for the purpose of impersonating the husband of, and to, any wife other than one's own he may (if successful) be guilty of rape; and it is not wise to rely upon being able to prove that one's histrionic powers are too poor to deceive an unbiased audience.

OF RIOTOUS BEHAVIOUR

A *riot* is the assembly of three or more persons with an apparent tendency to violence sufficient to inspire alarm or terror, even if only one person be in fact alarmed. If such an assembly consist of twelve or more persons the ensuing disturbance of the peace is a misdemeanour; and failure to disperse, after the reading of the Riot Act, is a felony.

To collect a crowd to the annoyance of the neighbours is a nuisance.

To join with others, by agreement, in hissing a performance is a conspiracy; but if a consensus of audible censure be not prearranged, it is lawful.

OF CURSING AND SWEARING

Indulgence in profanity by soldiers, sailors and navvies is punishable by a fine of one shilling; for other proletarians the fine is two shillings; but for gentlemen and those of higher station the scale is five shillings. This social injustice can no longer be defended on the ground that religion and morals are not taught in the elementary schools.

OF THE ENGLISH SUNDAY

If you belong to the Church of England, you are bound to go to church on Sunday, the penalty being "ecclesiastical censure". This is still important, because the duty to go is the foundation of the *right* to go, which you can enforce against a churchwarden who tries to keep you out—even if the church is full. If you are a dissenter, the law merely shrugs its shoulders about you.

But there are many things that you are not allowed to do. No public billiards (except in the club). No public stage plays. No fairs or circuses. No bear-baiting, bull-baiting, interludes or common players, even in your own parish. Outside the parish, no public games at all. No taking of any kind of game, whether with a dog, a net, a gun, or other instrument. No salmon-fishing. No bookmaking or "tote" betting. No boxing or all-in wrestling. But look at the things that *may* be sold and the business that *may* be done in shops: meals (this does *not* include fish and chips), newly cooked provisions and dressed tripe, sweets, minerals and ices, flowers, fruit and vegetables, milk and cream, new bread and rolls, medicines, cycle and motor accessories, smokers' needs, newspapers and magazines, books and stationery from main line bookstalls, guide books, postcards and souvenirs in the art galleries and parks, passport photographs, sporting requisites at a place where the sport is actually going on, fodder for horses, and post office business.

It is true that the only places of entertainment open to you are cinemas (where the local residents are in favour of Sunday picture-going), museums, waxworks, picture galleries, zoos, aquaria, lecture halls, and concert halls for the provision of "music with or without singing or recitation".

IN CONCLUSION

The law may be likened to a whimsical lady. It is an advantage to have a knowledge of her character, but her embraces are to be avoided, for they are apt to be both ill-timed and expensive. Remember, therefore, that, should you be haled before the magistrate, whether for a breach of public law or at the suit of some injured person for an infringement of a private right, it is no defence and will avail you nothing to plead ignorance of the law, for the law presumes that every man has full knowledge of his own duties and of the rights of others. This, as Euclid might have said, is absurd. Nevertheless it is the law.

ETIQUETTE

It isn't etiquette to cut any one you've been
introduced to. Remove the joint.

Lewis Carroll.

Etiquette

*'Of Courtesy, it is much less
Than Courage of Heart, or Holiness,
yet in my Walks it seems to me
That the Grace of God is in Courtesy.'*

LETTERS OF THANKS
(From "The Art of Letter-Writing", 1762.)

We should always endeavour to testify our Gratitude according to the Obligation we are under. Let us never be wanting to examine the Favour received and the Merit of the Person who conferred it. If a Friend has been of Service to us, we may thank him familiarly; but we must thank in very submissive Terms a great Lord, to whom we are indebted for a settled Condition of Life, or some considerable Present. Whatever may be the Quality of the Benefit and Benefactor, it is necessary we should seem sensible of it, and withal exaggerate its Circumstances, making appear the Utility or Honour that has accrued to us from it, and protesting, in concluding our Letter, that we shall preserve it in perpetual Remembrance.

An Example
LETTER OF THANKS FOR A SEAL

The Seal you sent me is the prettiest Thing I ever saw, and I am vexed I cannot praise it sufficiently. But, let me tell you, that the Poet who would fain seal up his Mistress's Mouth, because not very reserved in keeping his Secrets, ought to have had such an agreeable Seal, to be worthy of so nice an Application. The most excellent Engravers are Botchers to your's; nay, I must say, *Apelles's* Pencil never delineated any Thing with the Art and Delicacy of your Figures. But as I do not so much regard your Present as a Master-piece in its Kind, than as a Pledge of your Friendship; I cannot thank you enough for it, nor express to what a Degree I am, &c.

A MODERN BREAD AND BUTTER LETTER OR
COLLINS★

Dear Molly,

What a week-end! A household like yours shows us stuffy town-mice just what we miss. All those endless gossips over the washing-up! The romps with the children—dear things, so ready to accept one as their equal! The *smugness* of toasting one's toes at a blaze one has laboured to provide. Then that glorious windy climb to your quaint little market town and the lovely long *scribbler's eavesdrop* in the queue before plunging *headlong* home again! (Did I remember to tell you your back brake was broken?) And never did I *dream* I'd be present at the return of a real *prodigal*—so well-timed too, with Vicar there to tea!

Back in my little flat I realise how *right* my doctor was when he said I should enjoy life again after a complete change. Thank you a thousand times for that change.

Yours affectionately,
Margaret Usborne

ANOTHER EXAMPLE OF THE SAME

Dear Pandora,

I got back all right. That was the *slow* train. They took the fast one off last May. My wire hadn't arrived. So Jocelyn must have put "Highbury" instead of "Highgate" after all.

Excuse uneven writing—it's the bandage. Which reminds me, could you possibly see if I dropped my bangle in the wood-shed—either there or by the sink? Sorry—it was the rush at the end and the confusion of seeing Francis again after all those years. He's got very Australian, hasn't he?

Hope peace reigns in the nursery today. Sebastian and Sary Ann certainly are wonderfully lively! And I shall always remember my "Dick Turpin's last ride" on Saturday afternoon. And he wasn't carrying six of gran. and two of lump. Well, thanks so much, Pandora. It was sweet of you to ask me, especially with no help.

Love,
Audrey Morris

★ *"Collins": although letters of thanks are called after Jane Austen's character, in fact the terms of his letter are not given in "Pride and Prejudice".*

FROM A LADY RECENTLY MARRIED (1860)

My dearest Edith,

I have now been married six months, and not one little visit have you paid me yet! Do come and spend a fortnight with us, that you may see how happy we are. I am as happy as the days are long, and one look at dear Willie's face will satisfy you as to his contentment. He is the best and dearest of husbands, grants all my wishes, and loves me as foolishly as ever.

Our house is not a mansion, but happiness is not always found in splendid dwellings. I will not describe our little snuggery, as I wish you to come and judge for yourself if I have not every cause to be a happy woman. I have been so spoilt lately that I cannot bear a disappointment; so do not refuse my request. Hoping that you will come very soon (and with best love),

Believe me,

Your affectionate old friend,
Milly Le Briton

LETTER FROM A LADY TO HER HUSBAND
AT THE ARMY IN GERMANY

(From "The Art of Letter-Writing", 1762. N.B. Wife and husband should not use the same Letter Book.)

Dear Husband,

I cannot express how much I suffered when you set out for the Army in Germany. God alone knows the Grief my Heart has been pierced with. The Hopes of Peace we were flattered with, seemed to mitigate my Anxieties, and calm the Disturbances of my Mind. The Campaign opens, the War begins a-new; and I know not where I am, nor what I am doing. You might have lived happy and contented in the Bosom of your Country, with your Family and with your Friends, but you have preferred Troubles, Fatigues, and Alarms, to the Repose and Tranquillity of Life. What a cruel Destiny is this! How melancholy are the Reflections that weigh down my Heart! I spend the Days and Nights amidst continual Fears. Dread and Despair agitate continually my dejected Mind, and plunge me into an Ocean of Afflictions. Take Care of your Health, write to me often, love me as much as I love you; I cannot say more. Farewell, my dear Husband! I am the most disconsolate Wife living.

– AND HIS ANSWER

The Enemy does not give me half the Uneasiness you do, Madam! In the Name of God compose yourself, if you have any real Love for me. Misfortunes are only great in Imagination. I have happily passed through all former Campaigns; this will be attended with the same Success. Hardships and Labour are inseparable from a military Life; and it is at this Expense we must gather Laurels: Such is my State, such my Profession; I must gloriously discharge the Duties annexed to it. What are you afraid of? I am in perfect Health. Every Thing bodes us a favourable Campaign. We are almost sure of Victory. Cease your Alarms, my dear Spouse! I am sensible of your Tenderness; I love you to the Extent of your Wishes. Love, and a Husband's Fidelity, have the most engaging Charms, and afford the sweetest Consolation to your Sex. Hark! The drums now beat, and the Trumpets sound, *March!* Glory calls me forth. The Affections of my heart rest upon you: It is you alone that does possess it entirely. What will you have more? Farewell, my dearer Half; every Thing, I hope, will succeed to the Wish of, &c.

MODERN LETTERS TO CREDITORS

Dear Sirs:

It is with deep regret that I note the tone of your last ten communications. If you will be good enough to examine your books you will find that I have been a customer of some value to you for a matter of many years, and, though without commercial training myself, I cannot think that this policy of oblique insinuation and covert threat is the best way to insure the good will and continued custom of your patrons.

You hold me responsible for the purchase of 5 pairs of socks (or 5 tins of ginger biscuits, or 5 bottles of gin, as the case may be or may not be, as the case may be) in the year 1903 (or 1913, or 1923). It is not often that a firm of your standing commits itself to so gross an error, and I must request you to go into this matter of the socks (or biscuits or gin) at your leisure, as I have not the faintest recollection of having made any such purchase. Kindly acquaint me with the colour of the socks (or the brand of biscuits or kind of gin) with which you are under the misapprehension of having supplied me, and I will be glad to reconsider your uncouth demands for prompt payment.   Yours faithfully,

Dear Sir,

We beg to inform you that according to the Bank's Books, your account appears to be overdrawn to the extent of £1057s. 2d. We think it advisable to inform you of this, in case a remittance intended for your credit has not reached the Bank.

Yours faithfully,

Dear Sir,

I am greatly obliged to you for the information contained in your letter. I will hasten to glance through all the remittances intended for my credit and ascertain why they have not reached the Bank.

Yours faithfully,

Sir,

We have been instructed by our clients, Messrs. Clapperclaw and Carp, to apply for payment of £254s. 0d, the amount of their account against you.

Kindly see that this reaches us within five days of the date of this letter, failing which we shall instruct our solicitors to commence legal proceedings for the recovery of the debt.

We are,

Yours faithfully,

Sirs,

You are cordially invited to commence legal proceedings against me, as there is nothing which would give me greater pleasure than to expose to the British Bench the perfidy of Messrs Clapperclaw and Carp. Do you realise the nature of your clients? Debt collectors cannot be too careful in these matters, and it is

yours, which, I note on your letter head, was established in and has no doubt flourished since 1875, receiving instructions from Messrs Clapperclaw and Carp. Were I to describe in detail the shabby treatment and shabbier suiting which I have received at the hands of your clients, I doubt not that your Principal, as a man of judgment and respectability, would shudder away in horror at the very idea of acting on their behalf and would indeed reconsider the peremptory tone he pleases to take to me in his letter. No, Sirs. In withholding prompt payment, which is quite contrary to my usual custom, from Messrs C. and C., I am merely following the dictates of an outraged sense of justice and moral indignation. That they should have been able to impose upon so worthy a firm of debt collectors as yourselves is a matter for grave and disturbing reflection. My answer to them, as to you, Sirs, is, without hesitation, sue and be damned.

Yours faithfully,

THE BOOK-BORROWER

Charles Lamb was an honest borrower, returning the volumes as soon as he had read them. On one occasion he had borrowed from H.F. Carey a copy of Phillips' *Theatrum Poetarum* which he temporarily mislaid:

To Mrs George Dyer   Dec. 22nd, 1834

Dear Mrs Dyer,

I am very uneasy about a *Book* which I either have lost or left at your house on Thursday. It was the book I went out to fetch from Miss Buffam's, while the tripe was frying. It is called Phillip's Theatrum Poetarum; but it is an English book. I think I left it in the parlour. It is Mr Carey's book, and I would not lose it for the world. Pray, if you find it, book it at the Swan, Snow Hill, by an Edmonton stage immediately, directed to Mr Lamb, Church-street, Edmonton, or write to say you cannot find it. I am quite anxious about it. If it is lost, I shall never like tripe again.

With kindest love to Mr Dyer and all.
Yours truly,
C. Lamb

"To lend Bysshe a book," says Hogg, "was to bid it a long farewell, to take leave of it forever; but the pain of parting was often spared, for he bore away silently, reading it as he went, any work that caught his attention."

"Of those who borrow some read slow; some mean to read and don't read; and some neither read nor mean to read, but borrow to leave you an opinion of their sagacity."

Charles Lamb

Lady Dorothy Nevill, so Sir Edmund Gosse tells, preserved her library by pasting in each volume the legend: "This book has been stolen from Lady Dorothy Nevill".

The owner of a country house was showing some visitors over a superb library. "Do you ever lend books?" he was asked. "No," he replied promptly, "only fools lend books." Then, waving his hand to a many-shelved section filled with handsomely bound volumes, he added, "All those books once belonged to fools." *A correspondent to "The Times"*.

> Say, little book, what furtive hand
> Thee from thy fellow books conveyed?
> *W. Cowper.*

> Prince, hear a hopeless Bard's appeal;
> Reverse the rules of Mine and Thine;
> Make it legitimate to steal
> The Books that never can be mine!
> *Andrew Lang.*

RETORTS COURTEOUS

A *Blue-Mould Fancier*, by looking too long at a Stilton cheese, was at last completely overcome, by his Eye exciting his Appetite, till it became quite ungovernable; and unconscious of every thing but the *mity* object of his contemplation, he began to pick out in no small portions, the primest parts his eye could select from the centre of the Cheese.

The good-natured Founder of the Feast, highly amused at the Ecstasies each morsel created in its passage over the palate of his Enraptured Guest, and thus encouraged the perseverance of his Guest—"Cut away my dear sir, cut away, use no Ceremony, I pray: I hope you will pick out all the best of my Cheese—*don't you think that* THE RIND *and the* ROTTEN *will do very well for my Wife and Family?*"

William Kitchiner, MD, 1838.

As a matter of course young ladies do not eat cheese at dinner parties. *From "Manners and Rules of Good Society", 1888.*

By his host to Beau Brummel, who in his usual fashion arrived very late at dinner, which was not delayed for him: "I hope you like cheese".

When the Duke of Wellington was at Paris, as Commander of the allied armies, he was invited to dine with Cambaceres, one of the most distinguished statesmen and *gourmands* of the time of Napoleon. In the course of the dinner, his host having helped him to some particularly *recherché* dish, expressed a hope that he found it agreeable. "Very good," said the hero of Waterloo, who was probably speculating upon what he would have done if Blücher had not come up: "Very good; but I really do not care what I eat." "Heavens!" exclaimed Cambaceres, as he started back and dropped his fork, quite frightened from his propriety,— "Don't care what you eat! What *did* you come here for, then?"

From *Etiquette for Gentlemen, 1841.*

There was once-upon-a-time—or, because we have heard the story ascribed to three different Dukes, perhaps thrice-upon-a-time—a Duke who did not tolerate smoking during dinner, though he had many American acquaintances. Once, and once only, one of these lit a cigarette as soon as the soup-plates were removed. The Duke called his butler. "You will now serve coffee," he commanded, and that was the end of the meal.

1876 HINT ON TRAVELLING

For Ladies: In travelling, you need not refuse to speak to a gentleman who addresses you politely, as some foolish girls do. But by no means encourage random conversation in such a case. Your best plan, however, is to think as little as possible of gentlemen *as gentlemen*. Think of them as fellow-creatures of the same God, and treat them with respect and with self-respect. Your woman's heart should teach you the rest.

ON MUSIC AND WALTZING

A lady must never sing a song that is of a decidedly masculine character, nor if the words describe masculine action or passion. Imagine an interesting woman taking a part in "All's well", or "Here's a health to all good lasses", or singing "Pretty star of the night"; yet, can such things be, for they have been. Glees and catches should rarely be sung by a lady ... there is something so boisterous in the practice, most particularly of the latter, that, as a general principle, they ought to be avoided, especially at parties ... Choruses, in many instances, are still more objectionable. I can hardly imagine a chorus-loving lady, except, indeed, she be a listener only.

I will leave the subject of waltzing in the hands of my fair readers, with this simple request, viz., that whenever the waltz is proposed, they will think of its tendency, of the indelicacy of the exhibition; and then I am quite certain that this anti-English dance will very soon be banished from society. *From "The Ladies Pocket-Book of Etiquette", 1840.*

CONVERSATIONAL MANNERS: I

Table Talk is so natural to man, that the mouth is the organ both of eating and speaking. The tongue is set flowing by the bottle. Dr Johnson talked best when he dined; and Addison could not talk at all till he had drunk. Table and conversation interchange their metaphors. We *devour* wit and argument, and *discuss* a turkey and chine. That man must be very much absorbed in reflection, or stupid, or sulky, or unhappy, or a mere hog at his trough, who is not moved to say something when he dines. The two men who lived with no other companions in the Eddystone Light-house, and who would not speak to one another during their six months, must have been hard put to it, when they tapped a fresh barrel. To be sure, the greater the temptation, the greater the sulk; but the better-natured of the two must have found it a severe struggle on a very fine or very foggy day.

Table-talk, to be perfect, should be sincere without bigotry, differing ~~with~~ ... ~~discord~~ ... ~~something grave, always agreeable~~, touching on deep points, dwelling most on seasonable ones, and letting everybody speak and be heard. During the wine after dinner, if the door of the room be opened, there sometimes comes bursting up the drawing-room stairs a noise like that of a tap-room. Everybody is shouting in order to make himself audible; argument is tempted to confound itself with loudness; and there is not one conversation going forward, but six, or a score. This is better than formality and want of spirits; but it is no

293

more the right thing, than a scramble is a dance, or the tap-room chorus a quartette of Rossini. The perfection of conversational intercourse is when the breeding of high life is animated by the fervour of genius. Nevertheless, the man who cannot be loud, or even vociferous on occasion, is wanting on the jovial side of good-fellowship. Chesterfield, with all his sense and agreeableness, was but a solemn fop when he triumphantly asked, whether anybody had "ever seen him laugh?" It was as bad as the jealous lover in the play who says, "Have *I* been the life of the company? Have *I* made you all die with merriment?" And there were occasions, no doubt, when Chesterfield might have been answered as the lover was, "No: to do you justice, you have been confoundedly stupid."

Luckily for table-talkers in general, they need be neither such fine gentlemen as Chesterfield, nor such oracles as Johnson, nor such wits as Addison and Swift, provided they have nature and sociability, and are not destitute of reading and observation.

Leigh Hunt.

CONVERSATIONAL MANNERS: II

When there are no more than four people at table let there not be two conversations at the same time; for one of the four people will always want to forsake his conversation for the other. *F.M.*

CONVERSATIONAL MANNERS: III

Every denial of, or interference with, the personal freedom or absolute rights of another, is a violation of good manners. He who presumes to censure me for my religious belief, or want of belief; who makes it a matter of criticism or reproach that I am a Theist or Atheist, Trinitarian or Unitarian, Catholic or Protestant, Pagan or Christian, Jew, Mohammedan or Mormon, is guilty of rudeness and insult. If any of these modes of belief make me intolerant or intrusive, he may resent such intolerance or repel such intrusion; but the basis of all true politeness and social enjoyment is the mutual tolerance of personal rights.

(19th century).

CONVERSATIONAL MANNERS: IV

Conversation is but carving;
Give no more to every guest
Than he is able to digest;
Give him always of the prime
And but little at a time;
Carve to all, but not enough,
Let them neither starve nor stuff.
And that each may have its due,
Let your neighbour carve for you.

Sir Walter Scott.

ON THE HANDSHAKE

Have you noticed how people shake your hand? There is the *high-official*—the body erect, and a rapid, short shake, near the chin. There is the *mortmain*—the flat hand introduced into your palm, and hardly conscious of its contiguity. The *digital*—one finger held out, much used by the high clergy. There is the *shakus rusticus*, where your hand is seized in an iron grasp, betokening rude health, warm heart, and distance from the Metropolis; but producing a strong sense of relief on your part when you find your hand released and your fingers unbroken. The next to this is the *retentive shake*—one which, beginning with vigour, pauses as it were to take breath, but without relinquishing its prey, and before you are aware begins again, till you feel anxious as to the result, and have no shake left in you. Worst, there is the *pisces*—the damp palm like a dead fish, equally silent, equally clammy, and leaving its odour in your hand.   *Sydney Smith, 1820.*

ON SAYING GRACE

It is not creditable to a "thinking people," that the two things they most thank God for should be eating and fighting. We say grace when we are going to cut up lamb and chicken, and when we have stuffed ourselves with both to an extent that an ourangoutang would be ashamed of; and we offer up our best praises to the Creator for having blown and sabred his "images", our fellow-creatures, to atoms, and drenched them in blood and dirt. This is odd. Strange that we should keep our most pious transports for the lowest of our appetites and the most melancholy of our necessities! that we should never be wrought up into paroxysms of holy gratitude but for bubble and squeak, or a good-sized massacre! that we should think it ridiculous to be asked to say grace for a concert or a flower-show, or the sight of a gallery of pictures, or any other of the divinest gifts of Heaven, yet hold it to be the most natural and exalted of impulses to fall on our knees for having kicked, beaten, torn, shattered, drowned, stifled, exenterated, mashed, and abolished thousands of our neighbours, whom we are directed to "love as ourselves!"

A correspondent of *The Times*, who had of course been doing his duty in this respect, and thanking Heaven the first thing every morning for the carnage in the Punjaub, wished the other day to know "what amount of victory was considered, by the Church or State, to call forth a public expression of thankfulness to Almighty God." He was angry that the Bishops had not been up and stirring at the slaughter; that Sir Robert Peel was not as anxious to sing hymns for it, as to feed the poor; that Lord John Russell, with all his piety, was slower to call for rejoicings over the Sikh widows, than attention to hapless Ireland. *Leigh Hunt*.

THE LANGUAGE OF FLOWERS

In ancient Athens, the flowers consecrated to the gods were the symbols of their character and power; so that the Poppy was for Ceres, the Laurel for Apollo, the Ivy for Bacchus, the Cypress for Pluto and so on. The Romans used flowers for festive decoration even more than the Greeks. And in the mediaeval codes of chivalry, the language of flowers was developed as part of the ritual of courtship.

Fortunately the language of flowers and the etiquette of giving them are not too generally understood; and flowers today will be acceptable for themselves apart from their significance. But if, like a modern poet, you wish to indulge in a private meaning, these are the terms that you can use: *Acacia:* Platonic Love; the acacia was brought here from Canada, where it was venerated by the Indians as a symbol of chaste love. *Aloe*: Grief and Bitterness. *Amaranth*: Immortality; it was supposed to adorn the brows of the gods. *Amaryllis*: Pride; a meaning which comes from the nature of the flower for it is very difficult to cultivate. *Bramble*: Envy; because it hates its neighbours. *Carnation*: Pure

Love. *Columbine*: Folly. *Cypress*: Mourning. *Daffodils*: Regret. *Daisy*: Innocence. *Eglantine*: Poetry. *Fennel*: Strength; Roman gladiators mixed it with their food to give them more power. *Fern*: Sincerity. *Field Daisy*: "I will think of it"; a wreath worn round the head is an answer to a lover. *Gilly Flower*: Unfading Beauty; because they flower for so long, from early spring through the summer. *Hawthorn*: Hope. *Holly*: Foresight. *Holly-hock*: Fecundity; because of the great number of its flowers. *Honeysuckle*: The Bonds of Love. *Iris*: A Message; from its many colours resembling the rainbow, which was regarded by the ancients as a messenger of the gods. *Ivy*: Friendship. *Laurel*: Glory. *Lettuce*: Coldness; Venus, after the death of Apollo, slept on a couch of lettuce, to banish her passion. *Lilac*: First Emotions of Love: "I am falling in love with you." *Marigold*: Distress of Mind or Grief. *Orange Blossom*: Chastity. *Rose*: Beauty, Joy, and Fragrance; those who dream of roses will have especially good fortune. *Snapdragon*: Presumption; because it often goes where it is not wanted. *Snowdrop*: Consolation. *Thistle*: Fearlessness. *Tulip*: Intense Affection; "Will you marry me?"

But if you lack both flowers and the power of speech, here are two signs: A little shake of the left ear-lobe with the left hand means that the person or object under discussion is very nice indeed. A little shake of the right ear-lobe with the left hand (the left hand being taken over the top of your head) means that she, or he, or it, is superb, gorgeous, sonic.

Lady Mary Wortley Montagu reported that in Turkey in the eighteenth century the lover's sentiments were not written but expressed by gift:

Pearl: Fairest of the young. *Clove*: You are as slender as the clove; you are an unblown rose! I have loved ~~~~~~~~~~ ~~~~~~~~~~ *Jonquil*. Have pity on my passion! *Paper*: I faint every hour! *Pear*: Give me some hope. *Soap*: I am sick with love. *Coal*: May I die, and all my years be yours! *A Rose*: May you be pleased, and your sorrows mine! *A Straw*: Suffer me to be your slave. *Cloth*: Your price is not to be found. *Cinnamon*: But my fortune is yours. *A Match*: I burn! I burn! my flame consumes me! *Gold Thread*: Don't turn away your face from me. *Hair*: Crown of my head! *Grape*: My two eyes! *Gold Wire*: I die—come quickly.

A MIXTY MAXTY OF HINTS

PRECEDENT FOR THOSE ENTERTAINING
ROYALTY AT THE SEASIDE

"Weymouth. The King (George III) bathes and with great success; a machine follows the Royal one into the sea filled with fiddlers who play 'God save the King' as His Majesty takes his plunge." *Fanny Burney*.

OF CHILDREN'S RECITATIONS

A doting father once proposed to Dr Johnson, that his two sons should, alternately, repeat Gray's "Elegy", that he might judge which had the happiest cadence. "No," said the doctor, beseachingly, "pray, sir, let the dears both speak it at once, more noise will by that means be made, but it will be the sooner over." *From "Etiquette for Ladies", 1837*.

PUNCTUALITY

Punctuality to the hour of dinner cannot be too much insisted on ... "*Le grand Boileau*" has a shrewd observation on this subject. "I have always been punctual to the hour of dinner," he says, "for I knew that those I kept waiting would employ those unpleasant moments to sum up all my faults. 'Boileau,' they will say, 'is a man of genius—a very honest man; but that dilatory and procrastinating way he has got into would mar the virtues of an angel!'" *From "Etiquette for Ladies", 1837*.

Be punctual—especially for breakfast. Your hostess is almost certain to have much work to do and a breakfast later than she intended can dislocate the work of the day.

Do not put ash, and a *fortiori* cigarette ends, in your saucer or plate.

As a corollary, the hostess should see that there are ashtrays on the table.

Assemble your cocktail glasses and coffee cups to the general tray: it is tiresome to find strays after the washing-up has been done.

COMPLIMENTS

At thy friend's table forget not to praise the cook, and the same shall be reckoned unto thee even as the praise of the mistress. *Dr Kitchiner, "Etiquette for Ladies", 1837.*

In the old days a compliment to the cook was taken as a compliment by the hostess. Today a compliment to the hostess is almost always a compliment to the cook.

If you are being entertained by an Arab Sheik and he gives you, as in duty bound, his most beautiful horse because you admired it, remember to give it back to him forthwith. The eye of the sheep however has to be swallowed.

TIPS

English guests do not need to be told that it is customary to leave a tip for the hired help, even if she comes in only by the hour. But Americans will welcome the hint.

OF MEAN-NOTHING

Mere general invitations mean nothing; they are only the small coin of good society. "Sorry you're going. Hope we shall soon meet again. Hope we shall have the pleasure of seeing you to dinner some day", is a very common mean-nothing form of politeness. *From "Ask Mamma", 1858.*

OF DURATION

Don't presume on his (your host's) kindness by attempting to stay beyond what he presses you to do, for two short visits tell better than one long one, looking as though you have been approved of. You can easily find out from the butler or the groom of the chambers, or some of the upper servants, how long you are expected to stay. *From the same.*

TRUMPETERS

A valet is absolutely indispensible for a young gentleman. Bless you! you would be thought nothing of among the servants if you hadn't one. They are their masters' trumpeters. *From the same.*

OF STEALTHINESS

Goloshes are capital things. They keep the feet warm, and prevent your footsteps from being heard. *From the same.*

A POWERFUL NEW PROVERB

It's the careful step that makes the stairs squeak. *F.M. 1910.*

OF CARVING

"As it occurs at least once in *every day*, it deserves some attention. *It is ridiculous* not to carve well. A man who tells you that he cannot carve, may as well tell you that he cannot blow his nose: it is both as *necessary* and as *easy*." *Chesterfield, 1751.*

APOLOGIES

I : FOR MY DAUGHTER

You mustn't mind Caroline, she's—

   —going through a phase

   —taken a real liking to you

   —still got to learn there are things one doesn't say

   —all Audrey Hepburn just now

   —just read a book on your subject

   —going to bed soon, we hope

   —best if you just ignore her

   —always a one for the men

   —due to grow out of it soon

   —a bit uninhibited but we don't like to repress her

   —got very high standards

   —rather worried about her exam

   —going to fetch it in a minute, aren't you, darling?

   —just been promoted to grown-up dinner

   —never been able to resist a moustache

   —trying to be nice in her own way

   —got a very strong will of her own

   —never cared for milk, cocoa, fish, cake, green vegetables or anything but ice-cream

   —had such a good time, really.

II : FOR MY HOSPITALITY

I'm afraid it's only a scratch meal but—
  —my daily walked out on me
  —Caroline's been an absolute little devil
  —the butcher didn't send
  —I wasn't quite sure if we'd said tonight
  —when you think that, before the war, we—
  —I forgot it was half-closing
  —something went wrong with the stew
  —personally I can never manage anything before a lecture
  —there's plenty of macaroni; I've only to open a tin
  —we usually have our big meal at lunchtime
  —I simply loathe cooking
  —it's all the less to wash up
  —I do hope you can eat eel
  —we're vegetarians ourselves
  —what I say is, it's not the food but the company
  —home's always nicer than a restaurant
  —we *are* having it in the dining-room
  —the turnips are our very own
  —it won't be long now
  —I knew you wouldn't mind.

Margharita Laski.

DRIVING MANNERS
EASY GALLICO METHOD FOR DEFLATING
THE PUMPKIN AND RESTORING THE
HUMANITIES TO DRIVING

If you care to experiment with the Easy Gallico Method for Deflating the Pumpkin and Restoring the Humanities to Driving, you might try out some of these simple canons. They will kill you at first until you begin to get the hang of them but after a while you will find you will have no difficulty in becoming a member of the human race again.

1. When you come across a bunch of pedestrians trying to cross a street, come to a dead stop and wave them across, particularly if there are baby carriages, old people and fat women involved. Any chump can stop for a pretty girl, but try being kind

to a few scarecrows. Never mind the maniac behind you with his finger on the horn button. His blood pressure will eventually kill him and then there will be one less. If you have managed to contribute to this, it is your good deed for the day.

2. Slow down whenever you are in the vicinity of children. Pass them with your foot on the brake, not on the gas.

3. When a guy in a car is trying to enter a line of traffic from the side and nobody will let him in, giving him the old too-bad-for-you-Jack-hooray-for-me treatment, stop your car and let him in. The dazed expression on his puss will be worth the couple of seconds you lose. Again, you may help to kill off a couple of hysterics behind you.

4. If the light changes from red to green and pedestrians are caught in the middle of the street, wait until they are over before starting, instead of trying to unzip their garments with your wing. What great contribution to humanity are you making that demands that you save those extra three and a half seconds with a lightning getaway?

5. On the open road when somebody wants to get by, pull over and slow down. Make it easy for him instead of difficult.

6. If for any reason your jalopy won't do better than thirty on the open road, or you are a Caspar Milquetoast who likes to putter along on a Sunday, when you come to a straight stretch of road *pull over to the side, stop for a few seconds and let the queue go by.* This is the Millennium Department. It hasn't happened yet, but the blessings that would be impelled your way by the passing motorists would bring you good luck for a week.

7. Whatever the other monkey wants to do, let him do it. Give him a smile and wave him on. It won't cure him, but it *will* cure you.

8. Stop hating women drivers. Appreciate the miracle taking place before your eyes that this bundle of contradictions is actually handling a ton or so of complicated machinery and doing it darned well. There's nothing wrong with women drivers. The trouble goes much further back to their being women. You'll never fix that.

9. Stop hating other drivers, whether male or female, just on sight. Did you ever have the embarrassment of having a bumper hook or wing scrape, and you get out of your car jawing and

howling only to discover the driver of the other car is your best friend, a client, somebody you owe money to, or the wife of the boss? Think of other drivers as friend and not enemy. They could be someone just like you—God forbid.

10. Relax. Be grateful. Be humble. Be kind. Be human. Mind your manners. Enjoy this wonderful machine and help others to do the same. *Paul Gallico.*

PENMANSHIP

"It doesn't matter what you write but how you write it."

Let the "how" in this phrase refer not to the wording, the composition, of your thank-you letter but to its penmanship. Remember that Charles Kingsley once received a letter from Dean Stanley, the illegibility of whose hand was notorious, at a time when Mrs Kingsley lay very ill. Kingsley examined the letter for many minutes in vain. At last he said: "I have every reason to believe this is a very kind letter of sympathy from Stanley—I feel sure it is. Yet the only two words I can even guess at are 'heartless devil'. But I pause—I pause to accept that suggestion as a likely one under the circumstances."

We now have less excuse than ever for writing badly. The Italian Cursive, or Italic, Hand, first used by the Papal Chancery Scribes in the XV Century (see p. 305), is now widely used and properly admired. There are several books of examples and instruction, and a Society of enthusiasts; and there are fountain pens made specially without the usual bump on the underside of the nib, which must be flat. From the beginning to write with a flat, edged pen (or pencil) is pleasure, is fun. And anyone at any age can with a little diligence write a good hand at speed within six months.

To make a start all you need is paper and a pencil sharpened to a flat chisel edge. Now follow these few hints:

1. Hold the pencil lightly, the shaft pointing in the direction of the right forearm.

2. Make sure that the edge of the pencil is at the correct angle to the paper: it should make its thickest and thinnest strokes at a 45° angle to the writing line. The thickest stroke should be the downward diagonal stroke \ ; the thinnest, the

upward diagonal / . For the diagonal strokes practise 〰. The vertical and horizontal strokes will be slightly less thick than the downward diagonal.

3. The arches of "*m*" and "*n*" should be curved. Let there be no doubt as to whether you write *n* (joined, like *m*, at the top) or *u* (joined at the bottom).

4. Note that: (a) the key letters are "*a*" and "*m*". Begin the "*a*" with a push-stroke to the left at its top; (b) "*t*" is not a full ascender; cross it at the height of "*a*". (c) Turn the right-hand stroke of "*v*" in and of "*r*" out. As an aid to legibility it is as well not to join "r" to a following letter. (d) Capitals should be two-thirds the height of an ascender.

5. See that your letters are close one to the other: the italic is a compressed and cursive (that is running-one-letter-into-the-next) hand. Keep the space between words even and not too wide. Keep neat margins both left and right.

6. Now write out the alphabet; small letters and capitals. The example on p. 305 by Arrighi, the first Master Scribe to write a manual, should inspire you. But note that it is inevitably thickened in the reproduction, which is itself reproduced from an inevitably thickened 16th century reproduction.

7. After the week-end buy one or more of the excellent contemporary manuals on calligraphy—notably by Alfred Fairbank and Philip A. Burgoyne: they are not only excellent "tutors" but they also list the best makes of pens and nibs. *And resolve* that before the present season has twice changed you will be writing a fair italic hand.

P.S. To those who say that italic has no "character" point out (a) that Chinese faces look alike to a European only until he becomes familiar with the general physiognomy; and (b) that what is called "character" nearly always means illegibility, and is often begotten by swank (unsure or vain people tend to develop the most illegible secret signatures).

P.P.S. W.R. Lethaby once wrote: "A common interest in the improvement of ordinary handwriting would be an immense disciplinary force; we might reform the world if we began with our own handwriting but we certainly shall not unless we begin somewhere."

LITTERA DA BREVI

A a b c d e e' f g g h i k l m n o p q r s ſt u x y z

~: Marcus Antonius Casanoua :~
Pierÿ vates, laudem ſi'opera iſta merentur,
  Praxiteli noſtro carmina pauca date'.
Non placet hoc; noſtri pietas laudanda Coryti eſt;
  Qui dicat hæc; niſi vos forſan uterqʒ mouet ;
Debetis ſaltem Dÿs carmina, ni quoqʒ, et iſtis
  Illa datis, iam nos mollia ſaxa ſumus .

A A B B C C D D E E F F G G H H J J
K L L M M N N N O P P Q Q R R S
S T T U V V X X Y Z & e' ʒ &

Lud ... ...vuentinus ſcribebat Roma' anno
  ſalutis M·D·XXIII

GREAT POEMS

As certain also of your own poets have said.
The Acts of the Apostles.

… those brave translunary things
That the first poets had.
Marlowe.

Oft, in the public road
Yet unfrequented, while the morning light
Was yellowing the hill tops, I went abroad
With a dear friend, and for the better part
Of two delightful hours we strolled along
By the still borders of the misty lake,
Repeating favourite verses with one voice.
William Wordsworth.

The poetry of earth is never dead.
Keats.

Great Poems

'As certain also of your own poets have said'

O WESTERN WIND

O WESTERN wind, when wilt thou blow,
  That the small rain down can rain?
Christ, that my love were in my arms
  And I in my bed again!

Anonymous.

THE CONCLUSION

EVEN such is Time, that takes in trust
  Our youth, our joys, our all we have,
And pays us but with earth and dust;
  Who, in the dark and silent grave,
When we have wandered all our ways,
Shuts up the story of our days.
But from this earth, this grave, this dust,
My God shall raise me up, I trust.

Walter Raleigh.

A FAREWELL TO ARMS

MY golden locks Time hath to silver turn'd;
  O Time too swift, O swiftness never ceasing!
My youth 'gainst age, and age 'gainst time, hath spurn'd,
  But spurn'd in vain; youth waneth by increasing:

Beauty, strength, youth, are flowers but fading seen;
Duty, faith, love, are roots, and ever green.

My helmet now shall make an hive for bees,
    And lover's sonnets turn to holy psalms;
A man-at-arms must now serve on his knees,
    And feed on prayers, which are old age his alms:
But though from court to cottage I depart,
My saint is sure of my unspotted heart.

And when I saddest sit in homely cell,
    I'll teach my swains this carol for a song,
'Blest be the hearts that wish my sovereign well,
    Curst be the souls that think her any wrong!'
Goddess, allow this aged man his right
To be your beadsman now that was your knight.

George Peele.

SONG

TAKE, O take those lips away
That so sweetly were forsworn,
And those eyes, the break of day,
Lights that do mislead the morn:
But my kisses bring again,
    Bring again –
Seals of love, but sealed in vain,
    Sealed in vain!

Hide, O hide those hills of snow,
    Which thy frozen bosom bears,
On whose tops the pinks that grow
    Are of those that April wears.
But first set my poor heart free
Bound in those icy chains by thee.

William Shakespeare.

SPRING

SPRING, the sweet Spring, is the year's pleasant king;
  Then blooms each thing, then maids dance in a ring,
Cold doth not sting, the pretty birds do sing—
  Cuckoo, jug-jug, pu-we, to-witta-woo!

The palm and may make country houses gay,
  Lambs frisk and play, the shepherds pipe all day,
And we hear aye birds tune this merry lay—
  Cuckoo, jug-jug, pu-we, to-witta-woo!

The fields breathe sweet, the daisies kiss our feet,
Young lovers meet, old wives a-sunning sit,
In every street these tunes our ears do greet—
  Cuckoo, jug-jug, pu-we, to-witta-woo!
    Spring, the sweet Spring!

Thomas Nashe.

THE TRIUMPH

SEE the Chariot at hand here of Love,
  Wherein my Lady rideth!
Each that draws is a swan or a dove,
  And well the car Love guideth.
As she goes, all hearts do duty
  Unto her beauty;
And enamour'd do wish, so they might
  But enjoy such a sight,
That they still were to run by her side,
Through swords, through seas, whither she would ride.

Do but look on her eyes, they do light
  All that Love's world compriseth!
Do but look on her hair, it is bright
  As Love's star when it riseth!
Do but mark, her forehead's smoother
  Than words that soothe her;

311

And from her arch'd brows such a grace
    Sheds itself through the face,
As alone there triumphs to the life
All the gain, all the good, of the elements' strife.

Have you seen but a bright lily grow
    Before rude hands have touch'd it?
Have you mark'd but the fall of the snow
    Before the soil hath smutch'd it?
Have you felt the wool of beaver,
    Or swan's down ever?
Or have smelt of the bud of the brier,
    Or the nard in the fire?
Or have tasted the bag of the bee?
O so white, O so soft, O so sweet is she!

Ben Jonson.

THE ECSTACY

WHERE, like a pillow on a bed,
    A pregnant bank swell'd up, to rest
The violet's reclining head,
    Sat we two, one another's best.

Our hands were firmly cemented
    By a fast balm, which thence did spring;
Our eye-beams twisted, and did thread
    Our eyes upon one double string.

So to'entergraft our hands, as yet
    Was all the means to make us one;
And pictures in our eyes to get
    Was all our propagation.

As, 'twixt two equal armies, Fate
    Suspends uncertain victory,
Our souls—which to advance their state,
    Were gone out—hung 'twixt her and me.

And whilst our souls negotiate there,
   We like sepulchral statues lay;
All day, the same our postures were,
   And we said nothing, all the day.

If any, so by love refined,
   That he soul's language understood,
And by good love were grown all mind,
   Within convenient distance stood,

He—though he knew not which soul spake,
   Because both meant, both spoke the same—
Might thence a new concoction take,
   And part far purer than he came.

This ecstacy doth unperplex
   (We said) and tell us what we love;
We see by this, it was not sex;
   We see, we saw not, what did move:

But as all several souls contain
   Mixture of things they know not what,
Love these mix'd souls doth mix again,
   And makes both one, each this and that.

A single violet transplant,
   The strength, the colour, and the size—
All which before was poor and scant—
   Redoubles still, and multiplies.

When love with one another
   Interinanimates two souls,
That abler soul, which thence doth flow,
   Defects of loneliness controls.

We then, who are this new soul, know,
   Of what we are composed and made,
For th'atomies of which we grow
   Are souls, whom no change can invade.

But, O alas! So long, so far,
    Our bodies why do we forbear?
They are ours, though they're not we; we are
    Th'intelligences, they the spheres.

We owe them thanks, because they thus
    Did us, to us, at first convey,
Yielded their forces, sense, to us,
    Nor are dross to us, but allay.

On man heaven's influence works not so,
    But that it first imprints the air;
So soul into the soul may flow,
    Though it to body first repair.

As our blood labours to beget
    Spirits, as like souls as it can;
Because such fingers need to knit
    That subtle knot, which makes us man;

So must pure lovers' souls descend
    To affections, and to faculties,
Which sense may reach and apprehend,
    Else a great prince in prison lies.

To our bodies turn we then, that so
    Weak men on love reveal'd may look;
Love's mysteries in souls do grow,
    But yet the body is his book.

And if some lover, such as we,
    Have heard this dialogue of one,
Let him still mark us, he shall see
    Small change when we're to bodies gone.

                      John Donne.

THE ARGUMENT OF HIS BOOK

I SING of Brooks, of Blossoms, Birds, and Bowers;
Of April, May, of June, and July-Flowers.
I sing of May-poles, Hock-carts, Wassails, Wakes,
Of Bridegrooms, Brides, and of their Bridal cakes.
I write of Youth, of Love, and have access
By these, to sing of cleanly Wantonness.
I sing of Dews, of Rains, and piece by piece
Of Balme, of Oil, of Spice, and Amber-Greece.
I sing of Time's trans-shifting; and I write
How Roses first came red, and Lilies white.
I write of Groves, of Twilights, and I sing
The Court of Mab, and of the Fairy-King.
I write of Hell; I sing (and ever shall)
Of Heaven, and hope to have it after all.

Robert Herrick.

REDEMPTION

HAVING been Tenant long to a rich Lord,
   Not thriving, I resolved to be bold,
   And make a suit unto him to afford
A new small-rented lease, and cancel th'old.

In Heaven at his manor I him sought,
   They told me there, that he was lately gone
   About some land, which he had dearly bought
Long since on Earth, to take possession.

I straight return'd, and knowing his great birth,
   Sought him accordingly in great resorts,
   In cities, theatres, gardens, parks, and courts:
At length I heard a ragged noise and mirth
   Of thieves and murderers. There I him espied,
   Who straight, *Your suit is granted*, said, and died.

George Herbert.

SONG

ASK me no more where Jove bestows,
When June is past, the fading rose;
For in your beauty's orient deep
These flowers, as in their causes, sleep.

Ask me no more whither do stray
The golden atoms of the day;
For in pure love heaven did prepare
Those powders to enrich your hair.

Ask me no more whither doth haste
The nightingale when May is past;
For in your sweet dividing throat
She winters and keeps warm her note.

Ask me no more where those stars 'light
That downwards fall in dead of night;
For in your eyes they sit, and there
Fixed become as in their sphere.

Ask me no more if east or west
The phœnix builds her spicy nest;
For unto you at last she flies,
And in your fragrant bosom dies.

Thomas Carew.

I LAID me down upon a bank
Where love lay sleeping;
I heard among the rushes dank
Weeping, Weeping.

Then I went to the heath and the wild
To the thistles and thorns of the waste;
And they told me how they were beguil'd,
Driven out, and compel'd to be chaste.

William Blake.

JENNY KISS'D ME

JENNY kiss'd me when we met,
　　Jumping from the chair she sat in;
Time, you thief, who love to get
　　Sweets into your list, put that in!
Say I'm weary, say I'm sad,
　　Say that health and wealth have miss'd me,
Say I'm growing old, but add
　　Jenny kiss'd me.

Leigh Hunt.

WE'LL GO NO MORE A-ROVING

SO, we'll go no more a-roving
　　So late into the night,
Though the heart be still as loving,
　　And the moon be still as bright.

For the sword outwears its sheath,
　　And the soul wears out the breast,
And the heart must pause to breathe,
　　And love itself have rest.

Though the night was made for loving,
　　And the day returns too soon,
Yet we'll go no more a-roving
　　By the light of the moon.

Byron.

TO NIGHT

SWIFTLY walk o'er the western wave,
　　Spirit of Night!
Out of the misty eastern cave,
Where, all the long and lone day-light,
Thou wovest dreams of joy and fear,
Which make thee terrible and dear—
　　Swift be thy flight!

317

Wrap thy form in a mantle gray,
    Star-inwrought!
Blind with thine hair the eyes of Day;
Kiss her until she be wearied out,
Then wander o'er city, and sea, and land
Touching all with thine opiate wand—
    Come, long-sought!

When I arose and saw the dawn,
    I sighed for thee;
When light rode high, and the dew was gone,
And noon lay heavy on flower and tree,
And the weary day turned to his rest,
Lingering like an unloved guest,
    I sighed for thee.

Thy brother Death came, and cried,
    Wouldst thou me?
Thy sweet child Sleep, the filmy-eyed,
Murmured like a noontide bee,
Shall I nestle near thy side?
Wouldst thou me?—And I replied,
    No, not thee!

Death will come when thou art dead,
    Soon, too soon—
Sleep will come when thou art fled;
Of neither would I ask the boon
I ask of thee, beloved Night—
Swift be thine approaching flight,
    Come soon, soon!

P. B. Shelley.

WRITTEN IN THE FIELDS

TO one who has been long in city pent,
'Tis very sweet to look into the fair
And open face of heaven—to breathe a prayer
Full in the smile of the blue firmament.

Who is more happy, when, with heart's content,
Fatigued he sinks into some pleasant lair
Of wavy grass, and reads a debonair
And gentle tale of love and languishment?
Returning home at evening, with an ear
Catching the notes of Philomel—an eye
Watching the sailing cloudlet's bright career,
He mourns that day so soon has glided by:
E'en like the passage of an angel's tear,
That falls through the clear ether silently.

John Keats.

GO from me. Yet I feel that I shall stand
Henceforward in thy shadow. Nevermore
Alone upon the threshold of my door
Of individual life, I shall command
The uses of my soul, nor lift my hand
Serenely in the sunshine as before,
Without the sense of that which I forbore—
Thy touch upon the palm. The widest land
Doom takes to part us, leaves thy heart in mine
With pulses that beat double. What I do
And what I dream include thee, as the wine
Must taste of its own grapes. And when I sue
God for myself, He hears that name of thine,
And sees within my eyes the tears of two.

Elizabeth Barrett Browning.

From THE PRISONER

'HE comes with ~~western~~ ~~winds, with evening's wandering airs~~
With that clear dusk of heaven that brings the thickest stars;
Winds take a pensive tone and stars a tender fire
And visions rise and change which kill me with desire—

'Desire for nothing known in my maturer years
When joy grew mad with awe at counting future tears;
When, if my spirit's sky was full of flashes warm,
I knew not whence they came, from sun or thunderstorm;

319

'But first a hush of peace, a soundless calm descends;
The struggle of distress and fierce impatience ends;
Mute music soothes my breast—unuttered harmony
That I could never dream till earth was lost to me.

'Then dawns the Invisible, the Unseen its truth reveals;
My outward sense is gone, my inward essence feels—
Its wings are almost free, its home, its harbour found;
Measuring the gulf it stoops and dares the final bound!

'Oh dreadful is the check—intense the agony
When the ear begins to hear and the eye begins to see;
When the pulse begins to throb, the brain to think again;
The soul to feel the flesh and the flesh to feel the chain!'

Emily Brontë.

LOVE SIGHT

WHEN DO I see thee most, beloved one?
   When in the light the spirits of mine eyes
   Before thy face, their altar, solemnize
The worship of that Love through thee made known?

Or when, in the dusk hours, (we two alone)
   Close-kissed and eloquent of still replies
   Thy twilight-hidden glimmering visage lies,
And my soul only sees thy soul its own?

O love, my love! If I no more should see
Thyself, nor on the earth the shadow of thee,
   Nor image of thine eyes in any spring—
How then should sound upon Life's darkening slope
The ground-whirl of the perish'd leaves of Hope,
   The wind of Death's imperishable wing?

Dante Gabriel Rossetti.

SEED – TIME

FLOWERS of the willow-herb are wool;
Flowers of the briar berries red;
Speeding their seed as the breeze may rule.
Flowers of the thistle loosen the thread.
Flowers of the clematis drip in beard,
Slack from the fir-tree youngly climbed;
Chaplets in air, flies foliage seared;
Heeled upon earth, lie clusters rimed.

Where were skies of the mantle stained
Orange and scarlet, a coat of frieze
Travels from North till day has waned,
Tattered, soaked in the ditch's dyes;
Tumbles the rook under grey or slate;
Else enfolding us, damps to the bone;
Narrows the world to my neighbour's gate;
Paints me Life as a wheezy crone.

Now seems none but the spider lord;
Star in circle his web waits prey,
Silvering bush-mounds, blue brushing sward;
Slow runs the hour, swift flits the ray.
Now to his thread-shroud is he nigh,
Nigh to the tangle where wings are sealed,
He who frolicked the jewelled fly;
All is adroop on the down and the weald.

Mists more lone for the sheep-bell ...
Nights that tardily let slip a morn
Paler than moons, and on noontide's lap
Flame dies cold, like the rose late born.
Rose born late, born withered in bud!—
I, even I, for a zenith of sun
Cry, to fulfil me, nourish my blood:
O for a day of the long light, one!

Master the blood, nor read by chills,
Earth admonishes: Hast thou ploughed,
Sown, reaped, harvested grain for the mills,
Thou hast the light over shadow of cloud.
Steadily eyeing, before that wail
Animal-infant, thy mind began,
Momently nearer me: should sight fail,
Plod in the track of the husbandman.

Verily now is our season of seed,
 Now in our Autumn; and Earth discerns
Them that have served her in them that can read,
 Glassing, where under the surface she burns,
Quick at her wheel, while the fuel, decay,
Brightens the fire of renewal: and we?
Death is the word of a bovine-day,
Know you the breast of the springing To-be.

George Meredith.

MIRAGE

THE hope I dreamed of was a dream,
 Was but a dream; and now I wake,
Exceeding comfortless, and worn, and old,
 For a dream's sake.

I hang my harp upon a tree,
 A weeping willow in a lake;
I hang my silent harp there, wrung and snapt
 For a dream's sake.

Lie still, lie still, my breaking heart;
 My silent heart, lie still and break:
Life, and the world, and mine own self, are changed
 For a dream's sake.

Christina Rossetti.

I TASTE a liquor never brewed,
From tankards scooped in pearl;
Not all the vats upon the Rhine
Yield such an alcohol!

Inebriate of air am I,
And debauchee of dew,
Reeling, through endless summer days,
From inns of molten blue.

When landlords turn the drunken bee
Out of the foxglove's door,
When butterflies renounce their drams,
I shall but drink the more!

Till seraphs swing their snowy hats,
And saints to windows run,
To see the little tippler
Leaning against the sun!

Emily Dickinson.

WEATHERS

THIS is the weather the cuckoo likes,
    And so do I;
When showers betumble the chestnut spikes,
    And nestlings fly;
And the little brown nightingale bills his best,
And they sit outside the 'Traveller's Rest',
And maids come forth sprig-muslin drest,
And citizens dream of the South and West,
    And so do I.

This is the weather the shepherd shuns,
    And so do I:
When beeches drip in browns and duns,
    And thresh, and ply;
And hill-hid tides throb, throe on throe,
And meadow rivulets overflow,

And drops on gate-bars hang in a row,
And rooks in families homeward go,
    And so do I.

Thomas Hardy.

THE GOLDEN ECHO

    Spare!
There is one, yes I have one (Hush there!);
Only not within seeing of the sun,
Not within the singeing of the strong sun,
Tall sun's tingeing, or treacherous the tainting of the earth's
    air,
Somewhere elsewhere there is ah well where! One,
One. Yes I can tell such a key, I do know such a place,
 Where whatever's prized and passes of us, everything that's
    fresh and fast flying of us, seems to us sweet of us and
    swiftly away with, done away with, undone,
Undone, done with, soon done with, and yet dearly and
    dangerously sweet
Of us, the wimpled-water-dimpled, not-by-morning-
    matchéd face,
The flower of beauty, fleece of beauty, too too apt to, ah! To
    fleet,
Never fleets more, fastened with the tenderest truth
To its own best being and its loveliness of youth: it is an
    ever-lastingness of, O it is an all youth!
Come then, your ways and airs and looks, locks, maiden
    gear, gallantry and gaiety and grace,
Winning ways, airs innocent, maiden manners, sweet looks,
    loose locks, long locks, lovelocks, gaygear, going gallant,
    girlgrace—
Resign them, sign them, seal them, send them, motion
    them with breath,
And with sighs soaring, soaring sighs deliver
Them; beauty-in-the-ghost, deliver it, early now, long
    before death
Give beauty back, beauty, beauty, beauty, back to God,
    beauty's self and beauty's giver.

See; not a hair is, not an eyelash, not the least lash lost; every
    hair
Is, hair of the head, numbered.
Nay, what we had lighthanded left in surly the mere mould
Will have waked and have waxed and have walked with the
    wind what while we slept,
This side, that side hurling a heavyheaded hundredfold
What while we, while we slumbered.
O then, weary then why should we tread? O why are we so
    haggard at the heart, so care-coiled, care-killed, so
    fagged, so fashed, so cogged, so cumbered,
When the thing we freely forfeit is kept with fonder a care,
Fonder a care kept than we could have kept it, kept
Far with fonder a care (and we, we should have lost it) finer,
    fonder
A care kept.—Where kept? Do but tell us where kept,
    where—
Yonder.—What high as that! We follow, now we follow—
      Yonder, yes yonder, yonder,
Yonder.

Gerard Manley Hopkins.

THE idle life I lead
Is like a pleasant sleep,
Wherein I rest and heed
The dreams that by me sweep.

And still of all my dreams
In turn so swiftly past,
Each in its fancy seems
A nobler than the last.

And every eve I say,
Noting my step in bliss,
That I have known no day
In all my life like this.

Robert Bridges.

'HE KNOWETH NOT THAT
THE DEAD ARE THINE'

THE weapon that you fought with was a word,
And with that word you stabbed me to the heart.
Not once but twice you did it, for the sword
    Made no blood start.

They have not tried you for your life. You go
Strong in such innocence as men will boast.
They have not buried me. They do not know
    Life from its ghost.

Mary Coleridge.

LATE POEMS

And here the poet meets his favouring muse.
Crabbe.

It is a pretty poem, Mr Pope, but you must
not call it Homer.
Richard Bentley.

I wish you would read a little poetry sometimes.
Your ignorance cramps my conversation.
Anthony Hope.

Late
And here Poems
the poet meets his favouring muse'

IN THE POPPY FIELD

MAD Patsy said, he said to me,
That every morning he could see
An angel walking on the sky;
Across the sunny skies of morn
He threw great handfuls far and nigh
Of poppy seed among the corn;
And then, he said, the angels run
To see the poppies in the sun.

A poppy is a devil weed,
I said to him—he disagreed;
He said the devil had no hand
In spreading flowers tall and fair
Through corn and rye and meadow land,
By garth and barrow everywhere:
The devil has not any flower,
But only money in his power.

And then he stretched out in the sun
And rolled upon his back for fun:
He kicked his legs and roared for joy
Because the sun was shining down:
He said he was a little boy
And would not work for any clown:
He ran and laughed behind a bee,
And danced for very ecstasy.

James Stephens.

TO A POET A THOUSAND YEARS HENCE

I WHO am dead a thousand years,
 And wrote this sweet archaic song,
Send you my words for messengers
 The way I shall not pass along.

I care not if you bridge the seas,
 Or ride secure the cruel sky,
Or build consummate palaces
 Of metal or of masonry.

But have you wine and music still,
 And statues and a bright-eyed love,
And foolish thoughts of good or ill,
 And prayers to them who sit above?

How shall we conquer? Like a wind
 That falls at eve our fancies blow,
And old Maeonides the blind
 Said it three thousand years ago.

O friend unseen, unborn, unknown,
 Student of our sweet English tongue,
Read out my words at night, alone:
 I was a poet, I was young.

Since I can never see your face,
 And never shake you by the hand,
I send my soul through time and space
 To greet you. You will understand.
                              James Elroy Flecker.

ADDRESS TO MY SOUL

MY soul, be not disturbed
By planetary war;
Remain securely orbed
In this contracted star.

Fear not, pathetic flame;
Your sustenance is doubt:
Glassed in translucent dream
They cannot snuff you out.

Wear water, or a mask
Of unapparent cloud;
Be brave and never ask
A more defunctive shroud.

The universal points
Are shrunk into a flower;
Between its delicate joints
Chaos keeps no power.

The pure integral form,
Austere and silver-dark,
Is balanced on the storm
In its predestined arc.

Small as sphere of rain
It slides along the groove
Whose path is furrowed plain
Among the suns that move.

The shapes of April buds
Outlive the phantom year:
Upon the void at odds
The dewdrop falls severe.

Five-petalled flame, be nimble
Be firm, dissolving start:
Accept the stricter mould
That makes you singular.

Elinor Wylie.

THE HILL

BREATHLESS, we flung us on the windy hill,
Laughed in the sun, and kissed the lovely grass.
You said, "Through glory and ecstasy we pass;
Wind, sun, and earth remain, the birds sing still,
When we are old, are old ..." "And when we die
All's over that is ours; and life burns on
Through other lovers, other lips," said I,
"Heart of my heart, our heaven is now, is won!"
"We are Earth's best, that learnt her lesson here.
Life is our cry. We have kept the faith!" we said;
"We shall go down with unreluctant tread
Rose-crowned into the darkness!" ... Proud we were,
And laughed, that had such brave true things to say.
—And then you suddenly cried, and turned away.

Rupert Brooke.

NEW COUNTRYMAN

WHAT do I know now, that I did not know?
Cow does not smell of milk, milk smells of cow.
Stubble, the brighter for autumnal haze,
In half a summer's suns in afterglow.
Rain is a mortal friend, that was a foe.
"Sear", "rathe", "a—cold" are words of common grace.
Winter's thin landscape brings the beacon-brow
Comforting close, emptying the middle space
(A painter's trick): not features now, but face.
How quickly, quickly grass resumes its ways.

What eagers most the eye? Rain-gleam of plough.
What hurries, not harries, the heart? Fall, flow
Of leaves. Not mournful, no, no, no:
A sequined curtain shaken down to show
Singled twig, sprung branch, bough—
The bones of building sculptured into lace.
What heartens hope? Winter wheat in snow

Showing its ringes? But all, all the year's phase:
Charge, change, provision, deaths, decays,
The natural thrift: garner, store, stow
Of residue, each to its occasion, purpose, place
—So extending Time, his dear delays,
That I, growing old, have length, yes length, of days.
These things, before unknown to me, I know
                    And praise, praise.

                                        Francis Meynell.

FIFTH PHILOSOPHER'S SONG

A MILLION million spermatozoa,
    All of them alive:
Out of their cataclysm but one poor Noah
    Dare hope to survive.

And among that billion minus one
    Might have chanced to be
Shakespeare, another Newton, a new Donne—
    But the One was Me.

Shame to have ousted your betters thus,
    Taking ark while the others remained outside!
Better for all of us, froward Homunculus,
    If you'd quietly died!

                                        Aldous Huxley.

HAPPINESS

EVER again to breathe pure happiness,
The happiness our mother gave us, boys?
To smile at nothings, needing no caress?
Have we not laughed too often since with joys?
Have we not wrought too sick and sorrowful wrongs
For their hands' pardoning? The sun may cleanse,
And time, and starlight. Life will sing sweet songs,
And gods will show us pleasures more than men's.

Yet heaven looks smaller than the old doll's-home,
No nestling place is left in bluebell bloom,
And the wide arms of trees have lost their scope.
The former happiness is unreturning:
Boys' griefs are not so grievous as our yearning,
Boys have no sadness sadder than our hope.

Wilfred Owen.

ESSEX

'THE vagrant visitor erstwhile,
My colour-plate book says to me,
'Could wend by hedgerow-side and stile,
From Benfleet down to Leigh-on-Sea.'

And as I turn the colour-plates
Edwardian Essex opens wide,
Mirrored in ponds and seen through gates,
Sweet uneventful countryside.

Like streams the little by-roads run
Through oats and barley round a hill
To where blue willows catch the sun
By some white weather-boarded mill.

'A Summer Idyll Matching Tye'
'At Havering-atte-Bower, the Stocks'
And cobbled pathways lead the eye
To cottage doors and hollyhocks.

Far Essex—fifty miles away
The level wastes of sucking mud
Where distant barges high with hay
Come sailing in upon the flood.

Near Essex of the River Lea
And anglers out with hook and worm
And Epping Forest glades where we
Had beanfeasts with my father's firm.

At huge and convoluted pubs
They used to set us down from brakes
In that half-land of football clubs
Which London near the Forest makes.

Then deepest Essex few explore
Where steepest thatch is sunk in flowers
And out of elm and sycamore
Rise flinty fifteenth-century towers.

I see the little branch line go
By white farms roofed in red and brown,
The old Great Eastern winding slow
To some forgotten country town.

Now yarrow chokes the railway track,
Brambles obliterate the stile,
No motor coach can take me back
To that Edwardian 'erstwhile'.

John Betjeman.

Since we are what we are, what shall we be
But what we are? We are, we have
Six feet and seventy years, to see
The light, and then resign it for the grave.
We are not worlds, no, nor infinity,
We have no claims on stone, except to prove
In the invention of the human city
Ourselves, our breath, our death, our love.
The rocket was built, soars like an arrow
From the earth's rim towards the sky's,
Upwards-downwards in a star-filled pond,
Climbing and diving from our world, to narrow
The gap between the world shut in the eyes
And the receding world of light beyond.

Stephen Spender.

THE force that through the green fuse drives the flower
Drives my green age; that blasts the roots of trees
Is my destroyer.
And I am dumb to tell the crooked rose
My youth is bent by the same wintry fever.

The force that drives the water through the rocks
Drives my red blood; that dries the mouthing streams
Turns mine to wax.
And I am dumb to mouth unto my veins
How at the mountain spring the same mouth sucks.

The hand that whirls the water in the pool
Stirs the quicksand; that ropes the blowing wind
Hauls my shroud sail.
And I am dumb to tell the hanging man
How of my clay is made the hangman's lime.

The lips of time leech to the fountain head;
Love drips and gathers, but the fallen blood
Shall calm her sores.
And I am dumb to tell a weather's wind
How time has ticked a heaven round the stars.

And I am dumb to tell the lover's tomb
How at my sheet goes the same crooked worm.

Dylan Thomas.

THE ABANDONED SHADE

WALKING the abandoned shade
of childhood's habitations,
my ears remembering chime,
hearing their buried voices.

Hearing original summer,
the birdlit banks of dawn,
the yellow-hammer beat of blood
gilding my cradle eyes.

336

Hearing the tin-moon rise
and the sunset's penny fall,
the creep of frost and weep of thaw
and bells of winter robins.

Hearing again the talking house
and the four vowels of the wind,
and midnight monsters whispering
in the white throat of my room.

Season and landscape's liturgy,
badger and sneeze of rain,
the bleat of bats, and bounce of rabbits
bubbling under the hill:

Each old and echo-salted tongue
sings to my backward glance;
but the voice of the boy, the boy I seek,
within my mouth is dumb.

Laurie Lee.

WHISPERS OF IMMORTALITY

WEBSTER was much possessed by death
And saw the skull beneath the skin;
And breastless creatures under ground
Leaned backward with a lipless grin.

Daffodil bulbs instead of balls
Stared from the sockets of the eyes!
He knew that thought clings round dead limbs
Tightening its lusts and luxuries.

Donne, I suppose, was such another
Who found no substitute for sense,
To seize and clutch and penetrate;
Expert beyond experience,

He knew the anguish of the marrow
The ague of the skeleton;
No contact possible to flesh
Allayed the fever of the bone.

Grishkin is nice: her Russian eye
Is underlined for emphasis;
Uncorseted, her friendly bust
Gives promise of pneumatic bliss.

The couched Brazilian jaguar
Compels the scampering marmoset
With subtle effluence of cat;
Grishkin has a maisonette;

The sleek Brazilian jaguar
Does not in its arboreal gloom
Distil so rank a feline smell
As Grishkin in a drawing-room.

And even the Abstract entities
Circumambulate her charm;
But our lot crawls between dry ribs
To keep our metaphysics warm.

T. S. Eliot.

HATE POEMS

Up, Lord, disappoint him and cast him down.
Psalm XVII.

Hence, ye profane; I hate ye all;
Both the great vulgar, and the small.
Abraham Cowley.

The dupe of friendship, and the fool of love;
have I not reason to hate and despise myself?
Indeed I do; and chiefly for not having hated
and despised the world enough.
William Hazlitt.

Now hatred is by far the longest pleasure;
Men love in haste, but they detest at leisure.
Byron.

Hate Poems

up, Lord, disappoint him and cast   him down

ON ROBERT DUDLEY, EARL OF LEICESTER

HERE lieth the worthy warrior
Who never blooded sword;
Here lieth the noble councillor,
Who never held his word;
Here lieth his excellency,
Who ruled all the state;
Here lieth the Earl of Leicester
Whom all the world did hate.

Anon., 1588.

ON THE DUKE OF BUCKINGHAM

A MAN so various that he seemed to be
Not one, but all mankind's epitome.
Stiff in opinions, always in the wrong;
Was everything by starts, and nothing long;
But, in the course of one revolving moon,
Was chemist, fiddler, statesman and buffoon:
Then all for women, painting, rhyming, drinking:
Besides ten thousand freaks that died in thinking.
Blest madman, who could every hour employ,
With something new to wish, or to enjoy!
Railing and praising were his usual themes;
And both (to show his judgement) in extremes:

341

So over violent, or over civil,
That every man, with him, was god or devil.
In squandering wealth was his peculiar art:
Nothing went unrewarded, but desert.
Beggared by fools, whom still he found too late:
He had his jest, and they had his estate.

John Dryden.

ON A POET LAUREATE

HE had written praises of a regicide;
    He had written praises of all kings whatever;
He had written for republics far and wide,
    And then against them bitterer than ever;
For pantisocracy he once had cried
    Aloud—a scheme less moral than 'twas clever;
Then grew a hearty anti-Jacobin—
Had turn'd his coat—and would have turn'd his skin.

He had sung against all battles, and again
    In their high praise and glory: he had call'd
Reviewing "the ungentle craft", and then
    Become as base a critic as e'er crawl'd—
Fed, paid and pamper'd by the very men
    By whom his muse and morals had been maul'd:
He had written much blank verse, and blanker prose,
And more of both than anybody knows.

Byron.

TO EDWARD FITZGERALD

I CHANCED upon a new book yesterday:
I opened it, and, where my finger lay
'Twixt page and uncut page, these words I read
—Some six or seven at most—and learned thereby
That you, Fitzgerald, whom by ear and eye
She never knew, "thanked God my wife was dead."
Ay, dead! And were yourself alive, good Fitz,
How to return you thanks would task my wits:

Kicking you seems the common lot of curs—
While more appropriate greeting lends you grace:
Surely to spit there glorifies your face—
Spitting from lips once sanctified by Hers.

Robert Browning

A PORTRAIT

I AM a kind of farthing dip,
　　Unfriendly to the nose and eyes;
A blue-behinded ape, I skip
　　Upon the trees of Paradise.

At mankind's feast I take my place
　　In solemn sanctimonious state,
And have the air of saying grace
　　While I defile the dinner plate.

I am "the smiler with the knife",
　　The battener upon garbage, I—
Dear Heaven, with such a rancid life,
　　Were it not better far to die?

Yet still, about the human pale,
　　I love to scamper, love to race,
To swing by my irreverent tail
　　All over the most holy place;

And when at length, some golden day,
　　The unfailing sportsman, aiming at,
Shall bag me—all the world shall say:
　　Thank God, and there's an end of that!

R.L. Stevenson.

WISHES OF AN ELDERLY MAN
(WISHED AT A GARDEN-PARTY, JUNE ,1914)

I WISH I loved the Human Race;
I wish I loved its silly face;
I wish I liked the way it walks;
I wish I liked the way it talks;
And when I'm introduced to one
I wish I thought *What Jolly Fun!*
Walter Raleigh.

STATE POEMS

Permit the transports of a British muse
And pardon raptures that yourselves infuse.
> *Nahum Tate, Poet Laureate, to*
> *the new Parliament* (1701).

Praising all alike, is praising none.
> *John Gay.*

The world, we believe, is pretty well agreed
in thinking that the shorter a prize poem is,
the better.
> *Macaulay.*

State Poems

*'Permit the transports of a British muse
And pardon raptures that yourselves infuse'*

Robert Herrick on
THE KING (CHARLES I) AND QUEEN UPON THEIR UNHAPPY DISTANCES

WOE, woe to them, who (be a ball of strife)
Doe, and have parted here a Man and Wife:
CHARLS the best Husband, while MARIA strives
To be, and is, the very best of Wives.

Leigh Hunt addresses
THE INFANT PRINCESS ROYAL

WELCOME, bud beside the rose,
On whose stem our safety grows;
Welcome, little Saxon Guelph;
Welcome for thine own small self;
Welcome for thy father, mother,

~~Found the one and only the other,~~

Welcome to three kingdoms; nay,
Such is thy potential day,
Welcome, little mighty birth,
To our human star the earth.

Some have wish'd thee boy; and some
Gladly wait till boy shall come ...

347

Alfred, Lord Tennyson writes of
THE EXHIBITION, 1862

UPLIFT a thousand voices full and sweet,
　　In this wide hall with earth's invention stor'd,
　　And praise th' invisible universal Lord,
Who lets once more in peace the nations meet,
　　Where, Science, Art, and Labour have outpour'd
Their myriad horns of plenty at our feet.
O silent father of our Kings to be,
Mourn'd in this golden hour of jubilee,
For this, for all, we weep our thanks to thee!

Roy Dalziel celebrates
THE DIAMOND JUBILEE

QUEEN VICTORIA sixty years the Monarch of our Realm
Shows the grand old lady has kept a steady helm.
She often tacked, she never backed, she always heaved her lead,
And never turned into her bunk when breakers were ahead.

348

THE ZOO

The living creature after his kind.

Genesis.

Sporting the lion ramped, and in his paw,
Dandled the kid; bears, tigers, ounces, pards
Gamboll'd before them, th'unwieldly
   elephant
To make them mirth us'd all his might, and
   wreathed
His lithe proboscis.

Milton.

Cows are my passion.

Charles Dickens.

the Zoo

'the living creature after his kind'

THE TYGER

TYGER, tyger, burning bright
In the forests of the night,
What immortal hand or eye
Dare frame thy fearful symmetry?

Burnt in distant deeps or skies
The cruel fire of thine eyes?
On what wings dare he aspire?
What the hand dare seize the fire?

And what shoulder and what art
Could twist the sinews of thy heart?
And when thy heart began to beat
What dread hand and what dread feet

Could fetch it from the furnace deep
And in thy horrid ribs dare steep?
In what clay and in what mould
Were thy eyes of fury roll'd?

Where the hammer? Where the chain?
In what furnace was thy brain?
What the anvil? What dread grasp
Dare its deadly terrors clasp?

When the stars threw down their spears
And water'd heaven with their tears
Dare he laugh his work to see?
Dare he who made the lamb make thee?

Tyger, tyger, burning bright
In the forests of the night,
What immortal hand and eye
Dare frame thy fearful symmetry?

William Blake.

JONAH AND THE WHALE

HE sported round the watery world.
His rich oil was a gloomy waveless lake
Within the waves. Affrighted seamen hurled
Their weapons in his foaming wake.

One old corroding iron he bore
Which journeyed through his flesh but yet had not
Found out his life. Another lance he wore
Outside him, pricking in a tender spot.

So distant were his parts that they
Sent but a dull faint message to his brain.
He knew not his own flesh, as great kings may
Not know the farther places where they reign.

His play made storm in a calm sea;
His very kindness slew what he might touch;
And wrecks lay scattered on his anger's lee.
The Moon rocked to and fro his watery couch.

His hunger cleared the sea. And where
He passed, the ocean's edge lifted its brim.
He skimmed the dim sea-floor to find if there
Some garden had its harvest ripe for him.

But in his sluggish brain no thought
Ever arose. His law was instinct blind.
No thought or gleam or vision ever brought
Light to the dark of his old dreamless mind.

Until one day sudden and strange
Half-hints of knowledge burst upon his sight.
Glimpses he had of Time, and Space, and Change,
And something greater than his might;

And terror's leap to imagine sin;
And blinding Truth half-bare unto his seeing.
I was the living man who had come in ...
Jonah's thoughts flying through his being.

Viola Meynell.

THE COW

THE friendly cow all red and white,
    I love with all my heart:
She gives me cream with all her might,
    To eat with apple-tart.

She wanders lowing here and there,
    And yet she cannot stray,
All in the pleasant open air,
    The pleasant light of day;

And blown by all the winds that pass
    And wet with all the showers,
She walks among the meadow grass
    And eats the meadow flowers.

R.L. Stevenson.

THE RABBIT

THE rabbit has a charming face:
Its private life is a disgrace.
I really dare not name to you
The awful things that rabbits do;
Things that your paper never prints –
You only mention them in hints.
They have such lost, degraded souls
No wonder they inhabit holes;
When such depravity is found
It only can live underground.

Anon.: 20th Cent.

MAN AND BEAST

I AM less patient than this horse
And it is fleeter far than I.
Its hair is silky, mine is coarse;
Grasses have shaped that larger eye,
While to feed me live things must die.

The birds make little darts in air,
And fishes little darts in water,
Old sheep a silver glory share,
Peacocks are peacocks everywhere...
Man lies awake, planning the slaughter.

What woman has this old cat's graces?
What boy can sing as the thrush sings?
For me, I'd rather not run races
With dragon-flies, nor thread the mazes
Of a smooth lawn with ants and things.

Yet horse and sheep tread leaf and stem
And bud and flower beneath their feet;
They sniff at Stars-of-Bethlehem
And buttercups are food to them,
No more than bitter food or sweet.

THE ZOO

I, to whom air and waves area sealed,
I yet possess the human part.
O better beasts, you know must yield!
I name the cool stars of the field,
I have the flowers of heaven by heart.

Francis Meynell.

THE EAGLE

HE clasps the crag with crooked hands;
Close to the sun in lonely lands,
Ringed with the azure world, he stands.

The wrinkled sea beneath him crawls;
He watches from his mountain walls,
And like a thunderbolt he falls.

Alfred Lord Tennyson.

EPIGRAMS

A box where sweets compacted lie.
George Herbert.

What is an Epigram? a dwarfish whole,
Its body brevity, and wit its soul.
Coleridge.

O be less beautiful, or be less brief.
Sir William Watson.

And if you find it wond'rous short,
 It cannot hold you long.
Oliver Goldsmith.

Epigrams

"A box where sweets compacted lie"

THE BALANCE OF EUROPE

NOW Europe balanced, neither side prevails;
For nothing's left in either of the scales.
Alexander Pope.

ON A CERTAIN LORD'S GIVING SOME
THOUSAND POUNDS FOR A HOUSE

SO many thousands for a house
For you, of all the world, Lord Mouse!
A little house would best accord
With you, my very little lord!
And then exactly match'd would be
Your house and hospitality.
David Garrick.

YOU beat your pate, and fancy wit will come:
Knock as you please, there's nobody at home.
Alexander Pope.

SWANS sing before they die—'twere no bad thing
Should certain persons die before they sing.
S. T. Coleridge.

LIE on! While my revenge shall be
To speak the very truth of thee.
Robert, Earl Nugent.

A TRUE MAID

NO, no; for my virginity,
When I lose that, says Rose, I'll die:
Behind the elms, last night, cried Dick,
Rose, were you not extremely sick?
Matthew Prior.

THE POWER OF TIME

IF neither brass nor marble can withstand
The mortal force of Time's destructive hand;
If mountains sink to vales, if cities die,
And lessening rivers mourn their fountains dry;
When my old cassock (said a Welsh divine)
Is out at elbows, why should I repine?
Jonathan Swift.

ON A BEAUTIFUL YOUTH STRUCK BLIND
WITH LIGHTNING

SURE, 'twas by Providence design'd
Rather in pity than in hate,
That he should be, like Cupid, blind,
To save him from Narcissus' fate.
Oliver Goldsmith.

UPON A GENTLEWOMAN WITH
A SWEET VOICE

SO long you did not sing, or touch your lute,
We knew 'twas Flesh and Blood, that there sat mute.
But when you playing, and your voice came in,
'Twas no more you then, but a *Cherubin*.
Robert Herrick.

ON THE TOILET
TABLE OF
QUEEN MARIE-ANTOINETTE

THIS was her table, these her trim outspread
Brushes and trays and porcelain cups for red;
Here sate she, while her women tired and curled
The most unhappy head in all the world.

J.B.B. Nichols.

MY OWN EPITAPH

LIFE is a jest, and all things show it;
I thought so once, but now I know it.

John Gay.

SUFFOLK EPITAPH

STRANGER pass by and waste no time
On bad biography and careless rhyme.
For what I am, this humble dust encloses;
And what I was is no affair of yourses.

1870.

THE MORON

SEE the happy moron,
He doesn't give a damn!
I wish I were a moron—
My God! Perhaps I am!

Anonymous.

A RIDDLE SOLVED

KIND souls, you wonder why, love you,
When you, you wonder why, love none.
We love, Fool, for the good we do,
Not that which unto us is done!
Coventry Patmore.

EMINENT PHYSICISTS

I

NATURE, and Nature's laws, lay hid in night:
God said, *Let Newton be!* And all was light.
Alexander Pope.

II

IT did not last: the Devil, howling *Ho!*
Let Einstein be! restored the status quo.
J. C. Squire.

RELATIVITY

THERE was a young woman named Bright
Who travelled much faster than light.
   She started one day
   In a relative way,
And returned on the previous night.
Anonymous.

"COME, come," said Tom's father, "at your time of life,
There's no longer excuse for thus playing the rake—
It is time you should think, boy, of taking a wife."
"Why, so it is, father—whose wife shall I take?"
Thomas Moore.

ETERNITY

HE who bends to himself a Joy
Doth the winged life destroy;
But he who kisses the Joy as it flies
Lives in Eternity's sunrise.

William Blake.

The publishers would like to thank:

Francis Meynell and Vera Meynell for the original idea of *The Week-End Book*; Francis Meynell for his poem 'New Countryman', reprinted with the kind permission of Benedict Meynell.

★

'All Creatures that on Earth do Dwell', 'The Green and Pleasant Land' & 'The Fields and the Beasts Thereof' by John Moore from The Week-End Book (Copyright © The Estate of John Moore 1924) are reproduced by permission of PFD on behalf of the Estate of John Moore.

★

'Starshine at Night' authored by Sir Fred Hoyle, reprinted with the kind permission of Barbara Hoyle.

★

'Architecture' authored by J.M. Richards, reprinted with the kind permission of Victoria Gibson.

★

The contribution of Eleanor Farjeon to 'Games', reprinted by kind permission of David Higham A̶

★

Permission for the use of 'Food and Drink' is granted by arrangement with the Estate of Louis Untermeyer, Norma Anchin Untermeyer c/o Professional Publishing Services. The reprint is granted with the expressed permission by Laurence S. Untermeyer.

365

366

367

"QUALITIES" OR THE NEW CONFESSIONS BOOK	BEAUTY	BRAINS	CHARM	TASTE
No one should assess other people before he has assessed himself. Full marks are 20 for each quality.				
_____ on _____				
_____ on _____				
_____ on _____				
_____ on _____				
_____ on _____				
_____ on _____				
_____ on _____				
_____ on _____				
_____ on _____				
_____ on _____				
_____ on _____				
_____ on _____				
_____ on _____				
_____ on _____				
_____ on _____				
_____ on _____				
_____ on _____				
_____ on _____				
_____ on _____				
_____ on _____				
_____ on _____				
on				